# SPORT,
## *Philosophy,*
## and Good Lives

# SPORT,
## *Philosophy,*
# and Good Lives

RANDOLPH FEEZELL

University of Nebraska Press
Lincoln and London

© 2013 by the Board of Regents of the University of Nebraska

The following chapters originally appeared in the *Journal of the Philosophy of Sport*, www.tandfonline.com: Chapter 1, "A Pluralist Conception of Play," vol. 37, no. 2 (2010): 147–65. Chapter 2 originally appeared as "Vulgarians of the World Unite: Sport, Dirty Language, and Ethics," in vol. 35, no. 1 (2008): 17–42. Chapter 6 originally appeared as "Celebrated Athletes, Moral Exemplars, and Lusory Objects," in vol. 32, no. 1 (2005): 20–35.

Library of Congress Cataloging-in-Publication Data
Feezell, Randolph M., 1950-
Sport, philosophy, and good lives / Randolph Feezell.
pages cm
Includes bibliographical references and index.
ISBN 978-0-8032-7153-1 (pbk.: alk. paper)
1. Sports—Philosophy. 2. Sports—Moral and ethical aspects. 3. Sportsmanship. I. Title.
GV706.F4 2013
796.01—dc23      2012050400

Set in Adobe Garamond Pro by Laura Wellington.
Designed by J. Vadnais.

# Contents

# Introduction

This book discusses sport in the context of some traditional philosophical questions. What is a good human life? To whom do we
look for ethical guidance? What is the meaning of life? (What is a
meaningful life? What makes human activities or projects meaningful?) These are big questions that have been important in the
history of philosophy. I first considered referring to "sport and big
questions" in the title, since the notions of good lives, ethical guidance, and meaning are central in the book. I came to see that a
reference to good lives was the unifying motif, and even the issue
of meaning in life could be understood to be part of a larger reflection about how to live well, what are the constituents of good
human lives, and how sport might fit into the picture. Also, whereas
the consideration of the ethics of swearing, for example, might
seem to be a puzzling addition to a book about sport and "big
questions," the arguments involved in considering whether we
ought to cuss, inside and outside of sports, involve issues about
how best to live.

In relation to these unifying questions and issues, some of the
specific topics in the book are less surprising than others. When
thinking about the attraction and value of sports, some have empha-

sized the role of play, as I do. Some have stressed the importance of our sport heroes as role models who can have a positive influence on others. In contrast, it is less common to consider pessimistic views of sports that stress sport participants' vulnerabilities, the ethics of swearing, coaches who use their authority to offer sage advice to their players about how to live well (coach as sage), and the conditions on the basis of which we consider lives and activities meaningful—with an eye toward the contribution of sports to meaningful lives.

In the first part of the book, I begin by examining the extensive literature on play. I show that play resists a simple or parsimonious reduction to an attitude that engages an activity for its own sake (the common view among philosophers of sport). A pluralistic conception of play illuminates the relation between sport and play and the contribution of playful activities to good human lives. Next, I examine various reasons for pessimistic views of sport. I contrast an optimizing view of happiness, which stresses desire satisfaction, and the strategy of adaptation found in Stoicism, Buddhism, and Taoism, which recommends wisely adapting one's desires to the world in order to avoid unhappiness. Given the ways in which sport is a locus of vulnerability for participants, I argue for a moderate form of desire adaptation, including the moderation of fans' passionate desires for the success of their teams. This discussion leads naturally to a more extended examination of the ethics of supporting sports teams, which I offer in chapter 4. In the last chapter of part 1, I examine the ethics of using dirty language, an unusual but fascinating topic. Because some of the common arguments for the elimination of cussing appeal to prudence, social good, and virtue, it is appropriate to examine this issue in the context of references that presuppose elements of living well. Furthermore, because dirty language is so prevalent in the world of sports, it is appropriate to focus on sport examples. The relevant arguments obviously extend beyond sports, however. I distinguish two extreme positions, the puritan rejection of swearing and the vulgarian unqualified acceptance of potty mouth. I defend a position I call "moderate vulgarianism." I end the chapter with some practical suggestions.

In part 2, I critically examine the common view that celebrated athletes are role models. I argue that the term *role model* is ambiguous, as are judgments that involve this notion. Once we distinguish being a role model in a narrow and a broad sense, and the difference between making a descriptive or a normative claim about role models, we are in a position to sort out the strengths and weaknesses of various claims about sports heroes as role models. I end the discussion by suggesting that we should think of our sports heroes as fictional objects that are imaginatively constructed in the context of the sports world, rather than everyday individuals like you and me. In this part I also examine another relatively unusual topic. Many view coaches as particularly well suited to offer various kinds of advice about how to win games, leadership, management skills, and so forth. Some coaches seem to think they are in a position to offer sage advice about how to live, as if they are more interested in the ethical development of the whole person, not simply developing the person qua athlete. Although many have bemoaned contemporary athletes' sense of entitlement (to act boorishly, selfishly, even violently), few have questioned coaches' sense of entitlement to offer ethical instruction to athletes, especially in the context of college athletics. In this chapter I offer a discussion of a recent coach book whose pretensions are immoderate, especially when we think about such issues against the background of thoughtful advice offered in the history of philosophy, both Western and non-Western, about how to live well. After considering an alternative model of coaching and ethical guidance, I offer some conclusions about the proper use of coaches' authority.

In the final part of the book I examine a topic that requires a wide-ranging examination of the recent literature, especially in analytic philosophy, about the question of the meaning of life. It seems to be intuitively plausible to think of sports activities as meaningful and to believe that such activities contribute to meaningful lives. It is not at all clear, however, what such claims mean. It is rare, in popular sports-talk discourse, to raise the possibility that sports participation is attractive and that it is so difficult for athletes to give up their involvement in sports, because such involvements are meaningful. The common view is that athletes are motivated by a thirst for competition. I examine the less common view that sports contribute meaning to lives. I discuss attempts to provide general accounts of meaningful lives in terms of conditions that must be met in order for lives to be meaningful. I do this in order to generate a broader view of the meaning of meaning in judgments about meaningful lives and activities. I offer a somewhat paradoxical view that the question of the meaning of life (or, rather, the conditions under which activities and lives are meaningful) is much less important than one might think. Meaning is everywhere. On the other hand, sport is more important than some think because it provides a significant space of meaning in life.

I hope the book effectively balances topics that have been a part of scholarly philosophy of sport discussions (play, the ethics of supporting sports teams, the role-model argument) and more unusual topics (sport and unhappiness, swearing, coach as sage, sport and the meaning of life) that may raise new questions for both scholars and generalists. My purpose is not only to raise questions, but also to offer alternative ways to look at sports and different ways to understand our attachments to these activities. As with my previous work, I confess that these philosophical reflections are personal, in the sense that I attempt to understand my own lifelong love affair with sport and my dissatisfaction with typical ways of talking about and understanding sports found in our commercial culture. There is more to sport than is suggested by the ethos that seems to be the common denominator expressed on sports-talk radio, on ESPN, and in other popular media outlets. There is more to sports than winning, competition, and money. We need alternative vocabularies in order to understand ourselves as well as our involvements. In stressing my existential connection to these issues, I also assume that my own experiences as a player, coach, and fan (and university professor) have not been wholly idiosyncratic. For example, it may be unusual yet illuminating to attempt to develop attitudes toward sport that involve patterns of desire adaptation described in non-Western approaches to life, or to understand part of the attractiveness of sport by using the category of meaning rather than the usual suspects.

Some might complain that in some cases my discussion displaces sport as the central topic and uses it merely as an occasion to raise questions about traditional philosophical issues (the meaning of life) or topics that are larger than sport-specific issues (the ethics of speech). I do not see the alternatives as mutually exclusive. In much of the book sport is the central object of philosophical reflection. In some cases sport is used to occasion reflection on traditional philosophical issues, yet the ultimate goal is to illuminate sport, albeit in a somewhat more indirect way and in a manner that has implications for life outside sport. The chapter on sport and the question of the meaning of life requires an extended discussion of the types of answers that have been given by philosophers. Although the topic of sport may seem to be largely absent in that chapter (ignoring the introductory remarks and sport-related counterexamples), the point is to provide the philosophical background for an account of sport found in the final chapter. There, I suggest that sport is a significant "space of meaning" in life.

I direct my book toward a diverse audience. Perhaps scholars will find in this book something worthy to consider, and both undergraduates and graduate students might find interesting topics here. I would be disappointed, however, if the book proved to be less than accessible to a broader, literate audience. The Barnes and Noble crowd will find the writing clear, and some of my examples from contemporary sports will be familiar. They may have to work in places to follow my arguments, but there is nothing particularly esoteric in any of my discussions. If you play or have played or coached these games, or if you find yourself often watching, listening to, or reading about these activities, I suspect you will find something of interest here, or at least something to think about and even contest. All of us, including sports geeks, are philosophers.

# Part One.
## Sport and Good Lives

# 1 A Pluralist Conception of Play

The philosophical and scientific literature on play is extensive, and the approaches to the study, description, and explanation of play are diverse. In this chapter I intend to provide an overview of approaches to play. My interest is in describing the most fundamental categories in terms of which play is characterized, explained, and evaluated. Insofar as these categories attempt to describe what kind of reality we are talking about when we make claims about play, I hope to clarify the metaphysics of play. Once this categorical scheme is made clear, we will be in a better position to evaluate the task of definition, claims about the relation of sport and play, and assertions about the significance of play. First, I place the discussion in the context of Bernard Suits's account of play and some other recent approaches to play. Next, I distinguish the following approaches to play: play as behavior or action; play as motive, attitude, or state of mind; play as form or structure; play as meaningful experience; play as an ontologically distinctive phenomenon. There is a natural progression in the way the analysis unfolds. In the final section I argue that my analysis generates a pluralist, nonreductive account of play.

## 1. The Question of Play

It may appear that there is very little new under the sun for a philosopher to say about play. This is in striking contrast to the growing science of play. In various scientific fields there are lively and ongoing debates about the evolutionary and neuroscientific bases of play, occasioning numerous research programs and new theories about what is going on when animals and children, especially, engage in playful behavior. Scientists seem not to be as worried about the kinds of questions that worry philosophers, yet such questions cannot be ignored, except by stipulation. What *is* play? Can it be defined? How is it recognized? Is it good? Why is it good? How is play related to other significant cultural activities, like art or religion? What is the relation between sport and play? How does play contribute to a good life?

I have been impressed recently by the differences between more simplified accounts of play and the enormous diversity of play phenomena that are mentioned and studied outside of philosophy of sport by scholars in various fields. Whereas some philosophical discussions have focused on the canonical texts written by Johan Huizinga and Roger Caillois,[1] and have generated relatively broad notions of play involving a variety of characteristics, others have been suspicious of the supposed scope of play. Yet when some scientifically informed scholars have been forced to offer a definition or a philosophical account of play, they inevitably turn to Huizinga and offer at least a variation on a theme described in *Homo Ludens*. Bernard Suits, eminent philosopher of sport and "*paidiatrician*," has produced an account of play that some philosophical scholars of sport have largely taken for granted. His "words on play" have been taken to be the final words, so to speak. It is against the background of his provocative early essay on play (as well as some later comments) that I wish to rethink some issues concerning the unity and diversity of play, its relation to sport, and its value.[2]

In his essay "Words on Play," Suits combines his interest in pursuing the traditional philosophical task of definition with his suspicion about claims concerning the scope of play phenomena. Why look for a definition of play? Why attempt to overcome Wittgensteinian objections to such a task? Suits responds: "chiefly because a definition is a kind of restriction or limitation, and I believe that, ever since Huizinga began to find play under nearly every rock in the social landscape, quite a bit too much has been made of the notion."[3]

Early on Suits offers three claims that are particularly relevant for this discussion. First, he agrees with the common view that play involves activities that are ends in themselves or desired for their own sake. All play is autotelic, as opposed to instrumental. Autotelicity is a necessary condition of play, but he denies that all autotelic activities are instances of play. "In other words, I regard autotelicity as necessary but not sufficient for an adequate definition of play." Next, he denies that there is a logical relation between playing and playing games. Despite the fact that we speak of "playing" games, he considers such usages to indicate merely that we are participating in a game; we may or may not be playing. For example, when we speak of playing a musical instrument, we are indicating performance, not necessarily play. Sometimes game playing is playing, but it may not be, because of the autotelicity requirement. This leads Suits to say the following (which many take to be obvious—I don't): "That one has to be playing in order to be playing a game seems equally implausible. When professional athletes are performing in assigned games for wages, although they are certainly playing games, we are not at all inclined to conclude from that fact that they are without qualification playing. For we think of professional athletes as working when they play their games and as playing when they go home from work to romp with their children." Third, Suits recognizes that his account of play (which I will mention in a moment) is at odds with a variety of common usages, yet he insists that such figurative or metaphorical usages are nonetheless valuable. If we combine an account that places a boundary on the concept of play and an awareness of the vast array of ordinary usages of the word, we identify a helpful avenue of inquiry, "since an explanation of *how* they are figurative requires a sorting out of the respects in which the thing at issue is, and the respects in which it is not, play or a game."[4]

For Suits the sorting is relatively simple, because we merely have to relate autotelicity (a genus) to the way we use resources in certain activities (a specific difference). For example, little Johnny is rebuked for playing with his food, a resource normally used for nutrition. Here is Suits's definition of play: "X is playing if and only if x has made a temporary reallocation to autotelic activities of resources primarily committed to instrumental activities."[5] According to Suits, when we temporarily reallocate *any* resource to intrinsically valued activities, including time or energy, we are playing.

For now, let's turn from Suits's words on play to some other recent words, written by, respectively, Colin McGinn, a very fine philosopher; Diane Ackerman, a very fine essayist and poet; and Stuart Brown, a very fine (I presume) medical doctor, psychiatrist, and clinical researcher. First is a comment from McGinn, in a book about sport and a discussion of his attempt to improve his tennis game:

> Certainly, tennis, like other sports, is a form of play. . . . Play is a vital part of any full life, and a person who never plays is worse than a "dull boy": he or she lacks imagination, humour and a proper sense of value. Only the bleakest and most life-denying Puritanism could warrant deleting all play from human life. . . . Play is part of what makes human life worthwhile, and we should seek to get as much out of it as we can.[6]

In a beautiful book-length meditation on "deep play," the most deeply absorbing and "ecstatic" form of play, Diane Ackerman writes:

> The spirit of deep play is central to the life of each person, and also to society, inspiring the visual, musical, and verbal arts; exploration and

discovery; war; law; and other elements of culture we've come to cherish (or dread). . . .

This book is not a conclusion but an exploration. It invites you to look closely at the human saga, and consider how much of it revolves around play. . . . Indeed, it's our passion for deep play that makes us the puzzling and at times resplendent beings we are.[7]

Finally, Stuart Brown, founder of the National Institute on Play, expresses thoughts based on forty years of conducting play studies and taking more than six thousand "play histories" of all kinds of people:

I have found that remembering what play is all about and making it part of our daily lives are probably the most important factors in being a fulfilled human being. . . .

I don't think it is too much to say that play can save your life. It certainly has salvaged mine. Life without play is a grinding, mechanical existence organized around doing things necessary for survival. Play is the stick that stirs the drink. It is the basis of all art, games, books, sports, movies, fashion, fun, and wonder—in short, the basis of what we think of as civilization. Play is the vital essence of life. It is what makes life lively. . . .

The world needs play because it enables each person to live a good life.[8]

The contrast between Suits's attitude and approach and these enthusiastic claims about the value of play is noteworthy. When Suits considers play, he thinks there is much less there than meets the eye. He offers a tidy conceptual analysis that attempts to deflate the Huizingian notion that there is "play under nearly every rock in the social landscape." On the other hand, these contemporary playologists (if I may coin a term) do see the pervasive influence and importance of play in human life. Huizinga was right, they tell us. Play is under a lot of rocks. Diane Ackerman makes the influence of Huizinga explicit: "From time to time, this book becomes a fantasia on a theme by Huizinga, in which I play with some of his ideas, amplify them, follow their shadows and nuances." Brown gets no further than chapter 2 before he brings his own "foundational definition" into relation with Huizinga's famous discussion. Although McGinn does not explicitly mention Huizinga, his comments about entering a magical world with its own rules and goals, play and seriousness, freedom, and ridding ourselves of ordinary existence are well-known elements in Huizinga's analysis.[9] One problem with Suits's approach is this: Should we accept his definition, we would have no idea, based on his account, why so much has been made of making a "temporary reallocation to autotelic activities of resources primarily committed to instrumental activities." We are left in the dark about the common forms and experiences of activities that typically involve such reallocation and why our neo-Huizingians value it so highly.

Now contrast Suits's definition with Huizinga's frequently cited words on play summarizing his account. (This will be a useful reference for the following discussion.)

> Summing up the formal characteristics of play we might call it a free activity standing quite consciously outside "ordinary" life as being "not serious," but at the same time absorbing the player intensely and utterly. It is an activity connected with no material interest, and no profit can be gained by it. It proceeds within its own proper boundaries of time and space according to fixed rules and in an orderly manner. It promotes the formation of social groupings which tend to surround themselves with secrecy and to stress their difference from the common world by disguise or other means.
>
> . . . Play is a voluntary activity or occupation executed within certain fixed limits of time and place, according to rules freely accepted but absolutely binding, having its aim in itself and accompanied by a feeling of tension, joy and the consciousness that it is "different" from "ordinary life."[10]

It is evident from this brief overview of claims about play that there are different approaches to the study, description, and evaluation of play. Undoubtedly, there is a startling diversity of phenomena associated with play. A noted scholar of play, Brian Sutton-Smith, refers to the "ambiguity of play" in his important book, but he is most interested in what he calls "the ideological underpinnings of play theories." My focus will be on the attempt to understand the diversity of play phenomena rather than the diversity of play scholarship and what he calls the "rhetorics," or rhetorical underpinnings, of different theories of play.[11]

## II. Approaches to Play

### A. Play as Behavior or Action

Diane Ackerman begins her book by saying, "Everyone understands play." In one sense that is not quite right, because there is considerable controversy about the question of definition. We can, however, wield the concept and recognize paradigm cases of play. That is because play is initially categorized as a kind of behavior. It is something we can see or observe. It has been and continues to be extensively studied by scientists who are interested in both animal and human play. My son picks up our dog's chew toy, and she immediately perks up, exhibits the "play bow," paws outstretched on the floor with her rump raised in the air, and wants the toy to be thrown, after which she sprints to the toy, then coyly brings it back, waiting for it to be tossed again. Chimps exhibit a "play face," analogous to the look of the joyous, smiling faces of children playing at the playground, running, jumping, skipping—spontaneous, improvisational, vigorous, unrestrained. Scientists tell us that play is prominent throughout the animal kingdom, not just in mammals. We are told that "animal play researchers have established specific criteria that define play behavior," and that "most species have 10 to 100 distinct play signals that they use to solicit play or to reassure one another during play-fighting that it's still all just fun."[12] In more primitive forms, play is pure movement and motion, for no apparent reason. When animals are playing in the wild, they are not looking for food or being attentive to threats from the environment. When children are playing, they are not living under the constraints of material needs or desires. They are "just playing," freely and exuberantly. They appear to be enjoying themselves immensely, like the two juvenile grizzly bears in the Alaskan wilderness observed by Stuart Brown and Bob Fagen, an expert on animal play behavior. Brown asks why the bears are playing. Fagen replies, "Because it's fun." Brown says, "No, Bob, I mean from a scientific point of view."[13]

The exchange between the two is interesting because it both separates and connects the notions of animal behavior and human activity, or play as behavior and play as activity. Play behavior in animals is "apparently purposeless," as biologists claim.[14] When animals are playing, they are not, apparently, engaged in any kind of instrumental activity associated with their survival needs. Their play may be "fun," as the animal behavior scientist claims, but there must be something biologically deeper going on. Because of the prevalence of play in animals there is the presumption that there must be some adaptive advantage associated with play behavior. This generates scientific theories about the biological usefulness of "apparently" biologically useless behavior. When pushed, Fagen says, "In a world continuously presenting unique challenges and ambiguity, play prepares these bears for an evolving planet."[15] Other scientists have added to or revised the play-as-preparation hypothesis, arguing that play contributes to neural development (the growth of the cerebellum and the development of the brain's frontal cortex) and more flexible and responsive brains.[16]

When we turn to human play, especially the play of children, we can ask the same sort of questions about such behavior. Play is unproductive, insofar as it is not obviously pursued for the sake of satisfying material needs. It seems as wasteful and superfluous as animal play, a useless squandering of energy. We are animals, of course, so play can be studied from the standpoint of understanding the paradox of behavior that is both apparently useless yet has some adaptive advantages. But behavior may now be thought of as action, which humans may explicitly and self-consciously choose to engage in at least at some point in development. It is still pre-conscious and preverbal in certain contexts and to a certain developmental stage, as Brown says,[17] and extremely varied, but now it may be approached in terms of its unique phenomenology, which is described as extending from children to adults. The concept of "apparent purposelessness" in animal behavior leaves open the issue of play's biological usefulness and allows the scientist to speculate about animal psychology. The bears certainly *appeared* to be having fun. For human play, the concept of "apparent purposelessness" leads naturally to the issue of what it means to choose an action for its own sake, or what it means to desire an activity as an end rather than as a means to some further end. It leads inevitably to considering psychological elements that are involved in playing, that is, engaging in intrinsically valued activities.

B. *Play as Motive, Attitude, or State of Mind*
For some philosophers of sport, like Bernard Suits (as we have seen) and Klaus Meier, it is a bit of a truism to say that play essentially involves an attitudinal component. The key to play is autotelicity, engaging in activities for their own sake or as ends in themselves. This involves the question of the de facto motives, reasons, or purposes involved when activities are undertaken. According to Suits, play requires that an activity is valued for itself. Meier holds that "autotelicity is both a necessary and sufficient trait" for play. As he says, "I wish to provide a definition based on the orientation, demeanor, or stance of the participants." Play requires intrinsic reasons, and if our reason (exclusive? predominant?) for doing whatever we choose to do is intrinsic to the activity, it is play. "Consequently, if games or sports are pursued voluntarily and for intrinsic reasons, they are play forms; if they are pursued involuntarily or engaged in predominantly for extrinsic rewards, they are not play forms."[18] Angela Schneider echoes these views when she claims that judging an activity to be play "is determined not by the nature

of the activity itself . . . but rather by the attitude of the player toward the activity." As she says, "Playing is not a type of activity, but rather a mode of performing any activity."[19] These comments distinguish play as an attitude (or having an essential attitudinal component), and classifying an activity as play depends on the context within which it is performed in specific circumstances, rather than its structure.

This way of approaching play raises the issue of the relation between claims about play as an activity and play as attitudinal. Stuart Brown describes cases of golfers he has seen playing Pebble Beach who, instead of enjoying the experience of playing one of the most famous and spectacular golf courses in the world, transform what should be a highlight of their golfing experiences into misery and unhappiness. Brown denies that they are playing. "They are self-critical, competitive, perfectionistic, and preoccupied with the last double bogey. These emotions don't allow them to feel the playful, out-of-time, in-the-zone, doing-it-for-its-own-sake sensation that accompanies joyful playfulness." From our tennis matches to our pickup basketball games, most of us have encountered the tortured player whose misery and unhappiness infect all those with whom he is playing. This leads Brown to say the following: "Sometimes running is play, and sometimes it is not. What is the difference between the two? It really depends on the emotions experienced by the runner. Play is a *state of mind*, rather than an activity."[20]

This emphasis on the attitudinal component of play may be misleading. It may lead to a confusion between an activity and an attitude. To say that play "is a state of mind," as Brown does, does not really make sense if we interpret the claim literally. Play is an activity that may or may not require a certain kind of attitude, but the attitude is not the activity itself. Would it make sense to say that we are playing when in fact we are doing nothing, perhaps paralyzed in a drug-induced but affirmative haze of consciousness, glad to be experiencing paralysis for its own sake? (Assume no "play of ideas" going on in the mind of person.) If a person were hooked up to an experience machine (in Robert Nozick's famous thought experiment), electrodes attached to his brain, giving him mental states ("experiences") while he is floating like a blob in a tank, it would make no sense to say that the person could be playing. (Let's say he is being fed the joyful experience of winning the U.S. Open in golf.) It would make more sense to say that the person has playful attitudes, or the "state of mind" associated with play. The miserable golfers are doing something—they are playing golf, unhappily and without any joy. Better to say, as Suits, Meier, and Schneider do, that play is an activity that requires a certain kind of attitude, or is defined in terms of the attitude we take toward the activity, that is, an activity engaged in as an end in itself or for intrinsic reasons.

Despite the fact that many philosophers of sport take this position to be obvious, some puzzling questions arise. If autotelicity is sufficient for play, as Meier insists, does this mean that we could, in principle, transform *any* activity into play? Would Sisyphus's interminable rock rolling be magically transformed into play if the gods injected a magic potion into his veins that caused him to identify with his pointless toil? How about an apolitical functionary who spends his free time volunteering at Auschwitz, enjoying the unpaid activity of marching the Jews to the gas chambers? Fun? Is he playing? We may say that these activities are play for these persons, but, at the least, it strikes us that these are not the *kind* of activities that are either commonly or even appropriately categorized as play, as they would have to be if autotelicity were sufficient for play. This raises the question of whether certain kinds of formal requirements might be, if not necessary, at least typical and causally relevant for appropriateness. It would be helpful to be able to say more about the form or structure of activities for which it would be appropriate to have intrinsic reasons to perform them. Recall Colin McGinn's comment that tennis, like other sports, is a form of play. If I understand his claim, he holds that tennis, as such, is play, or sports, as such, are play activities. Suits finds these claims to be ridiculous. He says, "I have never—anywhere—made, or even entertained, the ridiculous assertions that some games or sports *as such* are play or that some *as such* are not."[21] It is not clear to me why it is ridiculous to assert that play activities may have formal or structural requirements. It is also unclear what sort of argument is offered for the view that autotelicity is necessary and sufficient for play, other than the claim that it is just obvious in paradigm cases. If the argument is ultimately a phenomenological one, the phenomena require a more nuanced and thicker description.

This line of argument leads to questions about mixed motives. Suits also seems to think it is obvious that when professional athletes are playing games, they are not really engaged in play because they are being paid. They are working, not playing. As we will see, they are engaged in activities that have a certain structure, but if play requires autotelicity, professional game playing is instrumental, not autotelic. Furthermore, Suits offers the provocative thesis that Olympic athletes, "amateurs" in some sense, are not playing when participating in Olympic events, because they are acting under a compulsion to win the gold medal rather than being motivated to engage in their Olympic athletic activities simply for the sake of participation. Pickup games are autotelic; highly competitive Olympic events are not. Suits says, "I am suggesting that acting under such a compulsion, rather than the desire to win simply because winning defines the activity one is undertaking, is what turns a game that could be play into something that is not play."[22]

The problem is that when we engage in certain activities, we may have a variety of motives. Even if autotelicity is necessary for play, it is not clear why an activity that has some external end could not also be desired for its own sake. Suppose I love to throw a rubber ball against a wall and catch it with my bare hands. I then develop some rules. I throw at certain angles, at certain spots, with certain velocities, and I see if I can catch the ball before it bounces a specified number of times within a defined space. I establish a point system. I love playing wall ball! I tell my good friend how much fun I have playing wall ball, and he joins me. We develop our skills, play tense and competitive games, and deeply enjoy our encounters. Our friends hear about wall ball and want to watch, but we decide to make them pay for the pleasure of being spectators. Now we are professional wall ballers! We are admired. We establish a league. More people want to watch . . . According to Suits and many others, it makes no sense to ask whether wall ball, as such, is a playful activity, since it depends on participants' attitudes. Was wall ball transformed into "work" as soon as I was paid? Suppose that I was extremely happy to be paid for playing wall ball, grateful that I could play my game for money, and hopeful that I could continue to play and that I never lost my love for the game. In fact, my attitudes could be quite complex. My desires could be characterized as conditional or hypothetical. I am happy to be paid for playing wall ball, but I would play even if I did not get paid.

Consider another example, somewhat closer to home. My job is to teach and engage in philosophy. As an undergraduate I received no compensation for this. As a graduate student I received a stipend to study and teach. At one point philosophy became my job, my work, yet *doing* philosophy is, in an important sense, something I do for the immense satisfaction it gives me. It is valued as an end, despite the fact that the activity can also be characterized instrumentally. It is something I would continue to do whether or not I am paid to do it. My motives are mixed; my attitudes are complex.[23]

Play is attitudinally more complex than Suits and others seem to think. Consider another aspect of this complexity. Wall ball, like other games, is strictly conventional. It is made-up. Its rules are imaginative constructions that are the conditions for a certain kind of activity to occur, that is, conditions for playing wall ball. It is not work, art, science, religion, poetry, war, or anything else. As Huizinga says, "It's not 'ordinary' or 'real' life. It is rather a stepping out of 'real' life into a temporary sphere of activity with a disposition all of its own." He is talking about play. I am talking about wall ball as a form of play. Huizinga continues by giving the example of the young child playing "trains," pretending that chairs are something else than "real life," and urging Daddy to act accordingly. He says, "This 'only pretending' quality of play betrays a consciousness of the inferiority of play compared with 'seriousness,' a feeling that seems to be something as primary as play itself." Here I would speak of a distinctive attitude toward playful activities. They are not "serious," yet they can be wholly absorbing and engaged in quite seriously. I have called such an attitude "serious nonseriousness."[24] Even professional athletes are sometimes pushed in times of crisis to admit the "nonserious" character of their activity. A young Major League Baseball pitcher is killed in a car crash. One of his teammates sadly comments, "This is real life, not baseball." The attitude taken by the professional baseball player is essentially related to the form or structure of the activity, as if such an attitude is appropriate because baseball, as such, is not "real life." Play is structurally nonserious.

One other element of attitudinal complexity is important. When the scientist is asked why the bears play, he says, "Because it's fun." We may not be sure about bear phenomenology, but when we consider the play of children and adults, when we think of our youthful and grown-up play, it is natural to speak of fun, joy, enjoyment, or satisfaction. Brown says his miserable golfers did not feel the "playful, out-of-time, in-the-zone, doing-it-for-its-own-sake *sensation* [emphasis added] that accompanies joyful playfulness." The pleasure of play, however, is not like the pleasure of sensations in which we take delight—the pleasurable sounds, tastes, smells, and feel of ordinary experiences, such as the pleasurable sensation of orgasm. Fred Feldman's recent defense of hedonism makes explicit what has been implicit in important historical accounts of the value and kinds of pleasure, including Epicurus's account of the good life. Feldman distinguishes sensory pleasure and attitudinal pleasure. Sensory pleasures are feelings, that is, pleasurable sensations. Attitudinal pleasures need not be felt. "A person takes attitudinal pleasure in some state of affairs if he enjoys it, is pleased by it, is glad that it is happening, is delighted by it." Feldman gives the example of a person being pleased by the fact that there are no wars going on in the world. I may be pleased by Barack Obama's being elected president, or I may enjoy the company of a good friend. Attitudinal pleasures are intentional, and they need not have the "feel" of sensations. "We know we have them not by sensation, but in the same way (whatever it may be) that we know when we believe something, or hope for it, or fear that it might happen."[25] (These are propositional attitudes.)

For many, sport is a rich source of attitudinal pleasure. It was for me. It is also clear that there is a close relationship between enjoying an activity and desiring to engage in it for its own sake. If we add that certain kinds of activities are such that their form or structure occasions an attitudinal recognition of being set apart from "real life," then we have arrived at a more complex attitudinal account of play, whose elements may have an equal claim in locating or categorizing an activity as play. Why shouldn't we take the attitudinal recognition of the conventional nature of certain kinds of activities as sufficient for play? But now more needs to be said about the formal or structural elements in play activities. Whatever other motives or attitudes a person might have, if an activity is enjoyed, attitudinally recognized as not "real life," and intrinsically attractive, regardless of other motives, then there are good reasons to categorize it as play—independent of whether a person is also being paid to perform the activity.

*c. Play as Form or Structure*

The emphasis on form or structure redirects our attention to features of the activity itself rather than the subjectivity of the player. It also makes way for an approach that emphasizes relational elements or the interplay between subjectivity and features of the activity. The emphasis on form or structure—here, lack of form or structure—first appeared in the description of animal behavior and children's play as improvisational and spontaneous rather than mechanical and determined. Suits distinguishes primitive play—the baby splashing water in the bathtub—and sophisticated play, which involves rules and the development of skills. Kenneth Schmitz categorizes play in terms of a continuum from the least formal to the most formal types: frolic, make-believe, sporting skills, and games. Play need not be formal, but it often is. It is especially the gamelike elements of formal play that are relevant when considering whether it is reasonable to claim that sports or games as such are play—despite the fact that Suits and others may believe such assertions are "ridiculous." This is because it is plausible to claim, as Suits does, that "the elements of sport are essentially—although perhaps not totally—the same as elements of game."[26]

Suits's insightful and familiar account of the elements of playing games provides the basis for an emphasis on play as activity having a certain form or structure and the claim that sport as such is activity having this structure. First, games are means-ends activities; they have a structure in which means are related to ends in a specified manner. There are goals that may be described independently of the respective games, like a golf ball coming to rest in a cup, a basketball going through a hoop, a soccer ball entering a netted goal, or a football being carried beyond a certain point. But these goals may be brought about in a variety of ways. I may place the golf ball in the cup with my hand, climb a ladder to put the basketball through a hoop, and so forth. Games are developed when means are limited by specific rules that prescribe and proscribe the ways in which goals may be brought about, transforming prelusory goals (pregame goals) into lusory ends (ends intrinsic to the game), one of which is to win the game by achieving certain lusory goals. Since the means specified by the rules always rule out the most efficient way to achieve a prelusory goal, games are quite unlike real life, in which efficiency is often the hallmark of rationality. Hence, because of their structure, games do require an attitude that allows for the injection of gratuitous difficulty into life simply for the sake of the occurrence of the activity itself. Suits summarizes the elements of playing games in the following definition: "To play a game is to attempt to achieve a specific state of affairs (*pre-lusory goal*), using only means permitted by rules (*lusory means*), where the rules prohibit use of more efficient in favor of less efficient means (*constitutive rules*), and where such rules are accepted just because they make possible such activity (lusory attitude). I also offer the following only approximately accurate, but more pithy, version of the above definition: Playing a game is the voluntary attempt to overcome unnecessary obstacles."[27]

To say, as Huizinga does, that play is not "ordinary" or "real life," or to claim, as Roger Caillois does, that play is both "separate" and "unproductive," is to acknowledge a formal or structural feature of play.[28] Formal play, by its very nature, is not instrumental, in the sense in which instrumentality is understood in everyday life. To say that play is "superfluous," as Huizinga does, or to claim that playing games involves gratuitous difficulty or the overcoming of unnecessary obstacles, affirms the difference between a world of play, with its own meanings—its own requirements and delimitations of space or time—and ordinary life. To say that games are not "serious" is to equivocate, unless it is clear that nonseriousness may be a claim about either the structure of the activity or the attitude of the player. Caillois says, "The confused and intricate laws of ordinary life are replaced in this fixed space and for this given time, by precise, arbitrary, unexceptionable rules that must be accepted as such and that govern the correct playing of the game."[29] When the professional baseball player speaks of death as a part of "real life" compared to baseball (not "real life"), he is recognizing the difference between ordinary means-ends activities in life and the structure of formal play, that is, the playing of games. Some play is improvisational and joyous; other forms of play express our attraction to gratuitous difficulty and the value we place on overcoming obstacles, even unnecessary ones. And many complex forms of play may well involve both: bursts of speed, creative physical movements, and spontaneity within the limits of the rules of the game or activity.[30]

Suits ends one of his influential essays on sport, play, and game by referring to a *New Yorker* cartoon in which an angry golfer is saying something to his partner: "The caption reads, 'Stop saying it's just a game! Goddamit, it's *not* just a game!' And he is quite right. For him, golf is not play, and so it is not, therefore *just* a game."[31] I would say that Suits's comment misleadingly reduces play to activity defined merely in terms of an attitude, ignores the formal aspects of the game of golf that are relevant in determining its character as play, and diminishes the experiential complexity of the activity, which may also be relevant in our judgments about play. For me, the cartoon suggests that the golfer has a rather shallow appreciation of the playful possibilities that are available in the experience of playing golf—at least in this particular example. How are such possibilities described?

### D. *Play as Meaningful Experience*

When we conceive of play as a certain kind of attitude that can be intentionally directed toward any kind of activity (object), or we think of play activity itself as having a certain form or structure, it is as if we are focusing on two poles or aspects of experience that are importantly related or whose interplay constitutes a richer account of play phenomena. For many descriptions of the features of play it is less misleading to speak of the lived experience of the player interacting with her environment or becoming experientially involved with something other than herself. When different aspects of play experience are described, at least some of these features are at the same time both formal elements of the activity and psychological features of the agent. To say that play is "uncertain," as Caillois does, describes both the course of undetermined events and the experience of the tension of not knowing what will happen or who will win. For these approaches, a dualism that abstractly separates subject and object is phenomenologically inadequate, although some features may seem to focus more on one aspect of playful involvement than another. In the following, I will mention various characteristics of play without taking the time to offer an extended analysis of each feature—which would require considerable space. My procedure illustrates the difference between a focus on attitude or state of mind, which subjectivizes play, and experiential properties that are occasioned by involvements that require an account of that with which one is involved or which cannot be reduced simply to states of mind. After mentioning various characteristics, I will refer to some lists of properties, including Huizinga's (as we have seen) and Caillois's, to make the discussion more manageable.

First, here are some features of play that have been emphasized and analyzed in the expansive literature on the subject: play is activity characterized by freedom, separateness, nonseriousness, illusion, unreality, delimitation of space and time, isolation, purposelessness, order, make-believe, a play world, superfluousness, suspension of the ordinary, internal or intrinsic meaning, inherent attraction, unalienated participation, internal purposiveness, serious nonseriousness, diminished consciousness of self, unselfing, absorption, responsive openness, attunement, experience of difficulty, overcoming obstacles, risk taking, finitude, narrative structure, unity, contingency, possibility, uncertainty, spontaneity, improvisation—and fun. I am sure I have not exhausted the possibilities!

Recall Huizinga's summary definition in which each part is significant and analyzed at some length. Huizinga insists that all "play means something," and later states, "We shall try to take play as the player himself takes it: in its primary significance." When we attend to the experience of play, parsimonious descriptions are impossible because of the experiential richness of these activities. The freedom of play is both attitudinal, in which a player deeply enjoys engaging in such activities, and experiential, in which involvement with a wholly conventional play world separates a player from the cares of ordinary life. The experience of "secludedness," "isolation," or even "tension" is the experience of structure, and it is attitudinally significant. "Experience" describes the abundant unity of meaningful activity (movement) and valuable intentional attitudes. Likewise, Caillois's list of the essential properties of play is best interpreted as an attempt to describe the essential experiences involved in the playing of games: play is free (not obligatory), separate (limited in space and time), uncertain (outcomes are not determined in advance and are due to players' innovations), unproductive (no new goods are created), governed by rules (conventional suspension of ordinary norms), and make-believe (an awareness of the unreality of the play world).[32]

Although Stuart Brown claims at one point in his interesting recent book that play is a "state of mind," when he initially and tentatively offers a "foundational definition" of play, in large part for heuristic reasons, the properties he mentions richly combine claims about movement, attitude, structure, and experience. Here are the properties he lists, along with a brief description of each:

- apparently purposeless (done for its own sake)
- voluntary ("not obligatory or required by duty")
- inherent attraction ("It's fun. It makes you feel good. . . . It's a cure for boredom.")
- freedom from time ("When we are fully engaged in play, we lose a sense of the passage of time.")
- diminished consciousness of self ("We stop worrying about whether we look good or awkward, smart or stupid. . . . We are fully in the moment, in the zone.")
- improvisational potential ("We aren't locked into a rigid way of doing things. We are open to serendipity, to change. . . . The result is that we stumble upon new behaviors, thoughts, strategies, movements, or ways of being.")
- continuation desire ("We desire to keep doing it, and the pleasure of the experience drives the desire. We find ways to keep it going. . . . And when it is over, we want to do it again.")[33]

Parts of Brown's list of properties are quite familiar after having considered briefly the seminal accounts of play found in Huizinga and Caillois. Some of the properties add additional or even new insights when we consider the experiential richness of play. The absorption described by Huizinga becomes "diminished consciousness of self" as players are fully involved in the activity of cycling, windsurfing, tennis, and the like. Improvisational potential connects the frolic of animals and children to the openness and free play of possibilities in rule-governed play. The category of improvisation describes the phenomenology of movement, a certain kind of kinesthetic freedom. Continuation desire is connected to attitudinal pleasure and the structure of repetition emphasized by Huizinga: "In this faculty of repetition lies one of the most essential qualities of play."[34] Games begin, are played out, even end, only to be repeated by players who want to continue playing, over and over. When Brown speaks of freedom from time, the language is experiential rather than structural. Time is experienced differently because the time internal to the game—due to the way that the game is temporally articulated according to rules—is often quite different from ordinary clock time. Play time starts and stops, speeds up and slows down, extends limitlessly, or is extinguished. Or, when we are absorbed in the activity, "in the moment," we lose our sense of the flow of time even when the activity itself is not articulated in terms of innings, periods, quarters, and so on.

A final approach to play deserves to be mentioned because the notion of play as meaningful experience, which unifies the different approaches to play as activity, attitude, and form, may be a derivative notion, dependent on an ontologically distinctive account of play that makes experiential accounts metaphorical rather than literal.

E. *Play as an Ontologically Distinctive Phenomenon*
In *Truth and Method*, Hans-Georg Gadamer is not primarily interested in the concept of play. He is centrally concerned with the

question of truth and understanding in the human sciences. He attempts to give an account of hermeneutical consciousness that describes the proper role of the historicity of existence in human understanding. Gadamer's discussion of play is merely a moment in his attempt to provide an analysis of aesthetic experience, an analysis that itself is a part of his monumental account of an experience of truth that cannot be reduced to scientific methods of understanding. Gadamer says, "The experience of the work of art includes understanding, and thus represents a hermeneutical phenomenon—but not at all in the sense of a scientific method."[35] His account of play is, however, significant.

Gadamer claims that play has its own mode of being and that play cannot be explained simply in terms of the subjectivity of the player. "Play has its own essence, independent of the consciousness of those who play." Gadamer argues that play is analogous to the way in which a work of art is fulfilled in the aesthetic experience of a spectator and is the real "subject" of the experience. Play requires a player with a certain attitude in order to come into being, but play is not reducible to the player's attitude; "play merely reaches presentation (Darstellung) through the players." For Gadamer, when we attend to apparently metaphorical usages of "play," when we speak of the play of light, waves, or natural forces, "what is intended is to-and-fro movement that is not tied to any goal which would bring it to an end." It is a mistake to think that these usages are figurative whereas our references to human or animal play are literal. The subject of play is play itself, not the subjectivity of the player. "Play clearly represents an order in which the to-and-fro movement of play follows of itself. It is part of play that the movement is not only without goal or purpose, but also without effort." The experience of freedom from the strains of ordinary life is the result of play playing itself through the player. "The structure of play absorbs the player into itself, and thus frees him from the burden of taking the initiative, which constitutes the actual strain of existence." For Gadamer, the mode of being of play is a "pure self-representation." Nature, in its unceasing, purposeless movement, renewing itself in "constant repetition," also exemplifies the being of mobility as self-representation. "Thus in this sphere it becomes finally meaningless to distinguish between literal and metaphorical usage."[36]

If Gadamer's approach seems unduly opaque and metaphysically obscure, consider the claim that his approach to play helps clarify the "playful character of the contest." For those who deny that contests or competitive games can be play, he reminds us that "through the contest arises the tense to-and-fro movement from which the victor emerges, and thus the whole becomes a game."[37] Gadamer's ontological approach clarifies the ordinary view that players (or spectators, for that matter) can develop a love or respect for "the game" as an independent phenomenon that is, in a sense, larger than the players, just as aesthetic appreciation or aesthetic experience recognizes the autonomy of a work of art standing over against the aesthetic consciousness as a demanding and authoritative presence.[38] The game or the work of art constitutes a reality in itself. "In cases where human subjectivity is what is playing, the primacy of the game over the players engaged in it is experienced by the players themselves in a special way." Gadamer's comment reflects the development of our discussion of the metaphysics of play, in which the subjective approach to play is corrected by references to form or structure. Gadamer's remarks ring true, both phenomenologically and ontologically, when he comments that the "attraction of a game, the fascination it exerts, consists precisely in the fact that the game masters the players." The player gives herself over to the game, or, if there is some dispute about speaking of a "game" in terms of the development of certain sporting skills, the player is taken up by her enjoyable experience of confronting gratuitous difficulties (or unnecessary obstacles). When the game is played, the "real subject of the game . . . is not the player, but instead the game itself. What holds the player in its spell, draws him into play, and keeps him there is the game itself." Attitudes are intentionally related to the nature of the task required for playing the game. "One can say that performing a task successfully 'presents it' (stellt sie dar)." Hence, we again arrive at the notion that playing games (or overcoming unnecessary obstacles), insofar as they are purposeless, that is, ends in themselves, shows that "play is really limited to presenting itself. Thus its mode of being is self-presentation."[39]

Gadamer summarizes his approach to play: "We have seen that play does not have its being in the player's consciousness or attitude, but on the contrary play draws him into its dominion and fills him with its spirit. The player experiences the game as a reality that surpasses him." Gadamer affirms the supposedly "ridiculous" notion that sport, as such, conceived broadly as game playing (in Suits's own sense), is play, ontologically interpreted as presenting itself in the tasks defined by the "make-believe goals of the game," in Gadamer's words.[40] Gadamer's account of play returns us to the first approach or moment in our discussion, when play is taken to be behavior or action, some observable natural phenomenon characterized, much as Gadamer describes, as spontaneous and purposeless "to-and-fro movement." The scientist then explains the phenomena biologically or in terms of neural development, the social scientist or humanist explains it in human terms, and we are led, dialectically, down a path that leads to Gadamer's interpretation of the original phenomena, in which play is "decentered" and taken to be ontologically distinctive, manifested in and through natural events, animals, children, and adults.[41]

Now we are in a position to bring these approaches together in order to offer some conclusions about the nature of play, its relation to sport, and its value and role in a good human life.

### iii. Play, Pluralism, and Good Lives

We began our discussion by attending to some of Bernard Suits's "words on play." Suits, always playfully provocative, voiced suspicions about attempts "to find play under nearly every rock in the social landscape," expressed doubts about those who make so much of the notion, offered his own attempt to place strict boundaries on the concept, and acknowledged that figurative uses of the word *play* force us to explain the relevant similarities and differences involved when we speak of the "play of light," the "playful dog," "child's play," "playing a game," and "playing professional sports." The upshot of our examination of approaches to play is evident. It is no wonder that play is found under nearly every rock in the social landscape, given the multiplicity of possible approaches and the legitimacy of each to tell us something important, even if incomplete, about the concept of play. Each approach picks out relevant properties generated by taking a certain descriptive or explanatory perspective on play phenomena. Each may claim to be a total account of play only by ignoring the legitimacy of other perspectives. Because of the plurality of the ways we can approach play, each should be taken to be a significant contribution to a nonreductive account of play.

The new prophets of play, Brown, Ackerman, and others, attempt to rouse us out of the doldrums of ordinary existence by awakening (or reawakening) in us moments of joy, exuberance, creativity, spontaneity, freedom, optimism, and fun—often associated with activities that are usually a part of early life but somehow get lost along the way. In attempting to enliven us to the possibilities of playful experience, they connect play to a notion of a good human life. Recall the initial comments by McGinn, Brown, and Ackerman. McGinn's comments on play are secondary; they arise in an intellectual memoir that is robust and confessional about the role of sports and games in his life, from childhood and adolescence through adulthood: marbles, trampolining, diving, pole vaulting, table tennis, bowling, pinball, fishing, squash, running, video games, lifting weights, skiing, kayaking, windsurfing, and tennis! Of course sport is play, he tells us. Brown and Ackerman are most interested in play, not sport, yet both assume in some of their comments that sporting activities are playful activities. Sport should be placed in the context of play and living well—joyously, freely, creatively. They call us to the possible enchantment of moments of our lives, when we are captivated by the absorbing activities that enable us to transcend everyday life, to "suspend the ordinary," as Kenneth Schmitz described the "essence" of play.[42]

So, is sport an expression of play? Should we understand sport in terms of the concept of play? As far as I can tell, there are two primary reasons given for resisting the relationship, one of which we have already examined. Both avenues of criticism claim that sport may be infected by desires that are incompatible with play. Many claim, as Suits does, that play for pay is not really play, that professional sport is instrumental rather than autotelic. As we have seen, this view falls prey to the problem of mixed motives and involves the reduction of play to attitudinal considerations, ignoring the relevance of other properties, both structural and experiential. Activities may be characterized in complex ways, and the rejection of professional sport as play on attitudinal grounds hides the ways in which such activities have playlike properties. Moreover, even if Suits and others are right about the dissociation of professional sport and play, in numerous instances in which people play sports, the activities embody many properties that are associated with play: freedom, separateness, absorption, purposelessness, and so on.

The other avenue of criticism stresses the role of the desire to win in sports, rather than the extent to which sporting activities may be infected by elements that make sports one's work or profession. Suits also argues that the compulsion to win, even for supposed amateurs like Olympic athletes, is incompatible with the notion that play must be engaged in as an end in itself. The stronger version of this criticism comes from Alfie Kohn, who insists that *any* desire to win, not simply an overarching compulsion, disqualifies an activity from being play. For Kohn, play and competition are incompatible. Since sport, by its very nature, involves competition, sport and play are incompatible. Because play involves the familiar idea of choosing an activity for its own sake, play can have "no goal other than itself." Competition is rule governed, often extrinsically motivated (by the desire for social approval), and goal oriented (a product orientation), rather than being a "process orientation." Therefore, because sport is competitive, "sports never really qualified as play in the first place. Although it is not generally acknowledged, most definitions of play do seem to exclude competitive activities."[43]

Kohn is undoubtedly correct to emphasize the dangers of competition, and the metaphor he uses is apt: "Clearly competition and play tug in two different directions. If you are trying to win, you are not engaged in true play."[44] Yet there is more insight in his view when he resorts to metaphor than when he engages in essentialist pronouncements. There is no essence of play. If we recognize the multiplicity of relevant considerations involved when we attempt to understand play phenomena, we should resist Kohn's view that play can be neither competitive nor rule governed. To say that play cannot be rule governed seems to reduce playful activities to frolic. However, there are more or less formal modes of play that many have pointed out. Rules may be formulated to create noncompetitive games (leapfrog) or games in which there is an internal goal (winning) sought by participants if they intend to engage in the activity. To say that play cannot be "goal oriented" either reduces it to frolic or equivocates on the notion of the "goal" of the activity in question. Certainly, playing a game, attempting to overcome unnecessary obstacles, or freely confronting gratuitous difficulty may be engaged in for the sake of the activity, even if the activity has an internal end that cannot be shared by the victor and the vanquished. Also, overcoming obstacles within the game means that sport, construed as game playing or skills development, is "goal oriented." The process itself has internal products. The process may or may not also have extrinsic motives, but those considerations must be placed along with others that count for or against our judgment about the way to categorize certain activities.

In the end, if we are reminded of the multiple approaches to play and the varieties of usages, both literal and figurative, that are involved when we refer to the concept of play, we are left with a framework within which to sort out relevant similarities and differences when we speak in terms related to play. I do not think that a pluralist account of play leaves things too open-ended, nor do I think that there are no constraints on what we call play. No doubt such an account does leave things more messy than Suits's essentialism suggests, but that is because of the complexity of the phenomena and the nature of the concept of play. Given what we have said about the variety of approaches to play, the fecundity of play phenomena, and the connection between play and a good human life, we should reinforce, whenever it is appropriate, the notion that sport is found in the neighborhood of play. And we should do this in order to encourage the enchanting possibilities of sport, play, and life itself. When we find that sport has strayed from its natural home, we must encourage the wayward child to come back from the world.

# 2 Sport, Vulnerability, and Unhappiness

## 1. Pursuing Happiness

The discussion of sport and play raises larger questions about sport and happiness, about the relation between sporting activities and good lives, and about sport and larger philosophies of life, such as hedonism. As I argued in the previous chapter, engaging in playful sporting activities can be a significant source of attitudinal pleasure. On the other hand, participating in sporting activities may involve failure and loss. Sport may promote unhappiness. Consider another important approach to life in light of the recognition that our happiness is fragile and we need some fundamental way to deal with what life throws at us. The Stoic begins with the notion that human beings are vulnerable and then develops a view of persons and their world to respond to such liabilities, with an eye toward advice about how to live well despite life's seemingly inevitable pitfalls. Some things are within our control; others are not. If we seek to make our happiness depend on things out of our control, on the satisfaction of desires that depend on the contingencies of the world, we will inevitably be dissatisfied—unhappy. The response? We should adapt.[1] Instead of attempting to make the world conform to our desires, we should reshape our internal economy; we should, in particular, remake our judgments and attitudes, and "master our desires," in the words of a contemporary scholar of desire.[2] We should make our desires conform to the world, or to those aspects of reality that we cannot change. Attend to what we can control. We should attempt to be a certain kind of invulnerable human being: a virtuous person, the Stoic sage.

The strategy of adaptation has a long and storied tradition in both Western and non-Western philosophy. It is said that Siddhartha Gautama left the sheltered world of palace life at age twenty-nine and first confronted inevitable and deeply disturbing facts about human existence: sickness, old age, and death. According to the young man who became the Enlightened One, the Buddha, life is characterized by suffering, by some disjointedness essentially related to our natures as creatures of desire, whose cravings and attachments leave us perpetually out of whack. His response? Adapt. Live in such a way that we undermine our cravings and attachments and live more satisfactorily by transforming ourselves psychologically and morally.

In mentioning Stoicism and Buddhism, I am merely gesturing rather loosely to a strategy that may be found in certain forms in other philosophies of life or religions, including Epicureanism, Taoism, Vedanta, and Christianity.[3] I am most interested in the general strategy and how it might be brought into relation with sports participation. It is interesting that passages in certain Stoic texts explicitly mention athletics (or what we would call sport), as if it might be important to show how a Stoic approach to happiness and the good life would apply to a significant aspect of ancient life. Given the importance of sport in modern life, it might be interesting to reflect on sports involvement, in all its forms, against the background of broader concerns about the good life judged from a number of different perspectives.

Let's distinguish two broad strategies used in pursuing happiness. Borrowing language from Steven Luper's valuable study, *Invulnerability: On Securing Happiness*, let's distinguish a strategy called "optimizing" and the adaptive strategy I have just sketched.[4] The

optimizing strategy should be immediately recognizable to the afflu-
ent and needy alike. We are bombarded with images of the "good
life" in which desires for wealth and celebrity are satisfied in the
lives of those lucky people we read about or watch on television.
Why not have it all? We could call them maximizers, satisficers, or
simply "desire satisfiers." Given the desires we have, a good life is
one in which we satisfy as many as we can in an efficient manner.
On the other hand, given the pitfalls of life, adapters are more
impressed by the way the world refuses to give us what we often
value and want and how unhappy we make ourselves by resisting
things over which we have little or no control. Of course, there is
also the issue of whether what we in fact want and value is what
we *should* want if we are pursuing happiness.[5] Here is how Luper
summarizes the different strategies:

> Adapting is quite a change in policy. Optimizing is an effort to trans-
> form the world so much that it gives us what we demand. It involves
> us in an attempt to subdue the world. Adapting, by contrast, would
> have us modify something that may be more tractable: ourselves. The
> idea behind the adapting of desire is to modify ourselves in light of the
> way the world is. In particular, adapting involves modifying our desires.
> Adapters of desire differ from optimizers primarily because adapters
> can drop fundamental goals for various reason [*sic*], such as that the
> goals are unattainable, and add fundamental goals, say because they
> *are* attainable.[6]

One might say, at this point, that I have stacked the deck against
the optimizers. Of course, the world does not always give us what
we want. It would be unwise or stupid not to recognize this fact.
Any reasonably wise approach to life must provide for a way to
respond intelligently to failures, disappointments, bad luck, and
all manner of misfortune. This may be obvious to some, but how
such insight is transferred to practical life is not so obvious. It certainly looks as if many people scramble toward bigger houses, more
expensive cars, more wealth and worldly success, more "hookups,"

social recognition, and fifteen minutes of fame, despite considerable growing empirical research and much anecdotal personal evidence that efficient desire satisfaction, in this sense, does not really
lead to long-term satisfaction or deeper happiness. It merely puts
us on a "hedonic treadmill," which, at some point, we want to get
off.[7] Also, there may be certain kinds of desires that are particularly
susceptible to the possibility of being unsatisfied, so if we seek a
happiness associated with desire satisfaction, or even wise pursuit
of goals, we may be wary of putting ourselves in a position where
we are particularly vulnerable. If we want to achieve happiness, or
at least maximize our opportunity to avoid unhappiness, we might
be wary of pursuing certain kinds of goals, or we may have to think
about them differently. One way the world may prohibit us from
achieving what we want is in situations in which we have competitive desires. These are desires that seek goals that cannot be
achieved or possessed by everyone, like being the best, being better
than, or winning games. As Luper says, "The general policy of ridding ourselves of unsatisfiable desires and adopting achievable goals
can be applied in various specific ways."[8] When we consider sports,
should we be optimizers or adapters? If adaptation is required, what
would an acceptable and wise strategy look like?

## II. Attitudes toward Sport

The previous comments suggest the beginnings of a case against
sports, or at least a hint that there is something essential to sport
that might be the ground for skepticism about its value or its role
in a good human life. Yet such creeping pessimism may seem inappropriate, given the pro attitudes common to so many. What's the
problem? I am most interested in the way that involvement in
sports may require adaptation and the notion that optimism must
be won. First, a brief reminder about basic attitudes.

"So the optimist is the guy who thinks this is the best of all possible worlds, . . . the pessimist is the guy who fears the optimist is
right."[9] Some are glass-half-full people; others are glass-half-empty

sourpusses. In some cases, optimists and pessimists do not disagree about the facts; rather, they respond differently. They take different attitudes toward the facts. Some respond cheerfully; others find reasons for concern. Other things being equal, it is better to be cheerful, although such an attitude might be purchased at the expense of having true beliefs. (More about wishful thinking later.) Here is how the distinction is explained in light of the initial joke about optimists and pessimists who agree about the facts:

> They differ, though, in their framework attitude to what is the case. Of course there are facts they may disagree about. One can imagine contexts in which the optimist and the pessimist disagree about what is possible, or likely, or both even if they agree about what is the case. But in this particular joke, they agree about what is possible too. They both agree that it just doesn't get any better than this. One takes consolation in that fact, and the other feels bad about it not being able to get any better. From this perspective, the pessimist regrets what is unavoidable. By their own lights, pessimists set terms for being happy, demanding from reality that it be different from what it possibly can be.[10]

What should be our framework attitude toward sports? When we consider sports, should we be optimists or pessimists? There is another option, I suppose, and it pops up in writing about sports. Typically, the writer is a male sports optimist. He mentions his wife, who is utterly indifferent to the writer's serious concerns about the nature and value of sport.[11] The undercurrent seems to be to produce an apology for intense interest in sports in the face of serious unconcern or outright hostility on the part of a person who is both loved and respected by the writer. At some point it may occur to the optimist that indifference, even if it is based on ignorance, lack of experience, or more sophisticated judgments about the triviality of winning games or trying to be good in a sport, is actually quite attractive, especially at moments in which failure or defeat is so painful. In this respect, indifference about sport may be aligned with a certain kind of pessimism that seeks to avoid involvement in sport for various reasons.

Sport optimists may defend their love in a variety of ways. They may focus only on the good things, provide new ways of conceptualizing the attractive features of sports, or remind us of what is really essential to sport. They may be aware of certain bad elements in sport, but insist on the preponderance of good elements over bad. One strategy is to insist that sport is closely related to play, so it shares with play valuable possibilities: diversion from worldly concerns (escape from worldly worries), freedom, zest, joy, lightheartedness, unity with the material world, and psychophysical affirmation.[12] Some emphasize the way in which sport can aid in the development of the self and self-knowledge as the participant is tested and required to confront her limitations and transcend these limits.[13] Some optimists emphasize the aesthetic possibilities of participating in and viewing sports,[14] while others are more impressed by the fact that sport has quasi-religious qualities. Michael Novak's passionate apology, *The Joy of Sports*, provides a kind of theology of sport, interpreting it as a civil religion for many Americans. Michael Mandelbaum's recent attempt to explain the meaning of sports, especially for fans (which seems to exclude his wife), emphasizes the shared features of sports and religion: "Team sports provide three satisfactions of life to twenty-first century Americans that, before the modern age, only religion offered: a welcome diversion from the routines of daily life; a model of coherence and clarity; and heroic examples to admire and emulate." Colin McGinn's exuberant philosophical memoir about his lifelong passionate involvement in numerous particular sports attempts to show why sport is valuable: "To me sport is an essential part of the good life, of the life worth living. Art, science, sport: all three matter (and more besides)."[15] Jan Boxill goes even further in the context of explaining why gender equity in sports is so important. Females must have equal opportunity to purse such significant human goods:

I maintain that sport is the single most available, unalienated activity that provides autonomous agents a vehicle for self-expression, self-respect, and self-development. An unalienated activity is freely chosen and exemplifies human creativity requiring both the energy of the mind and the body, in accordance with aesthetic standards. It is an activity designed to provide room to express and develop oneself. Though it may serve other purposes, it has as its end the activity itself. It need not have a product nor provide a service. Sports are such activities. Sports are ends in themselves, and as such are included in Marx's "realm of freedom."[16]

Sport optimist indeed!

Given this praise, how could one fail to love and respect such activities or fail to pass on such attitudes toward one's children? Michael Novak puts the issues in this way, in relation to the claim that sport is, "somehow," a religion. Novak declares his love and wants to pass it on. "I love sports, and I want to bequeath that love to my children—to that stranger with the mitt who is ten, and the two girls who are eight and three. It seems a precious gift to give. But why? Why do I love sports?"[17]

As one contemporary Sports Guy puts it, "Not so fast, my friend." One can appreciate Novak's sentiments, even if expressed with such soupy pathos. But is it so obvious that Novak's love, an apparent expression of passionate optimism, is appropriate? After all, sometimes love is blind, isn't it? Or naive? Shouldn't we seriously consider the case for pessimism before we bequeath this passion to our children?

### III. Sport: Some Arguments for Pessimism

It is possible to see involvement in sport as itself motivated by a desire for invulnerability, an attempt to escape from the complications of everyday life. I have called this an isolationist view of sport. It may be a unifying ground for certain kinds of sport optimism. If we can bracket the accidental from the essential, we will see that sport often creates an ideal space set apart from the world. Peter Heinegg briefly but beautifully captures this notion. Sport, he says, is a "mode of escape from life." "While life muddles along in opaque confusion, the ongoing action of sport is luminous." He speaks of the "soothing clarity of sport," insofar as it "eliminates the suffering caused by the randomness of existence." He says, "All men are aesthetes to some extent: they fly from the messiness of sick room, bedroom, factory, and market place to the artificial neatness of the playground." So, in fashioning a "separate universe," Heinegg claims that sport is a "flight from the pain of existence."[18]

I confess that I have been attracted to this charming view of sport, and I continue to hold it in a modified form, despite the obvious objections raised by social critics. Their criticisms, however, must be taken seriously. The isolationist view appears to be naive, ignoring plain social facts. To attempt to insulate sport from social reality distorts the truth, they say. Sport is a microcosm, sociologists of sport claim. We must put sport in the context in which it actually exists as a social phenomenon. If we do, it is impossible to sustain an optimism about sports. Infatuation, obsession, or love of sports should not overlook, as the title of a recent book calls it, "the sports industry's war on athletes."[19] The chapters tell a grim tale about modern sports: doping, eating disorders and playing hurt, cheating, dirty playing and on-field violence, recruiting scandals and academic fraud, racism, sexism, and classism. The section titles of each chapter provide the details for particular sports. The book is merely one of many written by sociologists and social critics who document the deplorable aspects of contemporary sports.[20] In addition, if spectators attempt to flee the "pain of existence" by attending to the magical world of sports, they will have to overlook or ignore the social and economic details that muddy their credulous fantasy.

Although sociological pessimism is weighty, the most obvious response from lovers of sport is analogous to believers responding to criticisms of religion. If we look at the sorry history of religious conflicts and the number of people who are killed, maimed, or caused to suffer, even today, in the name of God or Allah, or some other favored Divine Reality, or if we see the way in which religious believers attempt aggressively and sometimes violently to impose their worldview on others, we ought to be pessimistic about the role of religion in the lives of individuals and society—or so the skeptics argue. In response, defenders of religion insist that religion can be corrupted, a religion can be misunderstood or debased, but that need not affect our love or respect for the thing itself. Likewise, sport may be corrupted, but that need not affect our attachment to the elements of sport that are the basis for our love of these activities or our sense that involvement in sports may enhance our lives. Colin McGinn responds in this way to those who are bothered by all the negative aspects of sports: "My reply to these natural misgivings is simple: what we are describing here is the *corruption* of sport, not its *essence*. Yes, the sporting impulse . . . has been corrupted and debased; but this is not intrinsic to the very nature of sport. It's an imposition from outside, from extraneous sources." For McGinn, when you add money to the equation, whether it involves sport, sex, art, or politics, corruption is possible—even likely. But that does not mean that sex, art, and sport are inherently bad. For McGinn, "Sport is essentially innocent, in its primary nature."[21] What the sociological pessimist judges as a naive view of sport is simply the attempt to sort through the corrupting influences and connect with the nature of the thing. Optimism can be sustained. And, in fact, when sociologists resort to recommendations that involve reforming certain kinds of social realities involved in sports, their prescriptions must be grounded in some ideal vision of sport that guides such reforms. Realistically guided "naïveté" becomes the basis for reform.[22]

Should we agree with McGinn's judgment that sport is essentially innocent? His view is based on the possibility of identifying the "nature of sport," or what we might call the intrinsic features of sport, as opposed to corrupting "external" influences. Suppose we accept this internal-external distinction and speak of the sociological criticism as a variety of external critique. If the criticism is developed on the basis of external factors, then it is possible to distance our own involvement with sport from various kinds of corrupting external influences. Desires for money or social prestige may generate win-at-all-costs attitudes, but such attitudes may be resisted. Yet sport *is* competitive; it is about winning, isn't it? The problems with sports may be deeper, not merely based on contingent, corrupting external pressures, but based on the very nature of sporting activities. A deeper and more defensible form of pessimism may express an internal critique of sport.

According to Schopenhauer's famous account, we should be pessimistic about sport because we should be pessimistic about life, period. Confronting Schopenhauer's argument for global pessimism is instructive, even if flawed, because it challenges us to recognize the limitations of an optimizing approach to happiness and forces us to think carefully about a notion of happiness that is directly related to desire satisfaction and sport. Schopenhauer's argument is clear and seductive. Human existence is characterized by restless, ceaseless striving. Like Sisyphus, we are constantly rolling our rocks; unlike Sisyphus, our trips up the hill seemingly have some end points, since we seek goals in all manner of ways. We are apparently insatiable in our endless pursuit of goals in life. Desire is addictive. Insofar as we have desires, our lives are experienced as lacking or wanting in some respect. Yet when we satisfy ourselves, our happiness is short-lived. We become bored, until we move on to other ravenous strivings. Our lives, it seems, are perpetually swinging to and fro between the pain of unsatisfied desires and the boredom of fulfillment. Here is how Schopenhauer puts the argument in section 57 of *The World as Will and Representation*:

> We have already seen in nature-without-knowledge her inner being as a constant striving without aim and without rest, and this stands out much more distinctly when we consider the animal or man. Willing

and striving are its whole essence, and can be fully compared to an unquenchable thirst. The basis of all willing, however, is need, lack, and hence pain, and by its very nature and origin it is therefore destined to pain. If, on the other hand, it lacks objects of willing, because it is at once deprived of them again by too easy a satisfaction, a fearful emptiness and boredom come over it; in other words, its being and existence itself become an intolerable burden for it. Hence its life swings like a pendulum to and fro between pain and boredom, and these two are in fact its ultimate constituents. . . .

Now absolutely every life continues to flow on between willing and attainment. Of its nature the wish is pain; attainment quickly begets satiety. The goal was only apparent; possession takes away its charm. The wish, the need, appears again on the scene under a new form; if it does not, then dreariness, emptiness, and boredom follow, the struggle against it which is just as painful as is that against want.

. . . [E]very human life is tossed backwards and forwards between pain and boredom.[23]

There is clearly some truth in the gloomy picture painted by Schopenhauerian pessimism, which resembles, in various respects, the Buddha's notion that life is suffering, Kierkegaard's existential dialectic describing boredom as the inevitable outcome of an aesthetic approach to life, and even contemporary psychological research performed by Daniel Kahneman and others, suggesting that subjective well-being expected by dramatic examples of desire satisfaction (for example, lottery winners) is impermanent and disappointing.[24] Even when we consider sport, not as an arena of distinctive willing but simply as a representation of the general structures that characterize life, "tossed backwards and forwards between pain and boredom," there is something we must not ignore about Schopenhauer's analysis. There is pain in sports, as the will strives to satisfy itself, may be fulfilled momentarily, becomes bored, and then seeks further gratification. Here is a striking example of what Schopenhauer describes, in the words of an Israeli national squash champion who had achieved the goal for which he had worked so hard and long to achieve:

> After the night of the celebration, I retired to my room. I sat on my bed and wanted to savor, for the last time before going to sleep, that feeling of supreme happiness. Suddenly, without warning, the bliss that came from having attained in real life what had so long been my most cherished and exalted fantasy disappeared, and my feeling of emptiness returned. I was befuddled and afraid. The tears of joy shed only hours earlier turned to tears of pain and helplessness. For if I was not happy now, when everything seemed to have worked out perfectly, what prospects did I have of attaining lasting happiness?[25]

Schopenhauer's answer? None. But if we look more carefully at sports, we will see what is wrong with Schopenhauer's argument and what might be salvaged.

I remember a beautiful, warm spring day in my college years, waking up to the greening of the landscape, having trouble concentrating in my early-morning classes, rushing off to the locker room, where I dressed with teammates, taking the field for my warm-up lap, stretching, loosening the arm, and then taking my turn in batting practice. My experience that morning was one of splendid anticipation, looking forward to the baseball game that I would play later. I wanted nothing more than the end of pregame activities and the beginning of the game. I looked forward to the first at bat, the sweet pleasure of making solid contact, the anticipated feel of a line drive to right field, the distinctive crack of the ball striking the wood (not the "ping" we hear today), the smell of new pine tar on my bat, and the perfect fielding of a ground ball, where my infield action represented the seamless relation among feet, hands, glove, and ball. Perfect action. Nice rhythm. Delicate footwork. A delicious dance. Here the excitement of unsatisfied desire was hardly painful, as Schopenhauer insists. Moreover, the pleasures of anticipation are hardly unique to sport.

Schopenhauer's first mistake is to overlook pleasures of anticipation associated with attempts to satisfy all kinds of desires. This is the result of the way he models desires on the basis of natural or biological craving. Recall what he says about a person's desires: "Willing and striving are its whole essence, and can be fully compared to an unquestionable thirst." Hunger, thirst, or sexual desire may be experienced as uncomfortable lack, need, or want, but not all desiring is like this. Looking forward in anticipation may be connected with the notion that life is going somewhere, that it is not just "one damn thing after another"; it is often directed toward something good, pleasurable, or fulfilling. Pleasures of anticipation may sometimes be related to the notion that life or parts of life have a narrative structure that is appealing, that life is directed toward something that matters to a self.[26] The deeper problem is that not all unsatisfied desires are experienced in the way that natural desires are unfulfilled or thwarted. Luper makes this point also, insisting that it is important to make "the distinction between a desire we have not (as yet) satisfied and a thwarted one. Having a desire thwarted is almost always unpleasant, but being in the grip of a desire which has not been satisfied is unpleasant only in certain sorts of cases."[27]

Before we consider the issue of sport and thwarted desires, two other critical points are relevant. First, Schopenhauer overlooks details about the significance or importance of different desires. Not all desires are created (or discovered as) equal; some are more important than others. I may want to see a movie, take a vacation, receive a raise, find a new career path, patch up some fractured friendship, have my children graduate from college, get a dog . . . Schopenhauer is right about the pervasive character of desire, but it is not the case that all desires are of equal importance, nor is he right to suggest that the thwarting of all specific desires is equally painful. A recognition of these points is relevant for the evaluation and implementation of the two broad strategies for pursuing happiness: optimizing and adapting. Schopenhauer is right to insist that unqualified optimizing is deeply problematic. Despite his failure to appreciate the nuances of desiring, the pain of some thwarted desires is real. With this in mind, we should turn to sport. Isn't there something particularly troubling or worrisome about sports, because it is essential to competition that some fundamental desires of persons, qua sports participants, will inevitably be thwarted?

## IV. Further Arguments for Pessimism: The Problem of Competitive Desires

According to Alfie Kohn, sport is not innocent. His book *No Contest: The Case against Competition* attempts to provide a compelling case against all competitive activities, including sports. Marshaling powerful support from psychological research, Kohn argues that competition does not lead to better performance, make our play enjoyable, or build character. It is psychologically damaging, poisons our relationships, and is therefore morally problematic. The problem is structural, not attitudinal, because a competitive activity is characterized by what he calls "mutually exclusive goal attainment. This means . . . that my success requires your failure." In such an arrangement, "two or more individuals are trying to achieve a goal that cannot be achieved by all of them." Hence, the essence of competition, understood as mutually exclusive goal attainment, is as follows:

> One person succeeds only if another does not. From this uncluttered perspective, it seems clear right away that something is drastically wrong with such an arrangement. How can we do our best when we are spending our energies trying to make someone lose? Can this sort of struggle really be the best way to have a good time? What happens to our self-esteem when it becomes dependent on how much better we do than the next person? Most striking of all is the impact of this arrangement on human relationship: a structural incentive to see other people lose cannot help but drive a wedge between us and invite hostility.[28]

A discussion of sport figures prominently in Kohn's book because of his interest in education and the importance of competitive activities in the lives of children. Although sport is not unique as an arena for competitive desires, it may be particularly worrisome because of its cultural and developmental prominence. Kohn is mad as hell, and he's not going to take it anymore. "Competing drags us down, devastates us psychologically, poisons our relationships, interferes with our performance."[29] The book is full of complex analysis, social scientific and otherwise, offered to support the notion that we should reduce, as much as possible, the conspicuous role of contesting and competing in our lives. A more recent study of competition argues that Kohn's analysis is essentially correct. "Though his book is now dated (the revised edition was published in 1992), Kohn summarized a century of research on competition well, and more recent research has added additional nuances but nothing substantially different."[30]

Kohn's analysis suggests that we are particularly vulnerable to unhappiness—necessarily so?—when we involve ourselves in sport, because of the very nature of competition. But this conclusion did not await the findings of social science. We may need social scientists to investigate cherished assumptions about whether we need competition in order to perform or learn better, or whether, in fact, certain character traits are typically developed in those who compete in sports. We do not need them to tell us that competition leaves us vulnerable to unhappiness because our passionate desires to win or succeed are thwarted. Let those who compete describe the phenomenon of losing. (The references are unimportant. Take these comments to be cultural artifacts.) "Losing is like death." "The thrill of victory, the agony of defeat." "Losing tears you apart." "Losing tears your heart out." "Every time you win, you're reborn; when you lose, you die a little." "In sport, there's happiness and there's misery. That's all. You win or you lose." The great basketball coach Bobby Knight comments on the interesting asymmetry of winning and losing: "As long as I've coached, winning never did anything for me or to me that in any way compared to what losing did. The loss was far, far worse than the win was good. The two never evened out in terms of the emotions involved or emotions spent."[31] Upon failure or loss, some are called "losers" or "chokers." The vocabulary of competing, failing, and losing includes *embarrassment, humiliation, bitterness, despair, shame, depression, anguish, self-doubt, lack of self-esteem* or *self-respect,* and *anxiety.*

The joy of sports? If we think that it is only unbalanced players, coaches, or fans who utter these over-the-top lamentations, consider this comment by Michael Novak, unabashed lover of sport, who wants to pass his passion on to his children:

> For the underlying metaphysic of sports entails overcoming the fear of death. In every contest, one side is defeated. Defeat hurts. No use saying, "It's only a game." It doesn't feel like a game. The anguish and depression that seize one's psyche in defeat are far deeper than a mere comparative failure—deeper than recognition of the opponent's superiority. That would be a simple emotion to handle. Even before a game, one might be willing to concede that much; one might already *know* that the other is better. But in a game, the more talented do not always win. A game tests considerably more than talent. A game tests, somehow, one's entire life. It tests one's standing with fortune and the gods. It can put one almost in a coma, slow up all of one's reactions, make the tongue cleave to the mouth, exhaust every fount of life and joy, make one *wish* one were dead, so as to be attuned to one's feelings.[32]

I want to say two things about Kohn's view of competitive activities and Novak's mythopoetic expression of the "losing is like death" view. First, I think they may agree about the psychological impact of failure and loss, but differ radically in how to respond. Kohn's view is straightforward. Sport is not worth the psychological toll it may inflict. Because it is neither instrumentally good nor morally probative, we should reduce or eliminate the competitive aspects of the games we play. As an optimizer who understands the problems associated with competitive desires, he wants to change the world, that is, he wants to change social arrangements so the world will conform to our desires for enjoyable play, psychological health, moral character, and satisfying relationships with others. Given the fact that the problems are structural and not within ourselves, we should attempt to eliminate competitive structures in our lives. Competition necessarily produces desires that cannot be satisfied, so we should do away with competition.

On the other hand, Novak's view is more subtle. The agony of defeat takes place in a religiously charged, symbolic world. Sport affirms the struggle that is at the heart of human existence. "Misfortune has its uses," as Schopenhauer said. Lurking on the horizon of Novak's love of sport is an essentially religious view of the world, in which our struggles are necessary but ultimately worth the effort. As he says, "Sports are mysteries of youth and aging, perfect action and decay, fortune and misfortune, strategy and contingency. Sports are rituals concerning human survival on this planet: liturgical enactments of animal perfection and the struggles of the human spirit to prevail."[33] Symbol. Ritual. Liturgy. Novak's strategy is to place competitive desires in a larger context of religious and mythic beliefs and concepts that assuage our pain.

Second, it is not at all clear what it means to say, "Losing is like death." When Novak says, "Defeat hurts like death," perhaps he means that it is painful like the loss of a loved one. But why? The death of a loved one thwarts the desire to be with someone, to sustain a friendship or loving relationship, or even the desire we have for other persons to have *their* deepest desires satisfied in order to be happy or fulfilled. If losing is like death, as some coaches say, it may be because of the thwarting of the sport participants' fundamental desire to win, analogous to our fundamental desire to live— not to be annihilated. Death thwarts desire, as does losing. If the desire to win is essential in sports construed as competitive activities, then unhappiness is inevitable when that desire is unfulfilled.

### v. Modes of Vulnerability

We are particularly vulnerable when we participate in sport as a player, coach, fan, or any kind of interested person who thinks that what happens in a sporting contest or activity matters. The modes of vulnerability are not difficult to describe.

### A. *Injury*

Since sports are physical activities, there is an ever-present possibility of injury, from minor impairments to major harms that may impair one for life or even cause death. Injury thwarts desires to play and succeed.

### B. *Alienation*

Social scientists, philosophers, and ordinary people are unanimous in realizing the threats to interpersonal relationships endemic to competitive activities. Kohn's chapter "Against Each Other" documents the research well.[34] Luper puts it nicely when discussing our propensity to judge our talents or qualities in relation to others. We want to be or judge ourselves to be smarter, richer, or better than others. "Such comparative desires—desires that call for our possessing features that cannot be possessed by everyone—can be called *competitive* desires since they tend to lead us to regard others as threats." Drew Hyland has stressed this aspect of sport. While arguing that friendship is a possibility, even the true telos of competing against (with) others, we risk alienation from others when we play.[35] Because of the comparative and competitive pressures involved, problems may arise not only with opponents, but also with teammates, coaches, fans, officials—even parents with their children. The threat of alienation from others is pervasive.

### C. *Failure*

Here I mean not only the most obvious threat, which is to lose, but to fail in all sorts of ways that thwart desires to make the team, play in the game, play more, effectively contribute, become better, become excellent, be recognized, be an all-star . . . the list is quite long. Sport provides pervasive opportunities to fail.

### D. *Psychological and Moral Dangers*

Again, social scientists have documented the possibilities; ordinary observation and anecdotal evidence agree. Sociological pessimists describe the disturbing facts, as do sport psychologists and researchers in moral development. We may insist that sport, while innocent, may be corrupted, yet Kohn's emphasis on the structural depth of these problems must be addressed. Cheating. Violence. Aggression. Despair. How to respond?

*E. Defeat*

This is the ultimate failure, and unless a participant somehow avoids the competition—like playing tennis without keeping score, or becoming adept at a skilled physical activity, such as, windsurfing, without competing against another—then defeat is inevitable.[36] If it matters to someone who wins and loses, then sport must involve desires being thwarted—hence, unhappiness.

If our goal in life is to secure our happiness, then the question of significant involvement in sports is an important one. Notwithstanding his comments on death, Novak, like many lovers of sports, wants to pass on this passion to his children—despite the problems associated with competitive desires and despite leaving them vulnerable in significant ways. At least we should give them means to cope with these problems. How should this be done?

We began by distinguishing two broad strategies used in pursuing happiness: optimizing and adapting. It is clear that an unqualified optimizing strategy, in sports and elsewhere, leaves us particularly vulnerable to unhappiness. On the other hand, adaptation can come in a number of different forms. In his book Luper is critical of extreme forms of adaptation, like the attempt to eliminate desires altogether in life, because such forms end up being too life denying. He does defend a moderate form of adaptation, yet he is also wary of competitive desires. He distinguishes a "continuum upon which happiness falls," in which one extreme is what he calls "*felicity*, defined as a condition that cannot be improved upon, and *calamity*, a condition that cannot be worsened." On this continuum we move from what we might call superhappiness (felicity) through happiness to indifference, unhappiness, and calamity.

Luper thinks it is unwise to link competitive goals to either the most ideal form of happiness or even some lesser form of happiness on the continuum. On the basis of the previous discussion, it is not difficult to understand why he holds this view. If we aspire to goals that are extremely difficult or virtually impossible to achieve, because the goals in question either put us in opposition to others (such as the desire to be the world's best golfer) or demand extraordinary noncompetitive abilities that are scarce, we set ourselves up for failure—the unhappiness of thwarted desires. We can *wish* for these things, even put forth maximum effort to attain them, but we should not yield to massive disappointment when we fail. We should, he says, "try to arrange for our happiness to depend only on the attainable, and . . . these less ambitious goals should take a higher priority." Furthermore, if our goal is ideal happiness (felicity), we should not forget that competitive goals occasion "conflict among people, so that we are led to view the felicity of others as threats to our own felicity." The upshot seems to be that if we want to be truly happy, we should avoid arenas in life that force us to have competitive goals. "Avoiding competitive goals as a requirement for happiness is a good idea *both* because they are difficult to achieve *and* because they inspire aggression."[37]

I agree with Luper that happiness requires some strategy in which we wisely engage in desire adaptation. I do not agree, however, that such a strategy involves avoiding competitive goals. What would a wise adaptation strategy look like in relation to sports? In the following chapter I will examine various strategies that might mitigate the problem of competitive desires.

# 3 Losing Is Like Death

## 1. Can We Adapt?

Before we examine various ways in which we might alter our desires in order to reduce the possibilities of unhappiness in sports, we should first briefly raise a prior concern. Can we change our desires? My ultimate conclusion is not only that the mastery of desire is possible but that is the wise path for the sports participant.

Alfie Kohn insists that the problems associated with competitive activities, and thus sports, are rooted in the very structure of competition understood as mutually exclusive goal attainment. In my judgment, the problems are rooted in us. Kohn is right to call attention to the dangers inherent in competition, but such dangers are contingent. It is not the world we need to change; it is *ourselves*. We need to change our beliefs, attitudes, and desires. Yes, the structure of competition requires that there are losers, but the ways in which we respond to the competitive aspect of sport and frame our participation are up to us. At least to a certain extent, it is up to us to determine how we respond to the world, as adapters have emphasized.

Can we adapt? Can we really alter our desires to avoid the most unpleasant aspects of sports? Life? A complete answer would require a separate treatise, but some initial, relatively brief comments are useful. Recall that Schopenhauer develops his understanding of desire on the model of natural desires like hunger or thirst. These desires are based on biological needs and have a fairly distinctive phenomenology. When I am really hungry, there is a certain empty, gnawing feeling in my stomach as my desire for food becomes more intense. There is a natural object of this desire (food), and as long as I do not eat, the experience is uncomfortable or unpleasant. If someone wonders why I have this desire to eat, the appropriate answer (usually) is to provide some causal explanation in terms of bodily states and biological needs.[1]

In contrast, if we consider a wider range of human desires, most appear to be quite unlike the natural desires of hunger, thirst, elimination of waste, and (perhaps) sex. Since our interest is sport, consider certain kinds of wants or preferences specific to sporting activities. The desire to win is not related to biological need in any direct way, at least not in the way that our desires for food and water are. It does not have a distinctive phenomenology. I cannot describe and locate this desire in any way directly related to my body or certain distinctive feelings. The desire does not have a specific natural object, nor is the experience of the desire to win necessarily unpleasant as long as it is unsatisfied. As a matter of fact, the desire to win may produce an element of dramatic tension and excitement in experience, akin to the pleasures of anticipation that I previously described. The desire to win may, in fact, be more or less intense, but that seems to be a function of how disappointed I would be if I lost or how much I am willing to undergo (maybe in training or sacrifice) in order to fulfill the desire to win. If I am asked why I want to win, my answer will be in terms of reasons or motives I might have, not necessarily causal explanations of the desire itself. These various features of desires, like the desire to win a game or become better at a skilled, physical activity, have led most philosophers to what might be called the standard view, that desires are propositional attitudes, so "the correct form of desire sentences is 's desires (or maybe wants) that p.'"[2] Desire is akin to other propositional attitudes: belief, hope, wonder, and the like. I may want to win, hope that I win, expect to win, believe that I will win, and so forth.

Thomas Nagel draws an important distinction between "motivated" and "unmotivated" desires:

Many desires, like many beliefs, are *arrived at* by decision and after deliberation. They need not simply assail us, though there are certain desires that do, like the appetites and in certain cases the emotions. . . . The desires which simply come to us are unmotivated though they can be explained. Hunger is produced by lack of food, but is not motivated thereby. A desire to shop for groceries, after discovering nothing appetizing in the refrigerator, is on the other hand motivated by hunger. Rational or motivational explanation is just as much in order for that desire as for the action itself.[3]

Although the relevant desires in sports may not, in fact, be "arrived at by choice and deliberation" (I may unreflectively simply find that I have an overarching desire to win), they *may* be, insofar as such desires do not simply "assail us" in the way that hunger or thirst do. If we conceive of the desire to win, or the desires to become excellent, enjoy oneself, or be a good sport, as propositional attitudes, it is appropriate to think of them as possible objects of choice and deliberation, thus subject to adaptation. If the desire to win leads to unhappiness, then not only *can* we modify our attitudes to winning and losing, but perhaps we should.

## II. Strategies of Adaptation

In the following discussion I am most interested in the adaptation of desires, or what Martha Nussbaum has called, in her magisterial study of Hellenistic ethics, the "therapy of desire." We will start, however, with a strategy that primarily involves belief adaptation. Other strategies will involve belief, but are more explicitly directed toward modifying our desires. Given the vulnerabilities inherent in sport, including injury, alienation, failure, defeat, psychological damage, and moral failure, how should we cope? Put in the perspective of youthful participation in sports, how can we help our children to cope with the inevitable unhappiness experienced in sport participation? Should we steer our children away from sports, and seek "fun without competition," as Kohn argues?[4]

*A. Everything Happens for a Reason*
The first strategy I will discuss is familiar. As I write this, I am reflecting on a recent sports story featuring a college basketball player, much publicized coming out of high school, whose injuries transformed him from a lightning-quick point guard with exceptional offensive skills into a rather plodding ball handler—at least when judged in comparison with other major college point guards—who had become an offensive liability, yet preserved a starting role because of his intelligence and anticipation, both offensively and defensively. What started as a much-anticipated college career—maybe a prelude to professional basketball—ended in disappointment. When asked about his injuries, extensive rehabilitation, and frustrations, he responded: "Everything happens for a reason." (I will call this the EHFR Principle.)

The response, not uncommon, is one I have read and heard countless times in classroom discussions with college students about the problem of evil, as well as from other athletes. It is typically an expression of what I would call "theistic optimism," a strategy used to sustain a positive-framework attitude toward the world or to place pain, suffering, disappointment, and despair in a larger framework in order to make the events that occasion such experiences more "meaningful" or to help one make sense of the world. A child gets cancer. A best friend dies in a car wreck. A father has a debilitating stroke. A student fails organic chemistry. The graduate fails to get a job. An athlete blows out a knee. The team loses the championship game. Everything happens for a reason.

It is difficult both to understand how the strategy works and to evaluate its effectiveness. Is it an example of wishful thinking? Does it involve self-deception? As a possible strategy used to achieve happiness, here is how Luper defines wishful thinking: "the attempt to increase our happiness by subverting any available rational techniques for checking whether our beliefs are correct and changing our views until we believe that our desires *are* satisfied (or are eventually to be satisfied)."[5]

In paradigm cases of wishful thinking, it is fairly clear how the mechanism works. In one case, a college student who wants to become a physician believes she is quite good at mathematics and science—as she must be in order to be admitted to medical school—yet ignores the evidence of failed exams and courses, insisting that she is just not good at taking tests. In another case, a person wants to be loved and respected by his spouse, children, and friends, but ignores all the evidence to the contrary: disrespectful remarks, being ignored and made fun of, infidelity, and so on. In these examples, wishful thinking is motivated by a desire for happiness and does subvert rationality by ignoring the relevant evidence, as Luper insists. The student needs to believe that she is on her way to becoming a physician; the deceived person must believe that certain kinds of disrespectful and hurtful behaviors are benign. It is also evident that in both cases it will be hard to maintain the self-deception if the pattern of evidence is unassailable. The happiness involved is superficial and unstable, so the strategy is not as useful as one might suppose.

In the case of the college athlete, it is more difficult to understand, for a number of reasons, how the strategy of belief adaptation relates to desire satisfaction and happiness. His desires to perform at the highest level and perhaps play professional basketball were thwarted, so his belief that "everything happens for a reason" does not really function in the way it does in the previous examples, as a belief required for him to think his desires were satisfied or on the way toward being satisfied. One possibility is to distinguish long-term and short-term goals, so invoking his belief about the overall reasonableness of the world would be a way to conceive of his desires for superior athletic success as only short-term and apparent, open to correction by an appeal to deeper purposes—presumably God's purposes. Then he would (could) identify with these long-term desires. Perhaps God wants something else for him, and he can want what God wants. The problem here is to convince oneself that one's athletic desires are relatively unimportant on the basis of postulating an abstract metaphysical principle and that the unhappiness involved is a matter of the ultimate reasonableness of things, not simply bad luck. (To the young athlete, it does not *feel* like his disappointment is metaphysically positive.) The question is whether invoking the EHFR Principle is supposed to lead to adaptation of desires or simply to produce certain emotions (for example, resignation) that will dull the pain of disappointment in the face of thwarted desires.

It is also unclear whether the appeal to the EHFR Principle subverts rationality only in some specific cases, or whether it does so in principle. If it does express theistic optimism, then invoking the principle raises all of the difficult issues related to rationality and religious belief, as well as the problem of evil. Since we will not be able to resolve these issues here, I offer only some tentative comments. If the EHFR Principle is an expression of belief in theism, then the reasonableness of invoking the principle is a function of whether belief in theism is reasonable, presumably on the basis of some valid argument with reasonable premises, a relatively strong inductive argument, or some appeal to religious experience. It may be possible, in principle, to show that belief in theism is reasonable, but this is not the case for many people who have neither the time nor the motivation to engage these issues in a philosophically complex manner.[6]

Furthermore, a plausible way to interpret the principle is to understand it as a form of what Luper calls "conformism," one of whose types he calls "malleabilism." As a strategy for becoming invulnerable, conformism is where "we adjust our desire scheme in such a way that we want what is going to happen anyway. We *conform* our *will* to what will happen; we take the attitude: whatever happens is what I want." Let's say that the EHFR Principle can be either forward looking or backward looking. The college athlete may have carried this attitude into his confrontation with injury and disappointment, or it may have been occasioned by reflecting on his injuries. Malleabilism "results from internalizing the attitude that whatever happens is good. Just as it is, the world is good."[7] Not only does everything happen for a reason, that reason makes it good, apparently in an instrumental sense (or some sense of coherence). No doubt many people find such malleabilist conformism attractive, but there are problems.

The first thing that may occur to a reflective person is that it just does not *appear* to be true that everything happens for a reason. This thought is at the heart of some contemporary disputes about the problem of evil. It *may* be true, but we need independent evidence for supposing it is the case over a wide range of situations. Genocide. Infant or childhood suffering and death. Mass murders. Animal suffering. Extreme poverty and starvation. It is not unreasonable to expect the reasons for suffering to be more apparent than they are, and if there are no good, independent reasons for believing that theism is true, then the EHFR Principle *is* wishful thinking (or so one might argue).[8]

As a malleabilist form of conformism, the EHFR Principle also seems to require a peculiar set of attitudes and responses to the world. If we put these issues in a broader context, what would be the appropriate response to the Holocaust or more contemporary instances of genocidal slaughter? If everything happens for a reason and whatever happens is good (in the long run?), then there is no point in moral regret or resentment, is there? Moral indignation? These fundamental moral emotions would have to be significantly altered or interpreted differently if we must affirm that everything that happens is good. Moreover, it is not clear why we would be moved to reduce the suffering in the world if we embraced these attitudes, since in doing so we would evidently be reducing the amount of good instrumentally produced by apparent badness (or marring the overall moral coherence of things).[9] We would be upsetting the perfect moral equilibrium established by God. Oddly, it would not be altogether inappropriate to be cheerful in the face of suffering, grateful to be living in such a well-ordered moral universe! The consequences of such a malleabilist attitude might be disturbing to many.

Because the malleabilist must affirm whatever happens, she "must carefully avoid making any demands on the course of events," according to Luper. This suggests that malleabilists "are forced to develop a backward-looking perspective on life. They must wait for the future to reveal itself, then accommodate themselves to what happened." If this is the case, in order to avoid disappointment such a person "will have to cultivate no expectations or desires for the future at all (aside from desires whose satisfaction is guaranteed)." The consequence of such attitudes, as Luper insists, is "a radically passive approach to life"—much to the surprise of our disappointed athlete, I presume.[10] (I am supposing that he could work out the implications of the EHFR Principle reflectively.)

Given our discussion of the question of the meaning of life (later), even if theism is true, it might occur to some people that the EHFR Principle simply assumes that one could achieve happiness or meaningfulness by getting in line with God's plan, yet that might be rejected by persons who realize that a strongly meaningful life requires autonomy. God has his reasons, but they may not be mine.

For these reasons, invoking the EHFR Principle is not the best way to cope with the negative aspects of sports. It may be more reasonable and worthwhile to realize that sometimes injury is the result of bad luck; failure and defeat may be the result of a lack of athletic excellence rather than God's will. And invoking the principle, in itself, may do nothing to reduce the risks of alienation.

B. *Eliminating Desires*

The next strategy directly relates to desire. The most straightforward method to avoid the unhappy consequences of competitive desires is to eliminate them by avoiding competitive situations or activities. If we extract ourselves from situations that call for competitive desires, we can eliminate them altogether. This is the option that Kohn recommends, especially for children. If the desire to win is simultaneously the desire for others to lose, where one person's success entails the failures of others, then the solution is obvious (if we want to avoid unhappy consequences): do not engage in competitive activities; do not play competitive games. One can become invulnerable (qua possible competitor) by refusing to become involved in competitive situations, thereby avoiding the negative aspects of sports: defeat, psychological unpleasantness, alienation, and moral failure. What you will be left with is the fun of noncompetitive games. (Ignore for the moment broader implications.)

There is something to be said for this approach, perhaps analogous to the alcoholic avoiding bars and the addicted gambler avoiding the casino. For the lover of sports, however, going cold turkey gives up too much. To the extent that there is so much good involved in sports participation, avoiding sports throws out the baby with the bathwater (to mix our metaphors). When we consider the intrinsic joy of playing, the meaningfulness of giving oneself over to larger purposes, involvement in dramatic narratives, the satisfaction of overcoming obstacles, coming together with others to achieve a common goal . . . it is not clear that the bad aspects of sport are so bad that the only way to avoid them is not to participate, or that the strategy of social reform is the only way to ameliorate the situation. The better strategy would be to minimize the unpleasant or unacceptable elements while salvaging the good. Undoubtedly, part of the moral possibilities of sports would also be lost by Kohn's social reformist version of desire elimination. Sports participants should look elsewhere for ways to enhance their happiness (or avoid unhappiness).

Kohn's recommendation is limited and partial. It is only certain kinds of desires that we should attempt to eliminate by negating aspects of social life requiring mutually exclusive goal attainment. The strategy of desire elimination, however, has sometimes been recommended as a global policy used to secure happiness. Adaptation could be more far-reaching because of the ubiquity of desire. We began by considering sport and Stoic modes of adaptation. Some non-Western traditions also offer important alternatives to an optimizing approach to happiness. If we want to avoid unhappiness in sports, we might consider ridding ourselves of any desires—as far as it is possible. We could view sport in the larger context of a much broader goal: the elimination of desire in life.

Luper recognizes this as a distinctive strategy he calls "nihilism." A "way to become invulnerable is to will *nothing*, to be indifferent about all matters." He argues that both Taoism and Buddhism are nihilistic (in his sense) or have significant nihilistic tendencies. It would require a lengthy discussion to flesh out the implications of Buddhism and Taoism for sports. It would also require considerable space to respond charitably to Luper's interpretation of Buddhism and Taoism. Undoubtedly, the central message of Buddhism can be interpreted as Luper does, and there are numerous passages in the *Tao Te Ching* that sound nihilistic. For example, the author of the classic Taoist text speaks of "freedom from desire," says you should "make few your desires," and describes the Taoist ideal as "the sage desires to be without desires."[11] For our purposes, we can sidestep the difficult interpretive questions by taking Luper's comments as merely suggestive. Is there a way of interpreting these important and interesting approaches to life that might help us understand how to deal with sport and vulnerability?

If it was difficult to understand how the EHFR Principle functions to secure invulnerability, it is even more difficult to understand what it would be like to live without desires, period. And when we attempt to provide the details, the ideal is not attractive. As William Irvine says, "We are awash in desire at virtually every waking moment." Picture a state of desirelessness and what do we see? Unconsciousness? A meditative state? Some moment of self-conscious detachment from which one can observe one's mental life in repose? A life without desires, a life of complete indifference in which a person wills nothing, is a passive, lifeless shell. It appears to describe a life in which a person drifts and responds, but does not initiate anything, a life without direction or purpose. As Irvine says, "Banish desire from the world, and you get a world of frozen beings who have no reason to live and no reason to die." On the other hand, Irvine's fine book attempts to show the intimate connection between mastering desires and happiness. It is not the elimination of desire that is our goal. "What we should therefore seek is relative mastery: we should learn to sort through our desires, working to fulfill some of them, while working to suppress others." Irvine includes Buddhists and Taoists among "those who have thought carefully about desire" and says all "have unanimously drawn the conclusion that *the best way—indeed, perhaps the only way—to attain lasting happiness is not to change the world around us or our place in it but to change ourselves.*"¹² Is there a way of interpreting Buddhism and Taoism less nihilistically, more on the model of mastery of desire, rather than negation or elimination?

One way to salvage the elimination of desire strategy of adaptation is to note the distinction between desire in a strong sense and desire in a much weaker sense, where desires are more like preferences than cravings or passions. For example, I may want to go see a particular movie and find out, when I arrive, that all the seats are sold. In this case, mild disappointment might be appropriate. On the other hand, I might want, more than anything, to become a professional baseball player, or to become married to a particular person and start a family, or I may have an intense passion to pursue social justice. My desires may be intense and all-consuming. Joel Kupperman calls attention to this important distinction when he attempts to interpret the meaning of the Buddha's advice to lose our desires. He argues that the traditional meaning of "desire" is more narrow than simply having *any* wants or preferences. He says, "To desire something (in the traditional meaning) is to have a strong appetite or preference for it, so strong that you would feel deeply disappointed if things did not turn out as you wished." In this sense we can distinguish desires and mild preferences. When our desires are thwarted, we will suffer, as the Buddha claims. When the Buddha recommends that we lose all of our desires, Kupperman insists that "we need to bear in mind that a desire is an appetite or preference of a particularly intense and vulnerability-creating kind." Thus, on this reading, Buddhism is not nihilistic. It merely recommends that we "have mild preferences that lack the attachment and intensity characteristic of desire, and to have satisfactions that are not keyed to objects or to craving. These satisfactions will be more like joy than pleasure."[13]

Likewise, the distinction between desire in a strong sense and relatively weaker forms of preferences or inclinations may provide a way of charitably interpreting passages in the *Tao Te Ching* that recommend a life without desires as the ideal that places one in harmony with the Way (Tao). In Philip Ivanhoe's commentary on his recent translation of this masterpiece, he argues that the vision of the good life described there recommends the avoidance of both excessive and obsessive desire. The Taoist holds that "excessive desire per se is bad and the related belief that our 'real' or 'natural' desires are actually quite modest and limited. . . . The text claims that it is unnatural to have excessive desires and that having them will not only not lead to a satisfying life but will paradoxically result in destitution, want, alienation, and self-destruction."[14] "Excessive" may mean "too many" or "too intense." The text recommends that we pare down the range of our desires, and by doing so we will avoid obsessions about goals that are artificially promoted by society and whose importance is exaggerated.

If we combine these interpretations of Buddhist and Taoist modes of adaptation, the elimination of desire is transformed into the moderation of desire. What is eliminated is desire in the strong sense, as obsessive and addictive; what is retained is a smaller range of desires, less intense, more "natural." Ivanhoe says that the *Tao*

*Te Ching* "counsels everyone . . . to be humble, frugal, and modest." Kupperman's description of a person who has lost all desire is one who "would appear cool and detached . . . , never upset or worried." Also, the reduction of desire might change one's orientation toward time. Instead of obsessing about the future, one might be more appreciative of the present.[15]

If the sports participant took these recommendations to heart, if one succeeded in transforming more intense and obsessive competitive desires into something that looks more like mild preferences, then at least some of the problems of competitive desires would be reduced. Kohn says that we should avoid competitive activities. Luper says that we should avoid competitive desires—in order to avoid unhappiness and to dissipate the possibility of alienation from others. These responses to competition seem to presuppose that desires must be intense and passionate. They need not be, especially when moderation is combined with other adaptive strategies. We can first of all avoid the "losing is like death" view if we moderate our sports-related, vulnerability-creating cravings.

Before we turn to other adaptive strategies, I should also point out that both Kohn's view of competition as well as Luper's rejection of competitive desires appear to accept a certain socially sanctioned view of sport that is prevalent. In fact, I assume that many in the sports world would find it preposterous to recommend that athletes, coaches, and fans moderate their passionate desire for athletic and sport successes. The question is whether the moderation of passion is compatible with the achievement of the internal goals of sports participation. I believe it is. I do not think that exaggerating the value of victory, in particular, is required in order to acquire the goals that make sports activities worthwhile. My Taoist suspicions are put nicely by Ivanhoe's comments on the *Tao Te Ching*: "Socially sanctioned notions of beauty, music, good taste, and other sources of 'satisfaction' are portrayed as corruptions of natural preferences. Society isolates and exaggerates certain goods and elevates them to preeminent positions of prestige. This in turn leads people to clash and contend with one another in a mad dash to secure these goods."[16] In my view, the constant chatter about winning, the omnipresence of praise for the ultracompetitor for whom winning is everything, excusing shabby behavior in the context of the overriding value of "passion," and the attitudes that produce socially destructive behavior and interpersonal alienation are all of a piece—the social exaggeration of the value of victories in games and the supposed goods that go along with such embellishments, like prestige or material wealth.

## C. Redirecting Desires

My model for this adaptive strategy is found in another famous non-Western text, the Bhagavad Gita. Again, my interest here is the adaptive strategy described in the text and how it might be used to alter the psychology of action in the direction of a response to sport and vulnerability. The text can be read as a practical manual for living a satisfying human life, independent of deeper claims about the identity of Atman and Brahman, although the goal of losing the self (in some significant sense) is still paramount. The Gita tells the story of Arjuna, a young man of action, who has doubts about an upcoming battle that may involve friends and relatives. Arjuna is being counseled by Krishna, an incarnation of the God Vishnu. The famous passages on selfless action in chapters 2 and 4 recommend involvement in action without worry about results.

> You have the right to work, but never to the fruit of work. You should never engage in action for the sake of reward, nor should you long for inaction. Perform work in the world, Arjuna, as a man established within himself—without selfish attachments, and alike in success and defeat. For yoga is perfect evenness of mind. . . . Seek refuge in the attitude of detachment and you will amass the wealth of spiritual awareness. Those who are motivated only by the desire for the fruits of action are miserable, for they are constantly anxious about the results of what they do. When consciousness is unified, however, all vain anxiety is left behind. . . .

The awakened sages call a person wise when all his undertakings are free from anxiety about results: all his selfish desires have been consumed in the fire of knowledge. The wise, ever satisfied, have abandoned all external supports. Their security is unaffected by the results of the action. . . .

They live in freedom who have gone beyond the dualities of life. Competing with no one, they are alike in success and failure and content with whatever comes to them. They are free, without selfish attachments; their minds are fixed in knowledge.[17]

I call this strategy the redirection of desire (instead of elimination), because I assume that what is being called for is a change of attitude and attention in which a focus on absorption in the activity might still be characterized as involving at least certain kinds of wants or preferences. The Gita recognizes that focusing on outcomes produces worry and anxiety about the future. Attachment to results distracts one from being totally involved or absorbed in the activity itself. When one is totally involved or absorbed in certain kinds of activities, there is no worry about the self. The message of the Gita is not at all surprising to players and coaches, although they may sometimes have to be reminded that the best moments of sports participation are when participants are taken up as much as possible by full immersion in the game or activity, when present involvement in the flow of experience is extraordinarily satisfying.[18]

The message is similar to Buddhist and Taoist recommendations. Attachments produced by strong desires for outcomes lead to unhappiness; they occasion anxieties and the pain of thwarted desires when the outcomes involve failures and defeat. This undermines the gratifying possibilities of present experience. The advice is neither mysterious nor impractical. One may have a sense of the ongoing temporal movement of experience, but the focus is on the shape and complexity of the present. The message is simple although difficult to embody: Do not worry about winning or losing. Act for the sake of enjoyment and perhaps even better performance. In Joel Kupperman's commentary on the Bhagavad Gita, he insists that detachment is compatible with active engagement in the world, and even mentions the athlete as a prime example: "What is required is an overriding detachment, so that one will never worry about any form of failure or desire success. If we assume that this detachment does not preclude awareness of the likely shape of the future, it might actually improve performance. The result would be much like what athletes speak of as entering 'the zone.' There are comparable phenomena in relation to other kinds of performance. People are usually at their best when they become entirely absorbed in what they are doing and are not distracted by concerns about outcomes."[19] Redirecting desire in sports involves a fundamental change of attitude. If we can play in such a way as to avoid the anxieties associated with cravings for winning, thereby enhancing our enjoyment and even our performance, then there is no reason to say that "losing is like death." Detachment from intense desires for outcomes makes one invulnerable to the more extreme negative psychological consequences described by Kohn and others. When we redirect our attention to the activity rather than the outcomes, other important valuable possibilities become available.

D. *Multiplying Desires*

"Winning isn't everything; it's the only thing." Of course not. "It's all about winning." No, it isn't. "Life is about winning." How absurd. Despite the overcharged ethos of winning that pervades contemporary sports at virtually all levels, if we take seriously the view of sport and life expressed in these cultural clichés, it is plainly mistaken. Then why is it so prevalent? The view assumes that desire in sport is unified, as if the fundamental reason for playing sports is to win. What I have to say here is not new, it is not obscure, nor is it particularly contentious. If I am asked, "Why do you play sports?" or "Feezell, see here, why did you waste so much of your life playing and coaching games and teaching your children the intricacies of a good swing, good backspin on the jump shot, or proper preparation on the backhand?" my answer would not be, "Well, life is about winning, don't you know." There are numerous reasons for playing and coaching sports (later I will say more about fans), and to reduce the multiplicity of desires in sports to the hegemonic pursuit of victory is to ignore many of the elements that make sports worthwhile.

In no particular order, it is evident that one may play sports in order to find enjoyment; become better at some skilled, physical activity; seek to be really good, that is, to become excellent, judged by a relatively high standard; overcome obstacles that one has voluntarily placed before oneself; learn something important about oneself; practice developing not only sports skills but also traits of character that may help one succeed as a player and could be important in life—perseverance, courage, responsibility, and fair play; develop friendships with fellow participants; and to have something (so many things) to care about, in a sense related to meaningful activities and projects.

Multiplying desires—or simply recognizing that there are many reasons to play sports, many purposes involved, many things to want or care about—serves to undermine the supposed authority of the all-consuming desire to win and to undermine its power to disrupt our psychological well-being, moral character, and personal relationships. Losing is not like death in one obvious sense. Death extinguishes not only all present desires, including the desire to continue to live, but also all future desires. Losing thwarts the desire to win, but it does not extinguish ongoing desires to play, to become better, to challenge oneself, to be with others, and to have something to care about. In this sense, death is permanent, losing is impermanent, and the impermanence of loss is related to a further adaptive strategy.

*E. Trivializing Desires*
Multiplying desires may be enough to reduce the authority of the desire to win by making it appear to be one among many reasons to play sports, but some may still insist that it is the most impor-

tant desire among many desires. Because of its importance, it may trump other desires. According to this view, there is still a hierarchy of desires involved, with winning being the most important. So, "It's all about winning" means that the desire to win is not the only reason to play sports, but it trumps all other desires.

One response to this view is to remind people of the consequences of making the desire to win authoritative. That would subsume not only the moral goals of sport but also goals like enjoyment and friendship. In situations where conflicts of desires occur, the desire to win would always override, so all of the ethical issues emphasized by social critics could emerge: cheating, violence, gamesmanship, performance-enhancing drugs, and so forth. Making the desire to win authoritative is often a prescription for moral ruthlessness. If we find these consequences unacceptable or retain our intuitions that there are often more important ends in sport than winning the contest, we will be guarded in our judgments about the value of victory, thus changing our attitudes.

A more direct way to challenge this view is to insist that we think carefully about what we are doing in sports when we evaluate the importance of winning or even succeeding in all sorts of other ways involving the possibility of failure. Elsewhere I have attempted to defend the view that sport is *splendid triviality*, so I will not offer an extended defense here.[20] Susan Wolf has said this when reflecting on meaningful activities as "active engagement in projects of worth": "I have neither a philosophical theory of what objective value is nor a substantive theory about what has this sort of value." Neither do I. But I do think it makes sense, as she does, to relate judgments about good lives (for Wolf, meaningful lives) to "a distinction between more or less worthwhile ways to spend one's time, where the test of worth is at least partly independent of a subject's ungrounded preferences or enjoyment."[21] We do, in fact, quite readily recognize that "it's only a game," in situations in which severe injuries occur in sports, in which athletes devote themselves, outside of their sport, to enhancing the well-being or flourishing of other human beings. People play their games, involve themselves in skilled, physical activities, and invest these undertakings with utmost importance, while often recognizing that the pursuit of justice, social good, or knowledge may be more important in the grand scheme of things.

Reflective athletes are well aware of the modest value of the satisfaction of their athletic desires. In the following, Jim Bouton reflects on these issues in the introduction to *Ball Four*, one of the most insightful and honest books ever written about professional baseball. Writing in 1968, he wonders, why play baseball?

> I've heard all the arguments against it. That there are better, more important things for a man to do than spend his time trying to throw a ball past other men who are trying to hit it with a stick. There are things like being a doctor or a teacher or working in the Peace Corps. More likely I should be devoting myself full-time to finding a way to end the war. I admit that sometimes I'm troubled by the way I make my living. I *would* like to change the world. I *would* like to have an influence on other people's lives. And the last time I was sent down to the minor leagues a man I consider my friend said, only half-kidding, I guess, "Why don't you quit and go out and earn a living like everyone else, ya bum, ya?"[22]

Bouton is somewhat defensive in his response. He says, "What the hell, there are a lot of professions that rank even with baseball, or a lot below, in terms of nobility. I don't think there's anything so great about selling real estate or life insurance or mutual funds, or a lot of other unimportant things that people do with their lives and never give it a thought." But people need houses, ways to avoid risk, and financial security. They do not need to be able to strike out opponents or even appreciate the skill involved. Sport is superfluous, yet splendid. Bouton says, "The fact is that I love the game, love to play it, I mean." That is the fundamental desire, isn't it, despite the acknowledgment of its lack of "nobility" or importance? He admits, "A lot of it is foolishness, too, grown men being serious about a boy's game. There's pettiness in baseball, and meanness and stupidity beyond belief, and everything else bad that you'll find outside of baseball." For some, the pettiness and meanness are sufficient to cause one to avoid sports. Not Bouton. "Yet there's a tremendous lot of good in it for me and I wouldn't trade my years in it for anything I can think of." I could not agree more, yet when I think about my own love for baseball, in particular, it has little to do with how many wins or losses my teams racked up. "Losing is like death." No, it's not. It is not that important. And we should always remember that there is still the possibility of *playing*, in the broadest possible sense, after experiencing defeat. If Sisyphus does not quite get the rock to the top of the hill, it rolls back down, and he once again attempts to roll it to the top—more efficiently, faster, stylistically, or even beautifully—remember that if he is playing at rolling his rock, he is still enjoying his trivial and futile project.

It's only a game. Children must learn this lesson early on, as part of the education of their emotions and their relationships to their opponents. To learn that it is only a game and to embody that attitude in competitive play is at the same time a lesson in how to be a good sport. In this sense, trivializing desire also serves to civilize desire.

Trivializing desires is ultimately a matter of *playing as if*—playing as if the outcome of the game really matters, while realizing, as Bouton does, that there is something foolish about grown-ups taking children's games so seriously. We must take them seriously, in order to experience the possible goods and enhance our involvements, while sustaining an attitude that detaches the activity from matters of ultimate concern.

I mention, in passing, that it might be possible to conditionalize our desires in various ways.[23] For example, I may not care whether we vacation this summer, but if we do, I do not want to go to Disneyland again. Or, I do not want to go to Disneyland, but if we do, I will not be disappointed because it is better than staying home. Or, I want to go to Disneyland, but if we stay home, I will not spend time regretting my misfortune—perhaps we will take some local weekend getaways. The propensity to conditionalize desires depends on their strength or intensity and one's ability to adapt wisely and see alternatives. If we combine trivialization and conditionalizing, it is possible to develop an adaptive attitude that moderates disappointments. Is this possible in sports? The motto of an improvisational troupe called Comedy Sports is this: "We play to win but don't care if we lose."[24] No doubt there is some irony here, but there is some truth also. I recall moments in my life when I have badly wanted something, only to see my desires dashed. Even for relatively strong desires, in sports and in life outside of sports, it is possible to care deeply but move on, to look elsewhere for valuable possibilities and not to dwell on unsatisfied desires. This is one commonsense way of developing essentially Stoic attitudes in life. And when conditionalizing desire is combined with trivializing, it is much easier to turn despair into mild disappointment, especially when there are so many other elements involved that may be the basis for optimism, which is shown by redirecting and multiplying our desires.

### III. Adaptation, Moderation, and Fans

Sport, like life, offers ample opportunities for failure and disappointment. It distills in an interesting way the problem of making happiness depend on desire satisfaction. It shows the limits of optimizing and the dangers associated with competitive desires. It occasions the need for some kind of wise adaptation of desires, in order to make us less vulnerable to the "agony of defeat." More extreme forms of adaptation are unacceptable, however. Some people say we should avoid competitive activities or having competitive desires, but such people are too risk averse. They either exaggerate the importance of victory or underestimate the extent to which we can change our desires even when we seek success in sports. We do need something to push up against in life, in order to grow, develop, and learn, yet we have reflective resources to mitigate the supposed misery of confronting our limitations. The adapter is right to reject extreme forms of optimizing, in sports and elsewhere, but more extreme forms of adaptation overvalue negative forms of happiness, where the ultimate goal is to achieve a kind of tranquility associated with the avoidance of unsatisfied desires. We must learn to balance risk and the avoidance of unwise desires and attitudes.

The "losing is like death" view of sports—the notion that there is only the happiness of winning and the misery of losing—is unwise. It assumes that winning is the only good or the primary good in sports, and it is based on an optimizing approach to happiness that ignores what the adapter emphasizes—that avoidance of unhappiness, or at least its reduction, is possible by moderating our passions, refocusing our attention, and reshaping our attitudes.

For the most part I have been interested in those for whom involvement in sports is active and direct: players and coaches. What about fans? The lesson taught by the strategy of adaptation may be even more important for fans, whose relation to sport is external, not internal. I have changed my view of fans, in part because of my attempt to "externalize" (in Harry Frankfurt's sense)[25] the spectatorial desire for my team to win, in order to understand and evaluate that desire. Like many fans, I love the excitement of being caught up in the unfolding of sporting events, and I want my team to win. Yet I think of the experience in aesthetic terms. I want to see where the story is going, and I want the narrative to turn out a certain way. Yet when the story, book, or film does not turn out the way I desire, the disappointment is short-lived. Like the athlete and coach, aesthetic enjoyment arises in the absorption, yet here it is spectatorial rather than grounded in active engagement. So, the team loses. It's a game. Let's move on. There are more books to read, plays to attend, and games to appreciate. The end is relatively trivial, although the complexity of the unfolding process is quite fascinating.

At virtually all levels of sport, from crazed Little League parents and idiotic college boosters, to aggressive and violent fans of col-

lege and professional sports teams, the winning-is-everything attitude is a source of real problems. If it is possible for coaches and
athletes to become wise adapters, such strategies should be even
more available to fans who are not even directly involved in sports,
spectators for whom the phenomenon is representation rather than
movement, effort, sacrifice, confrontation with obstacles, overcoming limits—the joy of participation.

Colin McGinn, fine philosopher and lover of sports participation, does not suffer foolish fans gladly. Here is what he says about
fans:

> Most spectator interest in sports strikes me as tribal and nationalistic.
> You support "your" team, often hating their rivals and the rivals' sup-
> porters. I find this primitive and stupid, to be blunt, and we know
> where it can lead. I don't want to sully the page with reports of "foot-
> ball hooliganism" and the like ("savages at a soccer match" would be
> less euphemistic). Sport in this sense is largely of negative value, and I
> hold no brief for it. And isn't it clear that the interest in sport, here, is
> centred on winning and losing, not the appreciation of athletic excel-
> lence? This is why the typical "fan" is so downcast when "his" team
> loses, even if they put on a great show, only to lose to a team even
> greater. If spectators like the sport so much, I want to ask, why don't
> they play it themselves?[26]

Unlike McGinn, I think we may love a game without reducing it
to its "trappings and (dubious) symbolism," nor do I think that
being a fan is reduced merely to "sublimating his own thwarted
desire to be a sporting hero—to be *somebody*—into a passive experience of watching others, while relishing just a little too much the
victories of his team over other teams."[27] There are real dangers,
however. The screaming and uncontrolled fan, either in the stadium
or in front of his television, *is* pathetic—and sometimes dangerous.
Some of the most disturbing aspects of contemporary sports involve
fans whose "passion" has evolved into hatred and violence, whose
unreflective attachments have produced such ugly behavior toward

other human beings, and whose sense of identity and self-worth is tied to the victories of his team. (I need not "sully the page" with the more extreme examples: beatings and even death threats for coaches and . . . Steve Bartman.) In the next chapter I will examine more deeply issues associated with being a fan.

In my judgment the worst aspects of sports are deeply rooted in the all-consuming desire to win and an optimizing approach to happiness. We can learn much from the great traditions that emphasize mastery of desire and some ideal that prizes equanimity as well as modest and moderate desire satisfaction. I am saddened when I hear about athletes and coaches who have succumbed to the "losing is like death" view of sport, whose misery becomes unbounded. In the 1986 American League Championship Series, the California Angels were one pitch away from beating the Boston Red Sox and advancing to the World Series. With two strikes and two outs in the ninth inning, Angels' pitcher Donnie Moore gave up a game-tying home run to Dave Henderson, a hit that led to an extra-inning victory for the Red Sox and an eventual American League Championship. Donnie Moore was haunted by these memories, experienced constant booing by fans during the next three years, and began a "descent into despair." In 1989, after being released by a Minor League team, he shot himself. The joy of sports somehow led to suicide—and real death. It was called the pitch that killed Donnie Moore. Why do these games seem to mean so much to people? Why don't they change their attitudes and desires? Why do they make themselves so miserable? Are parents, coaches, players, and fans to blame when we do not actively promote alternatives to the win-at-all-costs attitude toward sport? I am haunted by the tragedy of Donnie Moore.

# 4 The Pitfalls of Partisanship

Issues associated with the ethics of supporting sports teams deserve more attention. In the last chapter I briefly examined the importance of adaptive strategies for fans whose overheated passion for their teams sometimes leads to questionable behavior and fragile judgments of self-worth. Despite the more extreme examples of stupid and even violent behavior, it is not clear that partisanship must be reduced to bad forms of tribalism and nationalism. Perhaps a more intelligent form of partisanship can be defended.

Nicholas Dixon has written the classic defense of what he calls the "moderate partisan," a fan whose "loyal support of a team is not only permissible but positively virtuous."[1] In the face of objections that might be mounted by a purist fan, who "supports the team that he thinks exemplifies the highest virtues of the game" (441), Dixon recommends a form of partisanship as the attitude ideal for fans.

Dixon's defense of the moderate partisan is both fascinating and apparently compelling, yet I remain less than fully convinced. In the following I construct an imagined dialogue between the partisan and the purist in order to raise some questions about the ideal fan attitude that Dixon defends. My sympathies are with the purist; however, the dialogue form may be appropriate, given the tentativeness of my views. I intend to sketch the contours of an attitude that Dixon fails to address. I hope that my reconstruction of Dixon's central arguments will be accurate and charitable, but I do not claim that the partisan in my dialogue exactly represents what Dixon might say. I will indicate the parts of the dialogue that make explicit reference to what Dixon says in his provocative paper. I leave it to the reader to sort out the strengths and weaknesses of the various arguments.

## A Dialogue between the Partisan and the Purist

PARTISAN:  As we are going to discuss and evaluate the central motivations of fans, let me begin by distinguishing two categories.

PURIST:  That's a good way to begin.

PARTISAN:  I distinguish the partisan and the purist. Both are supporters of a team, but their allegiances are motivated by quite different concerns. There are different kinds of partisan support, but the most basic kind arises when there is some personal connection with the players or coaches of a local, usually amateur, team.

PURIST:  Would it be correct to say that you use the model of a family or a circle of friends to characterize the partisan's motives?

PARTISAN:  That's correct, but these direct, local connections are not necessarily personal when we consider other kinds of fans. The followers of school or college teams may have direct connections with an institution. "Both of these two types of fandom are straightforwardly explicable by reference to a concern for the wellbeing of people for whom one cares or institutions with which one identifies" (441–42).

PURIST:  Yet when we consider rooting for high-profile college teams, especially after one graduates (even if one has attended the institution in question), the players aren't really friends, or even acquaintances. In this respect the players we're rooting for are more like athletes on professional teams. We don't know them. How could they be construed as our friends?

PARTISAN: Well, in many cases we simply become familiar with teams, because we watch them and read about them. Often we root for teams that represent our region or our country, whether they are college or professional teams. We may feel "enlarged" by the successes of the teams we root for.

PURIST: The family model scarcely accounts for such motives.

PARTISAN: We do support professional and college teams whose players have no local connections. "The basis for their support seems to be simple proximity and familiarity" (442).

PURIST: I reiterate. There's no family connection with players and coaches in a wide range of cases.

PARTISAN: In these cases I think the connections arise by adoption. We "adopt" them, as we do when we take people into our families in certain ways. "This process of adopting a team is no more mysterious than the increasing concern for the wellbeing of another that is central to the beginning and deepening of friendship" (442).

PURIST: Here's where the analogy breaks down. I suspect that you will defend partisanship on the basis of an analogy with a family or the kind of personal connections involved in friendship. It's virtuous to be concerned with the well-being of people for whom one cares. This strikingly contrasts with partisanship in sports. In most cases, not only do we not know whom we're rooting for, I'm not sure we're rooting for *them* at all. In many cases partisans seem to be rooting for themselves. When I consider most extreme partisans I have known, when their team loses they don't feel bad for the players; they feel bad for themselves. The partisan is miserable or happy because of a strong identification with a team. Fans are always talking about how "we" will do in the big game or what "our" prospects are for the coming season, as if they are actually members of the team. Where you see normal and virtuous concern for the well-being of friends, both real and adopted, I see this peculiar self-concern that is neither praiseworthy nor always psychologically healthy.

It's delusory. You see loyalty. I see, in its more extreme forms, a kind of tribalism. You see concern for others. I see self-interest and an obvious lack of concern for the well-being of the members of teams partisans root against.

PARTISAN: For me, familiarity, whether it's local or based on media coverage, is the basis for the growth and development of natural and praiseworthy connections with other persons who happen to be parts of teams and whose successes come to matter for people. I see nothing problematic about that. I do recognize that support for a team may be based on an appreciation of athletic excellence. The person I call a purist "supports the team that he thinks best exemplifies the highest virtues of the game, but his allegiance is flexible" (440). This kind of fan support is based on "admiration for a team's skill and style of play" (443). Would you call yourself a purist?

PURIST: I would say that sometimes I do choose my allegiances on purist grounds rather than on the basis of "local, regional or patriotic biases" (443). But it's more complicated. I do love a well-played game, and I support teams that play the game the way it's supposed to be played. As a matter of fact, I love baseball. I tend to support teams and players who hustle, are excellent base runners, can put down a bunt in a key situation, throw to the correct base—overall, who play smart baseball. In many cases I want the team who plays best to win a well-matched, skillful contest.

PARTISAN: I understand such matters. You seem to have "staked out the high moral ground" since your "choice of team is based only on sporting excellence" (443). I realize that purist ideals are important when we teach children that playing fairly and trying hard are more important than a "win-at-all-costs mentality" (443). But there's something missing in such purist attitudes.

PURIST: What?

PARTISAN: Consider a "surprising analogy with romantic love" (443). When we become attracted to another person, we are impressed by that person's good qualities. Over time, "our love becomes less dependent on our partner's qualities and fixes instead on their unique instantiation of those qualities: in other words, on their special identity" (443). Our love becomes "imprinted on the particular person" (443).

PURIST: That sounds plausible. How does this relate to the purist fan?

PARTISAN: Notice that, typically, "a person in love does not seek to 'trade up' to a different partner who scores higher than her current partner on the most significant evaluative scales" (443). Suppose another person has admirable qualities to a higher degree than our partner. This does not cause us to transfer our affections to a new love interest.

PURIST: Actually, it seems to me that *does* occur in many situations, but I'll grant you the point for now.

PARTISAN: In addition, "love can endure a considerable amount of change" (444). Our partner's qualities do sometimes dramatically change over time, yet love endures. I admit that some changes would be intolerable, but the identity of the object of our love may endure despite the fact that the original qualities that "led us to fall in love may diminish or even disappear" (444).

PURIST: Your point?

PARTISAN: My point is this: if we take the analogy seriously, the "purist barely qualifies as a fan at all" (444).

PURIST: Why?

PARTISAN: Because the purist's support for a team is "purely conditional" (444). It's too flexible. If some team plays better than the one he's rooting for, then the purist trades up. The purist is most interested in athletic excellence, defined by standards of good play within the game. The partisan is a loyal supporter of a team, despite the fact that the team may not play well. "Indeed, we regard the willingness to continue supporting a team despite hard times as a sign of admirable loyalty" (444). The purist has no such loyalty; she "lacks an allegiance that is imprinted on a given team and remains in spite of changing qualities. A loyalty that is so contingent is a fleeting tenuous type of support" (444).

PURIST: So far, I can agree with some of what you have said, but we need to make another distinction. When someone asks me, "Are you a fan?" I believe the question is ambiguous. You seem to think that the only person who qualifies as a fan is the partisan, as you have described such a person's motivations. Why not distinguish a team fan and a game fan? I'm more a fan of the game than I am a fan of a particular team. I'm a game lover rather than a team lover.

PARTISAN: In my judgment, "a certain amount of unconditional loyalty—the kind the partisan has—is essential to genuine support of a team" (444). You purists are too detached. You don't seem to want to indulge perfectly natural human responses to those with whom one becomes familiar. The loyalty of the partisan is virtuous. I do not think that the attitude of the completely purist fan is morally superior to the partisan's allegiance to his team. I'm defending "conventional fandom" (445), and I believe partisan loyalty is an "essential component" (445) of this desirable attitude toward teams.

PURIST: You have not quite accurately described my attitudes, but for now let me raise two problems. First, you say that loyalty is admirable, just as trust and forgiveness might be virtuous qualities in human relationships. If we're talking about supporting sports teams, there are situations in which teams do not deserve our support. If they cheat, they don't deserve our support. Or if they are too violent or extremely disrespectful to opponents or officials, we should not support them.

PARTISAN: I agree. That is why I defend the attitude of the moderate partisan. "A genuine fan may . . . withdraw her support if her team starts to engage in such indefensible practices as violent play or other forms of cheating, or even if it starts to use cynical, negative tactics, which may be within the letter of the law of the game, while violating its spirit" (445).

PURIST: These are purist attitudes. My love of the game prevents me from supporting such teams. Winning at all costs is a shabby ideal.

PARTISAN: I accept your criticism of the complete partisan who is blinded by prejudice and unmoved by ethical ideals. "A modicum of the purist's attitude will provide a healthy safeguard against any tendency the partisan may have toward blind allegiance to a team that is unworthy of such support" (445). I defend the moderate partisan whose allegiances are moderated by ethical commitments. I reject the 100 percent purist fan, who is not a fan at all, and I reject the 100 percent partisan fan, on the grounds you have staked out. "The ideal attitude for fans, then, appears to be the tenacious loyalty of the partisan, tempered by the purist's realization that teams that violate the rules or spirit of the game do not deserve our support" (445).

PURIST: I think you have failed to recognize another important attitude, which is, in fact, the attitude I want to defend. I'm not a complete purist; neither are you a complete partisan. My purist ideals have moved you toward a more moderate kind of fan. There are arguments that should move you further toward a purist attitude. First, I want to raise a second problem.

PARTISAN: What do you have mind?

PURIST: I'm still troubled by your use of analogies involving significant forms of human relationships: family, friends, even romantic love. You first wanted to use the model of a family to understand the nature of our connections with players and teams and to extol the virtues of loyalty and "concern for the well-being of people for whom one cares," as you said. When the connections are based on watching, attending, or reading about games and thus becoming familiar with persons who are strangers, our circle of concern is supposedly expanded by "adoption." Now, you criticize a completely purist fan by analogy with romantic love. A real fan doesn't trade up or change allegiances so readily, because the allegiance is "imprinted" on a team despite its changing qualities. The problem is this. You criticize the purist because the team she supports is replaceable. Her support for a team is too "ethereal" (444), as you say. However, for the partisan, especially when we focus on support for professional and high-profile college teams, the players are replaceable. For you, support is supposedly rooted in virtuous concern for the well-being of "friends," real or adopted on the basis of proximity and familiarity. But you're not really concerned with the well-being of particular players, who often have no connection with you, your city, region, or school. Professional players are traded. College players transfer. When they become members of opposing teams, you're not so concerned with their well-being when they attempt to defeat your team. Their relation to the team you support is contingent and, in the world of big-time commercial athletics, quite "ethereal." You are concerned with an abstraction, not Jones as a particular human being, as a friend, but Jones as a member of your favorite team. The bond between a team and its fans is quite unlike the bond between romantic lovers. If the zeal of the partisan is to be defended, even a fervent allegiance moderated by ethical commitments, I do not think the defense should be based on an analogy with real friendship, family connections, or romantic love. After all, you want to defend a zeal or fervent interest in certain teams winning games. I can understand an interest in athletic excellence and well-played, dramatic games. I fail to understand the basis for your enthusiasm.

PARTISAN: I don't think you appreciate the strength and legitimacy of "a perfectly natural human response that may be hard to suppress even in the case of the purist fan" (444).

PURIST: I do recognize this, even within myself. Yet I'm not sure it can stand up to critical reflection, and I'm not sure it can be defended by an appeal to an analogy with other significant human relationships.

PARTISAN: In developing my view I have considered "several arguments against loyal support for a particular team" (445). In my judgment, none of them is very strong. Since you are a purist, you may support such arguments. Perhaps we should consider criticisms of partisanship. I'll respond on behalf of the moderate partisan. I hope you'll see why I defend this attitude in the way I do. Even if you reject my claim that moderate partisanship is virtuous, you might come to see it as innocuous, hence morally permissible.

PURIST: That's an appropriate strategy.

PARTISAN: The first criticism that might occur to many people concerns the attitudes and actions of some partisans. I'll call this the Bad Attitudes–Immoral Actions Argument. From soccer hooligans to outraged Little League parents who assault umpires, some partisan supporters of teams engage in violent behavior and express hatred of their rivals.

PURIST: I think this is a serious issue.

PARTISAN: I do too. "However, there is nothing inherent in supporting a team that requires its fans to act violently and it would be unfair to tar all supporters, the vast majority of whom never act violently, with the same brush that we justly apply to hooligans" (446). In my view, fervent support for a team need not entail hatred, disrespect, or any negative attitudes toward rivals.

PURIST: I understand your point, and it is well taken. Yet you repeatedly speak in terms of "fierce allegiances," "zeal," and "fervent" support. In theory you are right. A partisan may enthusiastically support her team without hating or disrespecting rival teams. Yet you also speak of perfectly natural human responses that are hard to suppress. The "loyal support" that you defend is, above all, a fervent desire for the partisan's team to *win*. In practice, this identification with the success of a team often produces, perhaps "naturally," negative attitudes toward those who oppose your desires (opposing players and coaches) and those who make decisions that prevent your strong desires from being fulfilled (officials). And the opposing fans want your deepest, most fervent partisan desires to be unfulfilled. If the desire for a team to win were less fierce or fervent, or held with less zeal, we wouldn't have these problems. This is one of the reasons I support a moderate form of purism, not partisanship. If we're talking about the ideal attitude for fans, a more purist form of interest is less dangerous, morally speaking.

PARTISAN: You may be equivocating on the term *ideal*. I'm arguing that partisanship is perfectly compatible with respecting opponents and appreciating athletic excellence. It is ideal in the sense that partisan loyalty is also virtuous. For you, it is not "ideal" in the sense that, in practice, when partisanship involves strong desires, it may be dangerous. I admit that partisanship may lead to bad behavior, but it need not. Hence, moderate partisanship is permissible—and good.

PURIST: In my view, even moderate partisanship is not the ideal attitude for a fan, in the sense that, given the way the world is, given the actual psychology of fans, fervent interest in winning may and does lead to bad attitudes and bad behavior. Also, I still maintain that the family, friendship, and romantic-love analogies you depend on are misleading.

PARTISAN: Do you reject partisanship on the basis of an appeal to impartiality? The Impartiality Argument claims that partisanship violates a central moral requirement: to give equal consideration to the interests of everyone. Partisanship "involves giving special treatment to a favored group of people. And impartiality—giving equal respect to the interests of all people—is central to all non-egoistic moral theories" (446). Your purist interest in athletic excellence seems to appreciate an evaluative quality equally applicable to all teams.

PURIST: It does strike me that partisanship may be tribalistic in a bad sense, where arbitrary group membership or identification is the basis for not appropriately respecting the interests of others, but I don't hang my purist hat strictly on appeals to impartiality in a moral sense. This argument raises some deep issues in ethical theory about giving special preferences to some people—for example, members of one's family, friends, fellow citizens, and so forth.

PARTISAN: Yes, it does. I do not think that giving special preference to certain people—for example, family, friends, or even fellow citizens or a country—is, in itself, objectionable.

PURIST: I agree.

PARTISAN: In my view, "impartiality is primarily a restraint on our behavior that prevents us from harming those who are not part of our 'in-group'" (446). In pursuing our own interests and favoring the interests of some over others, we "may not trample on the rights of others" (446). This merely reinforces my view that partisanship does not necessarily involve bad attitudes, disrespect, or morally objectionable violations of impartiality. A special concern for our team is a prima facie good and need not involve "negative attitudes toward or violations of the rights of rival teams and fans" (447).

PURIST: My previous point remains. Although fervent partisanship need not violate the rights of rival teams and fans, it sometimes does. For that reason alone we should be wary of partisan zeal.

PARTISAN: On the contrary, the purist seems to have a disturbing detachment or lack of involvement when it comes to viewing sports. I admit that no one is obligated to support a particular team, yet "we have reason to be wary of the completely purist fan who has no lasting attachment to a single team" (447). Suppose someone regularly watches a local team and can generate only a detached, purist interest in athletic excellence or a well-played game. There may be something wrong with such a fan. It may express "an inability to develop empathy for other people. A person who lacks this ability may have difficulty forming friendships and lasting romantic attachments" (447).

PURIST: This is one of your weakest claims. You're speculating about the moral psychology of the fan. Since a local team may consist of strangers or people who are, at best, mere acquaintances, you have no idea whether a purist may have other significant relationships or is able to form such relationships. Purist detachment may be based on deeper reflective concerns about the value of winning games. Since the partisan may fervently root for a nonlocal high-profile college team or some professional team, I do not see how you're in a position to speculate on that brand of partisanship. But the deeper problem is this. At various points you have criticized the "completely purist" fan or the "100 percent purist" fan. We started with the distinction between the partisan and the purist fan, in relatively pure motivational senses. You admitted that purist attitudes concerning the ethics of competition must temper the "tenacious loyalty of the partisan" (445). Now you talk as if there are simply two attitudes: moderate partisanship and the completely purist fan whom you have just criticized as possibly cold and uncaring. This is a false dilemma. In fact, I'm neither a moderate partisan nor a complete purist. I am a moderate purist, in a sense I will explain. You have failed to consider this as the ideal attitude of fans. I appreciate athletic excellence. I love the game. I also think that teams that cheat or violate the "spirit of the game do not deserve our support," as you have said. On the other hand, fervent or zealous support for a team, which expresses an extremely strong desire for a particular team to win, is neither a virtuous concern for the well-being of others, admirable loyalty toward friends, nor wholly innocuous. You admit that extreme partisanship can't survive some forms of ethical reflection. I'm not sure it can withstand scrutiny about the value of its object. After all, we are talking about the desire for a chosen team to win games.

PARTISAN: Are you suggesting that the goal of winning games is trivial, or doesn't matter in some important sense?

PURIST: That's exactly what I'm suggesting.

PARTISAN: I call this the Triviality Argument. "Isn't sport too trivial an entertainment to justify making teams of highly-paid professionals the object of fans' devotion" (447)?

PURIST: I would add support for high-profile college teams. Actually, I would add support for any team, at any level. I don't think any team deserves "fervent" support, if by that you mean an extremely strong desire for a team to win. I just don't think that the outcome of sporting events should matter so much to fans.

PARTISAN: "In the absence of a morally worthy object of allegiance," you find partisan support to be "a form of tribalism: the division of sports fans into arbitrary opposing factions" (447)?

PURIST: Something like that.

PARTISAN: I have three responses to the Triviality Argument. First, you don't support your claim that "pursuits of sporting teams are too trivial to make them a suitable object of fans' allegiance. Teams provide entertainment and excitement for spectators, which is already enough to take their enterprise out of the category of the mindless" (447).

PURIST: Just because some spectators find an event exciting or entertaining doesn't make it worthwhile. Some people find cockfighting or dog fighting exciting and entertaining. Nonetheless, they are cruel and morally reprehensible practices. Suppose the gods set up grandstands for people to watch Sisyphus roll his rock up the hill, time after time, and also had the power to manipulate their interests in such a way that they found rock rolling exciting and entertaining? That wouldn't make the object of their interest any less meaningless. Winning a sporting contest is trivial, especially to the fan, in the clear sense that the outcome of an artificially constructed competition, in principle, doesn't affect the well-being of a fan in any significant way. It doesn't involve suffering, disease, death, achievement, self-realization, self-expression, knowledge, or even virtue—for the fan. We read books and watch films. We're interested in how the narrative unfolds. We become fascinated by representational details and narrative drama. The story ends, and we walk back to real life and the possibility of attaining important human goods, one of which is not the success of your favorite team.

PARTISAN: Not only do teams provide entertainment and excitement, but "their displays of physical excellence—skill, conditioning, etc.—can be comparable to those performers, such as ballet dancers, whom we are far less tempted to dismiss as unworthy of devotion" (447). Athletes also exhibit praiseworthy mental qualities that we admire. These factors, including aesthetic elements, are worthy of admiration. "Supremely fit and skillful athletes who perform efficiently and gracefully seem to be ennobling of human nature and hence worthy of admiration and support for similar reasons as artistic performers" (447).

PURIST: I agree! Yet all of these elements you refer to are precisely the ones that generate *purist* motives or admiration! You attempt to defeat the triviality objection by referring to purist concerns. Admiration for athletic excellence, cunning strategy, psychological strength, and aesthetically efficient and graceful movement—such forms of interest are not team specific. They are independent of who wins and loses or support for a particular team. Ethical and aesthetic appreciation and admiration are central to a purist's motivation and her attraction to sports.

PARTISAN: The purist's interests are still too detached.

PURIST: The fan *is* detached. The fan is not involved in the way that players and coaches are. They are the ones who are involved in the joy of play, the pursuit of athletic excellence, the possibility of success and failure in their artificially constructed world. It may and does matter greatly to them whether they win or lose or play as well as they can. To us, the fans, who often scarcely know much about the members of the teams we root for, who seem unconcerned about the failures of rival teams and players, and who replace our allegiances when players change teams, our interests are more passive. I do not see why outcomes should matter so much to the partisan.

PARTISAN: "The purist shows a commendable appreciation for the fine points of the game but seems to lack the passion and commitment that is the lifeblood of competitive sport" (447).

PURIST: It's the lifeblood of competitive sport for the players and coaches! *They* are the ones who are competing. Fans are watching. It's as if the voyeur watches two strangers having sex and then expresses great satisfaction with his romantic attachments and erotic activities. That's a better analogy.

PARTISAN: Your "criticism unfairly singles out support of sporting teams when many other allegiances would be vulnerable to the same objection, if we were willing to describe them in similarly unfavorable terms" (448).

PURIST: For example?

PARTISAN: Again, consider romantic love. Often, it is "an arbitrary, irrational attachment to a person" (448). Recall how I described the way that romantic love may begin with admiration of certain qualities and be sustained despite the fact that the qualities of a person may undergo considerable change. We think of these attachments as good; "we do not normally regard such love as groundless or undesirable" (448).

PURIST: Again, I just don't find the analogy convincing. In cases of love, we are talking about profoundly important relationships between particular individuals. Rooting for players on a team isn't remotely like that. Within the world of sports, players as members of teams are more like fictional objects who contingently acquire certain descriptions, that is, a Yankee, a Packer, a Bull. We usually know little about them.

PARTISAN: I insist that a fan's allegiance to her team is virtuous, not "an empty-headed, blind affiliation. Such dedication is no more inherently divisive or tribalistic than is people's devotion to their romantic partners" (448).

PURIST: You have provided two responses to my triviality objection. Your reference to possible aesthetic and moral value involved in viewing sporting events confuses aesthetic and moral admiration with evaluation of the value of the outcome and depends on a reference to purist concerns. Your second response makes use of a weak analogy. What's the final consideration?

PARTISAN: Remember that I am defending a moderate form of partisanship. You are concerned that "sport has too little value to justify the fierce allegiance of fans to their teams" (448). Partisan loyalty is not unconditional. As I have argued, a partisan should withhold support from a team whose violent or unethical behavior makes it an unworthy object of allegiance. "Moderate partisan fans' use of such moral and aesthetic criteria in determining whether to support a team helps ensure that even though their choice of allegiance may originally have been made on the arbitrary ground of familiarity, their continued loyalty depends on whether the team's actions are worthy of it" (449).

PURIST: I don't see how this addresses the original objection that the object of fans' allegiance is relatively trivial. That merely restates a point raised before we discussed the triviality objection. It doesn't respond to the objection, although it does attempt to allay other purist concerns.

PARTISAN: You have said that you are a moderate purist. Please explain this more fully so I can understand what you mean.

PURIST: I identify with your original characterization of the motivations of the purist. I am much more a game lover than a team lover. Perhaps my attitudes have developed over time. I appreciate athletic excellence, moral strength, and aesthetic grace. I do love to watch various games. In many cases I find myself drawn into the narrative unfolding of the game and the strategic details of competitive athletic contests. My attraction is a function of familiarity with the game, not merely with the players, because in many cases neither am I acquainted with the players, nor do I even know who is playing. Yet I'm drawn to a game with which I'm familiar. In many cases I become interested in who will win despite having little desire for a particular team to be successful. I don't really care which team wins, but I enjoy the dramatic unfolding that will be settled by a particular outcome. I want to see who wins, just as I want to see how a story turns out. I don't strongly desire a particular outcome.

PARTISAN: You say you're a moderate purist. Where's the moderation?

PURIST: First, I do find myself rooting for certain teams for a variety of reasons. Sometimes I'm attracted to various players and coaches, so I want their teams to succeed. In some cases my motives are exactly as you first described them. There are some partisan attachments, but they're quite mild. In rare cases I have some more personal connection with a team or its members. And I think you're right when you say, "The allegiance that arises from familiarity in the case of the partisan fan is a perfectly natural human response that may be hard to suppress even in the case of the purist fan" (444). One of the partisan motives you might have emphasized involves being part of a community with similar desires. Ask a fan of the Cubs.

PARTISAN: You do have partisan sentiments.

PURIST: Yes. Yet they seem to me to be quite unlike your moderate partisan's, whose allegiances you describe as fervent, fierce, and tenacious. Your partisan may recognize moral and even aesthetic ideals; nevertheless, for me, fierce or fervent allegiances are morally dangerous, lead to unhappiness when your team loses, and are absurd. You want to defend strong desires for a trivial object. That's absurd.[2] I recommend mild preferences. Allegiances arise with familiarity and are nourished by acquaintance and tradition. Critical reflection moderates natural partisan tendencies in the direction of purism. Buddhists teach that suffering arises from attachments, strong desires for objects (events, outcomes, states of affairs). Buddhists recommend that we give up strong attachments in order to avoid suffering.[3] So, I'm a moderate purist, in the sense that I do have allegiances, but they are moderated both by concerns that you recognize as well as by what I would call absurdist and Buddhist attitudes. I should also add that living for years with a person (my wife) who is completely indifferent to the outcome of sporting events has influenced me. She embodies a detached point of view. She doesn't really understand why the outcome of sporting events matters so much to people.

PARTISAN: Isn't your contrast between moderate versions of the two categories of fans a distinction without a difference? A partisan may recognize and appreciate much of what you admire in sport.

PURIST: There is a continuum from blind, fervent allegiance to complete purist detachment. As long as you defend conventional fandom in terms of fervent allegiance, there is a difference between your refined partisan and my reflective, detached purist who has some partisan sentiments.

PARTISAN: I don't accept your absurdist attitudes. Your quasi-Buddhist attitude seems flat and uninterested. Your moderate purist will miss out on all the fun of being a passionate fan.

PURIST: I immensely enjoy watching games and reading and thinking about sports. I'm a fan. What I do miss out on is the apparent misery of the fervent fan whose team loses. Reflection produces perspective. We should be fervently concerned about more important matters, as my wife has taught me.

PARTISAN: Where would we be without the loyal support of the partisan?

PURIST: You began by claiming that "loyal support of a team is not only permissible but also positively virtuous" (441). I wonder what "loyal support" amounts to. Let me make a final point. You suggest that in order for sports to flourish, we need a loyal fan base. There has been much written about the effects of commercialization on contemporary sports. Big-time college and professional athletics are Big Business. To the extent that the effects of commercialization are not positive, and to the extent that passionate fans contribute to this, perhaps we would be better off if fans adopted the attitude I endorse. This is very speculative, and I'm merely suggesting a further avenue of inquiry. Consider high-profile college athletics. Boosters who give millions to high-profile college athletic programs are not moderate purists who have mild preferences. They often don't really care about academic values and have no concern for the economic health of institutions of higher learning. Fervent allegiances are essentially related to skyrocketing coaching salaries, budgetary arms races among high-level programs, new multimillion-dollar athletic facilities, special treatment of athletes, and more. Even if teams don't overtly cheat, more subtle forms of corruption related to economic issues are closely related to passionate fans, even moderate partisans who disdain cheating yet support the machine. I find this troubling.[4] You may need to tell me more about the practical consequences of loyal support of sports teams.

PARTISAN: Another time. Thanks for an interesting discussion.

## Conclusion

I recommend a moderate form of the purist attitude of spectatorship. The dialogical form of the discussion should not mislead. The defense of moderate partisanship in the discussion is serious and interesting, and I do hope that its presentation has been charitable enough to allow the reader to sort out the strengths and weaknesses of the various arguments. My own view is squarely with the defense of the moderate-purist fan. The analogies used to defend partisanship are weak, there are moral dangers associated with any form of fervent allegiance, and the criticisms of the triviality objection are ineffective. A more detached form of interest may allow some inevitable partisan connections, yet the moderation of desire described in the last chapter is entirely appropriate, especially for fans. Love the game, feel the drama, appreciate athletic excellence wherever it occurs, be morally sensitive, admire and express virtue, and cheer for your team, mildly, if you do support one of the competitors. Losing is not like death, nor is it an occasion for misery, especially for fans.

# 5 Sport, Dirty Language, and Ethics

*Hell, no.*
Kofi Annan, 2005 (when asked whether he was going to resign as UN secretary-general)

*Go fuck yourself.*
Vice President Dick Cheney, 2004 (to Senator Patrick Leahy, at a Senate group photo session)

*I'm sorry if I offend you. But I don't swear just for the hell of it. You see, I figure that language is a poor enough means of communication as it is. So we ought to use all the words we've got. Besides, there are damned few words that everybody understands.*
Henry Drummond (the Clarence Darrow character in *Inherit the Wind*)

*Win or lose, Popeye, we're in the fuckin' greatest game ever played.*
Pete Rose, 1975 (to the opposing team's third base coach in the World Series)

We turn now to some more narrow concerns associated with sport and good lives. I focus on a relatively neglected area of ethical reflection, yet one that is particularly relevant when thinking about sports. The literature on cheating, sportsmanship, and performance-enhancing drugs is considerable. The literature on the ethics of speech, at least in sports, is sparse. Since sport is the locus for well-known vulgarians, and speech in sports is often profane (and we expect such coarseness), it might be interesting to examine the nature and value of dirty language against the background of its prevalence in sports. Because arguments against foul language are often based on appeals to prudence, virtue, or overall social good, reasons involved in evaluating bad language involve issues about how to live well. I confess that I am most interested in the fascinating (and even amusing) topic of vulgar language, yet the context in which I discuss these issues (sports) seems to me to be entirely appropriate.

From the distinguished to the dirtbag, cussing is ubiquitous, yet relatively few have attempted to understand this linguistic phenomenon, and fewer still have reflected on the ethical aspects of this type of speech.[1] In this chapter I will attempt just that. I will begin with some comments about the way in which Harry Frankfurt's notorious essay on contemporary culture occasions interesting questions about the use of taboo language and why scholars of sport might be particularly interested in these matters. After providing some descriptive details about the use of so-called bad language, I will consider the relevant arguments that might support various ethical judgments about cussing. The picture I will sketch will be rather messy, but if I am right, the messiness will favor the vulgarians rather than the puritans.[2] While my attention will be focused on cussing in sports, the implications of certain arguments for an ethics of speech in everyday life will be clear.

## 1. Frankfurt, "Bull," and Sports

I first read "On Bullshit" many years ago.[3] At the time my response to Harry Frankfurt's adventurous use of one of our favorite and familiar expletives was mild amusement, apart from the philosophical content of his conceptual analysis or the power of his cultural critique. He was on to something important, no doubt about that. The notoriety of the essay grew exponentially when Princeton University Press decided to print it as a stand-alone text and the sales took off. Here was a little book that had something significant to say about our cultural life, but . . . how could we talk about it in polite company? A *New York Times* review essay referred to "A Princeton Philosopher's Unprintable Essay Title," and politely demurred, referring to the phenomenon as "bull."[4] For me, the awkwardness associated with the title became as interesting as the analysis of sophistry that Frankfurt offers in the essay. The irony was delicious. He wanted to talk about "bullshit," but he could not talk about it without referring to it. The only way to avoid "bullshit" was to refer to it explicitly and truthfully. As reported in the *Times* article, Frankfurt says, "I used the title I did . . . because I wanted to talk about [bull] without any [bull], so I didn't use 'humbug' or 'bunkum.'" Since the essence of "bullshit," according to Frankfurt, is unconcern with truth, the very avoidance of the supposed obscenity stood condemned as a spurious attempt to uphold decorum at the cost of stating the obvious.

In Frankfurt's comments on the essay's title, we see a first line of defense of cussing, but the resources for a full-scale defense seem rather scant given the limited focus on the rather tame scatological reference involved. In the face of what many perceive to be the coarsening of our culture, it may seem better to bite the bullet and uphold the standards of more acceptable language. It is one thing to say that it might sometimes be more honest to refer to some speech as "bullshit"; it is quite another to defend the language of gangsta rap, ubiquitous bad language in movies and everyday life, immature adolescent and teenage cussing, and, for our purposes, the seemingly pervasive use of dirty language in sports.

Let's face it. There is a lot of cussing in sports. Thinking about Frankfurt's language raises some interesting questions, and these issues obviously extend beyond the world of sports. But they are distilled in a striking way when we consider the use of dirty language in sports. (In the next section I will say more about the meta-language associated with cussing.) Interview the CEO of Widget, Inc., about the first-quarter performance of his corporation, and it would be surprising to hear him utter an obscenity. On the other hand, the college or professional coach's press conference might be littered with various obscenities, and we would not be surprised. In Timothy Jay's valuable study *Cursing in America*, he reports data collected from an experiment with college students. They were asked to answer the question, what is the likelihood of hearing a dirty word in various campus locations? "Athletic field," along with two dorms and a pub, scored in a virtual dead heat as the most likely places to hear bad words. Students were also asked to make "likelihood judgments" about dirty-word usage among different campus occupations. Here "athletic coach" was the dramatic winner, far ahead of janitor, policeman, and groundskeeper.[5]

My own experience mirrors such data. On the field or court and in the locker room, I have heard bad language, "*F* bombs" and more, from people whose demeanor and speech in the everyday world seemed more like that of the smiling and unctuous television evangelist. And, of course, there have been and continue to be famous cussers from the world of sports: Ted Williams, Bobby Knight, Ozzie Guillen (now), and many more. My personal favorite (for purposes associated with this paper) is Bobby Knight, one of the greatest basketball coaches of all time, whose crude language has been repeatedly reported, as well as extensively documented in the book *A Season on the Brink*, a particularly useful source of material that will help us sort out various usages involved in the ethics of cussing.

The time may be ripe for considering these matters. In *Sports Illustrated*, Rick Reilly laments the prevalence of vulgar chants among student fans at college sporting events, and he notes that some colleges, including Boston University, have taken measures to curb swearing at athletic events. Reilly also comments favorably on James O'Connor's book *Cuss Control*, devoted to helping people reduce their cussing.[6] This assumes that we ought to curb our vile tongues, and it puts us in the arena of ethical reflection in a broad sense. Ethics is not simply about our duties or obligations. Ethical reflection also raises questions about how to live, what to do, and what kind of person we should be, judged from a standpoint that is broader than morality proper. Cussing may raise explicit moral concerns, but it may also involve questions of prudence, civility, manners, self-expression, politics, and aesthetic value.[7] It is surprising that so little attention has been given to the broader ethical issues associated with cussing. Social scientists who study dirty language are hesitant to make value judgments, but there seems to be an undercurrent of acceptance in their work: "It is prevalent. Therefore, it is permissible." On the other hand, it is natural for many simply to assume that cussing is wrong. After all, we are talking about dirty, offensive language, aren't we? First we need to pin down the linguistic phenomena at issue.

## II. The Metalanguage of Cussing, Dirty Words, and Usage

So far I have referred to our topic rather loosely and in various ways. We could be more precise. For our purposes, I will use the term *cussing* (and sometimes *swearing*) as the most general term to refer to a variety of linguistic phenomena: bad language, foul language, dirty language, blasphemy, cursing, profanity, vulgarity, obscenity, swearing, epithets, expletives, and offensive slang. Both Ruth Wajnryb and Timothy Jay begin their linguistic studies with attempts to offer an account of many of the central terms we use when referring to what I will call, in general, cussing. Wajnryb says "we need a meta-language that is precise and consistent," and Jay refers to "terms that 'the person on the street' uses to describe dirty words." For both, the initial glossary or classification scheme leads to a larger point concerning the ways in which various forms of cussing function in our language. As Jay says, "The purpose of the category analysis is to make the reader aware that historically and psychologically the use of offensive language is a coherent event, that such usage fulfills types of needs and intentions of the speaker and listener."[8] In this spirit I will focus on the purpose of the categories rather than the categories themselves, and some analysis of the way we traditionally refer to instances of cussing will naturally arise.

What about the words themselves? If the reader felt no shock or squeamishness in reading the initial references to Frankfurt's analysis of "bullshit," that is because the taboo associated with the use of this term is low or has been significantly reduced in our social context. Cussing is controversial because of the taboo associated with such words and phrases. We can speak of the taboo of a word to refer to the inhibitory power of cultural norms that work to lessen or reduce the use of a word or phrase. Such words have shock value, and they sometimes offend. Linguists have measured the effect of certain types of cussing in terms of the concept of "taboo-loading,"[9] or the level of offensiveness or shock value associated with instances of cussing.[10] A clear indication that the taboo of a word has been lowered, if not eliminated, is the extent to which it becomes acceptable to print it or say it in popular forms of media or polite company. A television show on Fox is titled *The Best Damn Sports Show Period.* A coach may now be reported as saying, "We played like crap," or "We got our butts kicked," or "They kicked our ass." Whatever scale is used, the concept of taboo-loading, the measure of the level of offensiveness, is useful for judging the possible effects of using such words and is therefore useful in making certain kinds of ethical judgments about cussing. At the least, the strength of the taboo will be relevant in most contexts, even if it is not decisive, as some might think.

A good test of taboo-loading will be the reader's reaction to less tame instances of cussing (an understatement indeed), where the shock value is undeniable in certain cases. At this point we need to mention a wider range of examples of dirty words.[11] Wajnryb says, "There are about a dozen of these (I like to think of them as the Dirty Dozen)—FUCK, CUNT, SHIT, PISS, BITCH, BASTARD, and

ASS (with DAMN, HELL, FART, CRAP, and DICK)—and they provide the resources for a number of different speech acts." Later, she speaks of the "Big Six, as they're affectionately called by some," and mentions that authorities generally agree that the Big Six include "FUCK, CUNT, COCK (or, if you prefer, DICK), ASS, SHIT and PISS."[12]

Once the words are explicitly mentioned, it is not difficult to construct some further useful categories. Some of them have to do with bodily functions or processes, in particular those having to do with sex (*fuck, screw, cocksucker, motherfucker*) or bodily products (*shit, piss, crap, fart*). Some have to do with bodily parts, probably associated with sexual functions or bodily processes (*cunt, dick, cock, prick, asshole, butt, tits*). Others, interestingly, have to do with religion (*damn, goddamn, hell*). *Bitch* and *bastard* may be hybrids. Thus, profanity (in a narrow sense) and blasphemy will usually involve secular uses of religious terms like *Jesus Christ* or *God* or *damn*. *Vulgarity* is a general term for cussing, but it often involves scatological references. *Obscenity* in a narrow sense is a legal term for unprotected speech (but may be used to refer more generally to cussing) and typically refers to words associated with sex.[13] Jay points out that in "American English obscenities are pointedly sexual in nature," and "Obscene words are considered the most offensive and are rarely, if ever, used in public media."[14] George Carlin's famous monologue on the seven words you cannot say on television included obscenities of a sexual nature, vulgar scatological references, and unmentionable female bodily parts.[15] Epithets or expletives have less to do with specific content references and more to do with how they function: emotional outbursts, sometimes abusive and usually venting negative emotions.

Given the taboo associated with these words, it is natural to attempt to explain the taboos, to understand why these words shock or offend or are prohibited. As Jay says, "One can see that what is considered taboo or obscene revolves around a few dimensions of human experience."[16] Historians, etymologists, psychologists, and psycholinguists have attempted to help us understand the historical and psychological sources of the taboos at work.[17] The explanation of such taboos or their relative strength is interesting and important, and such understanding may serve to reduce or eliminate our tendency to be shocked or offended by the use of such words. But it is clear that the way these terms are used in everyday language is, in some sense, independent of social scientific or historical accounts of taboos or taboo-loading. *That* these words do or may offend is ethically relevant. *Why* they offend is a separate relevant issue that I will briefly address later. Also, the issue of why they offend may be tied to a meaning that is of questionable relevance when we ask, "What is going on when people cuss?"

It is clearly ethically relevant to ask, "What are people *doing* when they cuss?" The critical perspective from which linguists like Wajnryb and Jay investigate "bad language" or "cursing" should be quite familiar to people who are familiar with the works of J. L. Austin, Wittgenstein, or John Searle's study of speech acts.[18] These philosophers of language taught us to attend carefully to what people *do* when they talk. The meaning of our words must be related to context, to the specific uses to which we put words to work. The concept of "speech acts" stresses the notion that we must be aware of actions, not simply words, when we attempt to understand meaning. Wittgenstein's well-known emphasis on language games reminds us of the vast array of purposes, embedded in our forms of life, that we actually have when we speak.

In a famous passage (section 23) from *Philosophical Investigations*, it is noteworthy that Wittgenstein mentions "cursing" as a kind of language game, one of the tools in our linguistic tool kit, and it is a game we play with numerous further purposes in mind. Wajnryb and Jay seem to accept Wittgenstein's reminder as a kind of truism underlying their linguistic investigations. Wajnryb says that swearers use the same words "in different circumstances and for different purposes. They dip into the swear bank and use words that may be similar semantically . . . but different pragmatically." Echoing my previous comments about the ambiguity associated with the question of what is going on when people cuss, she says, "Why do we swear? The answer to this question depends on the approach you take. As a linguist—not a psychologist, neurologist, speech pathologist, or any other -ist—I see swearing as meaningful verbal behavior; patterned; systematic; and readily lending itself to a functional analysis. Pragmatically, swearing can be understood in terms of the meanings it is taken to have in particular circumstances and what it achieves in any particular circumstance."[19]

Jay's comments are similar. He says that for his study of cursing, "the pragmatics of usage, or how the words function in use, is more important than fitting the words into grammatical or etymological categories." He also insists that a pragmatic perspective "can focus on how people actually curse in real world situations." Echoing Wittgenstein's attack on the reference theory of meaning, Jay emphasizes that "dirty words are used to express connotative meaning," and this contrasts with an exclusive emphasis on denotative usage. He comments that "connotation is conveyed meaning involved in irony, sarcasm, understatement, overstatement, humor, idiomatic usage and implied requests."[20]

If we focus on speech acts, that is, what we do when we cuss in particular contexts, it is obvious that we do an enormous number of things. I suspect any attempt to offer a tidy scheme whose goal is to describe in a relatively complete way the things we do when we cuss is bound to be incomplete. So we should charitably interpret any mapping scheme as a helpful or useful guide to common or prevalent usages, not the final word, so to speak. Wajnryb claims that there are three broad contexts in which we swear, three reasons people cuss, or what she calls "three broad domains of achievement—catharsis, aggression, and social connection—in which most uses of foul language can be classified." Generally speaking, cussing usually involves either venting our emotions, some form of abuse, or an attempt to connect with other people. Here are her initial examples: "It might be easier to think of the three components . . . as the three reasons people swear. The first is catharsis: the almost instinctive 'bastard' emitted when you stub your toe. The second is abusive: the 'bastard' that you snarl at the driver who just sneaked into your parking spot. The third is social: the 'bastard' in 'you old bastard' when you hail a friend you haven't seen for a while."[21]

With a nod to Wajnryb's initial useful scheme and the recognition that her book is full of specific examples of the enormous variety of usages associated with cussing, we need a more detailed account of the "reasons people swear," or what people are doing when they engage in these speech acts. It will also be useful to provide examples from sports.

### III. A Taxonomy of Usage

In the following I do not claim to provide an exhaustive account of types of cussing, but I do provide a more extensive set of categories than I have found in the linguists whose work I have consulted. (I invite the reader to find more categories.) Sport-related examples have been particularly useful in generating some of the types.

### A. *Cathartic*

I agree with Wajnryb when she claims that this kind of cussing is the most straightforward. She calls it the "stub your toe" variety. It involves venting or purging excess emotion, letting off steam in an immediate, brief, and usually explosive way. Such outbursts probably involve some attempt to restore one's psychological equilibrium in the face of negative things that happen to a person. Cathartic cussing is widespread in sports, when the player, coach, or fan responds to the strikeout, error, stupid foul, dropped pass, missed goal, and so on.[22]

### B. *Intensifying*

Although not as straightforward as cathartic cussing, this kind may be even more common in life and in sports. Wajnryb oddly discusses this under her category of "social connection," but it deserves its own status. Wajnryb and Jay refer to certain usages as "intensifiers" or "emotion intensifiers," but one might also highlight the way in which cuss words perform their tasks as exclamations or interjections. Add the well-chosen four-letter word in a sentence, and we know the speaker is emotionally involved in the situation. "Catch the ball" is relatively less intense than "Catch the fuckin' ball!" or "Catch the goddamn ball!" Wajnryb comments on the fact that *fuck* is "so effective as a general intensifier."[23]

c. *Expressive*

*Expressive* is a catchall term for various usages that function in ways that are not as explosive as cathartic cussing and do not function simply as intensifiers for what is expressed. No doubt all cussing is expressive, but we need a category describing the wide variety of specific feelings, emotions, or attitudes that might be expressed: discouragement, resignation, surprise, disbelief, and more. As I mentioned previously, Coach Bobby Knight's language has been well documented, and it might surprise some that he is reflective about his cussing.

> Much had been made over the years of Knight's use of profanity with the players. It is no exaggeration. Knight uses profanity when he is angry, when he is happy, and whenever he feels like it. He once taped an outtake for a TV show explaining why he used the word "fuck" so much. "I just think," he said, "that 'fuck' is the most expressive word in the English language. It can be used to express surprise as in 'Well I'll be fucked!' Or, it can be used to express anger, as in 'Fuck you!' Or, it can express dismay as in, 'Oh, fuck!'"[24]

D. *Abusive*

This kind falls under Wajnryb's category of aggression, but calling it abusive puts a more familiar face on it. Abusive cussing has an object, and when its target is another person (rather than an animal or some other kind of object), it involves insult, ridicule, some slur, or an expression of contempt. It may be cathartic (the categories may overlap), but it need not be. Here is an example from Coach Knight, when he recommends that a player tells one of his teammates, "Get in the f_____ game, . . . goddamn it. Quit playing like a pussy." Arguably, *f[ucking]* functions as an intensifier, *goddamn* functions as part of an expression of angry criticism, and *pussy* is abusive (and probably sexist as well). In the book he calls the media "assholes" and officials "a goddamned joke," "chickenshit mother_____," and "gutless sonofabitch[es]"; speaks of an opposing coach (as well as opponents) as a "sonofabitch"; and calls one of his players a "f_____ pussy."[25]

*E. Disparaging*

I confess that this category occurred to me because of my familiarity with the way in which a form of our favorite scatological reference is used in baseball. As Kevin Kerrane has described, *horseshit* is a "universal term of disparagement in baseball. Any baseball talent, body, body part, effort, action, player, team, city, or scouting assignment can be 'horseshit.'" Disparaging cussing has an object but is a broader mode of criticism than conveying abuse or ridiculing a person. It involves a negative evaluation of some state of affairs. The equine form is related to its bovine cousin, but in baseball at least, the horse variety "covers everything but the world of words—the world of stories, explanations, and scouting reports—at which point 'bullshit' takes over." Coach Knight refers to a "horseshit team," "horseshit defense," and bad playing as the "same old shit." At one point he says to his players, "This crap is no better than the crap I watched on Saturday. Get out of here. Go home. If you don't want to play any more than this then fuck it."[26] (Analysis: lower degree of taboo-loading in the first two instances of disparaging cussing, ending with an intensified expression of disgust.)

*F. Commendatory*

This category might be overlooked if we stress the negativity associated with predominant forms of cussing, but if we focus on usage in (at least) some sports, it is clear that our bad words can be used to commend or praise. In a later book on college basketball, John Feinstein says, "Like it or not, it is a simple fact of life that almost every coach on the planet uses profanity when talking to players." He continues with an excellent example of the way a word may commend. Coaches "understand that profanity is part of the language for most college athletes. The word 'motherfucker' is one coaches use often. It is considered a high form of praise. Every team needs a motherfucker, someone who is tough and mean and willing to do anything to win. That can mean getting in the other team's face or getting in the face of a teammate if necessary. Michael Jordan was a motherfucker, even if his college coach wouldn't use the term. Christian Laettner was a motherfucker and his college coach wouldn't hesitate to use the term."[27]

## G. Lubricating

We encountered this form of cussing in Wajnryb's initial account of the reasons we swear, where we reinforce social connections, as in greeting someone by referring to him as "you old bastard." This type of cussing "lubricates" social relationships, for example, when we use certain kinds of "swear intensives" that "slip comfortably into relaxed discourse among in-group members, imbuing their language with color and emotion and contributing to the general camaraderie." This is locker-room cussing, or cussing in contexts in which members of the team associate (the bar, a team member's room, house, apartment, and so on). Wajnryb refers to such social swearing as a "group lubricant, an indicator of in-group membership."[28]

## H. Comedic

Sometimes cussing is used in the service of comedy, quite explicitly by professional comedians and also by those who merely want to inject humor or playfulness into a situation. As intense and overbearing as Coach Knight apparently is, he has his playful side. Here is his response to a player who reaches for a pass with one hand: "Andre, there is no room for one-handed basketball on this team. If God had wanted you to play this game with one hand you would have an arm growing out of your ass." Or, "God grant me patience—and goddammit, hurry up."[29]

## I. Subversive

Because of the taboo associated with these words, cussing can be an attempt to subvert agreed-upon norms of politeness, civility, acceptable behavior, and more. The political and the comedic can be combined in the performances of people like Lenny Bruce and George Carlin, or the rebellion can take the form of the teenager carving out her personal space by using the words her parents restrict and condemn. We should allow for political or subversive cussing even in sports, and some contexts in which Knight cusses suggest this. Knight's rejection of politeness as a virtue might be interpreted along the lines described by Richard Dooling: "One should be careful to select an ambience with lots of decorum and plenty of politeness and good manners. This will nicely accentuate your own vulgar speech, your bad attitude, and your profound insensitivity to others—in short, it will make your swearing really count for something. And, of course, one must assiduously cultivate the previously mentioned habits of rowdy bars and slang dictionaries."[30]

## J. Self-Definitional

I believe there is an important form of cussing that has been largely missed by the linguists. This is swearing whose point is more dramatically self-referential and may, but need not, be related to the rebellious uses previously described. This is cussing that serves to define a person in a certain way, as having a certain identity, as being a certain type of person, as being from a specific place or affirming some background, or as being involved in life and with others in a way that expresses an act of reflective self-creation. (Think of the rough-hewn intellectual or the cussing cleric.) No doubt in interacting with certain people who do or do not cuss, or in reading about people whose language is crude or vulgar or pristinely polite and bland, we may learn something about the substance of a self, or, put differently, we may learn something about the narratives that have shaped a person or the stories within which selves have chosen to interpret and identify themselves. These speech acts may sometimes be particularly useful, in sports and in life, to express important aspects of self-definition.

## iv. Reasons Not to Cuss

So, what is wrong with cussing? When we move from descriptive concerns to normative issues, not surprisingly, things get muddier. We might start with the old adage that we are talking about mere words, "Sticks and stones . . ." and all that. Some might claim that words are ethically neutral because they cannot harm. But as we have seen previously, these words have a variety of functions and may have real consequences in life. J. L. Austin described the "perlocutionary force" of speech acts or "performative utterances" to point out that the things we say and thus do in particular contexts have causal consequences or effects.[31] Certain kinds of cussing may offend or harm because of the taboos involved and our normal reactions. The childhood admonition to ignore the hurtful effects of words contrasts sharply with the power of such words to express and provoke. Perhaps the place to begin is with the very taboos that are in play.

Cussing uses taboo language, as linguists point out and we all understand. Although there may be a more anthropologically distinctive and technical use of *taboo* in social scientific studies of certain cultural norms, as far as I can tell, there is nothing technical about its meaning when we describe cussing as the use of taboo words and phrases.[32] These words are inhibited by cultural norms and common negative emotional responses. If we are wondering whether we ought or ought not to swear, or whether we should teach our children how they should talk in sports and elsewhere, perhaps we should start with the obvious fact that these words are taboo. The burden of proof is shifted because the taboos involved exclude or inhibit such usage. To speak of such language as "dirty" or "vulgar" or "obscene" grounds a presumption against cussing, doesn't it?

That is much too simple. To say that cussing is taboo or subverts a taboo merely describes the fact that there are customs that inhibit the use of these words. To say that $X$ is taboo is to say that it is customary not to do $X$, and if we believe the normative sense follows from its descriptive meaning, then this expresses a simple form of ethical conventionalism or relativism, and it is apparently defeated by obvious counterexamples. In fact, counterexamples show the contingency of such norms both descriptively and normatively. Interracial relationships and breast-feeding in public may have once been taboo (and may still be for some people), but things change. Norms are subverted, and groundless taboos may diminish in their power to inhibit; they may even disappear. Colin McGinn comments on what he calls "taboo morality" as he introduces readers to the study of ethics and to reflections on moral issues associated with animals, violence, sex, drugs, and other topics:

> The approach I shall follow seeks to replace taboo morality with rational morality. Taboo morality tells you what to do and what not to do simply as a matter of decree. Certain things are deemed simply *taboo* and that is an end to it. Maybe some god or other authority has declared that the thing in question is taboo; in any case, no *reason* is given for the moral prohibition. "Thou shalt not eat cabbage on Wednesdays"— that type of thing. Rational morality, by contrast, seeks to give reasons for its judgements and prohibitions; nothing has to be taken on faith, as simply *so*.[33]

Are there reasons to stop cussing? In raising the topic with a friend, her first response was: it is not necessary.[34] That is a beginning, but not a very helpful one. First, we do not guide our lives by the underlying principle suggested by the response: "In life, engage only in actions that are necessary" (even if we assume that we could give some adequate analysis of what it would mean to engage in a "necessary action"). Perhaps the meaning of *necessary* in "it is not necessary" is this: one may choose to cuss; however, given the taboos in play, one should have good reasons to cuss—

and there are none. If that is what is being said, the appeal to "not necessary" is question begging. It is simply the claim that the taboos are sufficient to inhibit such speech. Why are they sufficient? Because they are sufficient.[35]

A more useful source to generate possible reasons not to cuss is James O'Connor's influential book. His self-help message is based on the notion that swearing, like other bad habits, can be dealt with using certain kinds of practical therapies. The therapeutic message, which has been communicated not only in the book but also on television shows, in newspapers and magazines, and in other venues, is based on evaluative judgments about cussing. In the book he lists "the top ten reasons to stop," comments on each, and then provides a more detailed list of "twenty-five reasons to stop swearing," using three larger categories: "Cursing Imposes a Personal Penalty," "Cursing Corrupts the English Language," and "Cursing Is Bad for Society."[36] The book is also full of personal testimonials about cussing. Although O'Connor's lists are suggestive and his compilation of personal data is useful, I think there is a better way of organizing various arguments against cussing, especially when we are most interested in the relative strengths and weaknesses of the arguments and how effective they are when we attend to sport-related cussing.

*A. Religious Arguments*
It is interesting that none of the reasons for not swearing listed by O'Connor has any obvious reference to religion, yet the twenty-two personal narratives included in the chapter "Why Don't These People Swear?" are full of references to God and religion (typically Christianity).[37] A typical reference to what God wants or requires appears to be an expression of the Divine Command theory of morality and has all of the philosophical problems associated with this approach. Even if we refrain from pointing out that the Divine Command theory makes morality arbitrary or makes God's supposed goodness redundant or vacuous, the reference to God as a

central premise in a moral argument will hardly be persuasive to those who do not share the religious assumptions involved in the assertion or who question the justification of the premise on rational grounds. McGinn's comments suggest that the reference to God without a claim about the reasons for God's injunction (does God prohibit cussing because it is wrong, or is it wrong because God prohibits it?) is a morally empty appeal to authority. If we do provide possible reasons for God's commands, then the appeal to God is superfluous.

When it comes to cussing in sports, one might deny the assumption that God cares about such speech. Bobby Knight's comment about athletes invoking the help of God is apt. After a college football player claimed that God helped him kick the field goal to beat Southern Methodist University, Knight says, "Does this mean . : . that God decided to screw SMU? God does not give a damn what goes on in athletics. Nor should he."[38] I assume that Knight would also say that God does not "give a damn" how coaches talk. Unless assumptions in religiously based moral arguments can be independently supported, such arguments are unpersuasive. O'Connor's omission of references to religion as reasons not to swear might be a rhetorical acknowledgment of these philosophical points.

### B. Prudential Arguments

Some of the "personal" penalties listed by O'Connor and mentioned by others involve what I would call, rather loosely, matters of self-interest. It is bad judgment to say certain things in your job interview or in the annual review with a censorious supervisor. You may not get the job or promotion if you have a potty mouth. O'Connor seems inordinately worried about how cussing makes you *appear* to others. He says that cussing "gives a bad impression," "reduces respect people have for you," "reflects ignorance," and is "immature."[39] Perhaps I should not underestimate the importance of the image we create for others, but we are talking about appearances here. One of the stereotypes that comes out repeatedly in comments from various people in O'Connor's book is that cussing shows a lack of education or is "ignorant" and indicative of a lower social class. I suppose we should be aware that there are these stereotypes, but it is obvious that there are numerous exceptions to such social judgments. (We shall return again and again to exceptions—they are everywhere.) Prudential arguments simply point to the need for good judgment in assessing the situation in which we speak, including an awareness of the relevant expectations and prejudices of those with whom we interact. In the two contexts with which I am most familiar, the academy and the ball field, there seems to be no interesting correlation between cussing and judgments of respect, intelligence, knowledge, and the like. If we acknowledge, as a plain, empirical fact, that there is a lot of cussing in sports, yet judgments of respect, intelligence, knowledge, and so forth are based on other factors, then such prudential concerns seem less weighty here than in other areas of life. In some workplaces, cussing makes you look bad. In others, such worries are minimal.

*c. Moral Arguments*

From the normative perspective there are morally deeper worries about cussing. Unlike appeals to self-interest and social appearances, to say that speech may harm, hurt, or even offend puts us squarely in the moral ballpark. If we have a duty not to harm, then foul language may violate this moral requirement. Abusive cussing is directed toward other persons and may involve insults or ridicule, so persons may be directly hurt by such language. There may be damage to a person's self-esteem, and this may undermine happiness.[40] Since sport involves competitive conflict and rather strict hierarchies of power and authority, abusive and socially aggressive cussing may be more prevalent here. The most disturbing aspect of Bobby Knight's treatment of his players involves this kind of personal abuse. Feinstein describes Knight's treatment of a player: "Knight's angry words hurt him." An assistant coach tells another team member, "When he's calling you an asshole, don't listen. But when he starts telling you *why* you're an asshole, listen. That way you'll get better." The two players responded to the coach's abusive language quite differently. "Thomas couldn't shut off some words and hear others. He heard them all, and they hurt." The other player's response to a vulgar characterization of his soft play was dissimilar. "Calloway laughed. He had learned quickly to shrug off most Knight insults."[41]

Sometimes the coach's words hurt; sometimes they do not. There is some ambiguity involved if we are thinking solely in terms of consequences that are morally relevant. Knight's intentions are also relevant, as well as the question of whether he can expect players to understand his long-term goals. Feinstein says this about one object of Knight's abuse: "Thomas was facing the same question everyone who comes in contact with Knight faces sooner or later: Is it worth it? Does the end justify the means? He knew Knight wanted him to be a better player." At the end of the book, Feinstein poignantly summarizes his impression of Knight after a season shadowing the coach: "The key for Bob Knight remains the same: He is as brilliant a coach as there is. He is an extraordinarily compassionate, caring, and sensitive person. No one has ever had a better or more loyal friend. And yet everyone who cares about him remains concerned about his ability to hurt and to cause pain. And the person he hurts most is Bob Knight."[42] To the extent that abusive cussing may harm or hurt, there is good reason to refrain from it.

We should not overlook other kinds of abusive cussing in sports. So far we have focused on coach-player cussing that may hurt or harm in some sense. But other kinds of cussing, like that of coaches and players directed toward officials, or coaches and players directing their abuse toward the opposition or even fans, may show a lack of respect for others and may produce a hostile or even violent situation. Such abusive cussing is unsportsmanlike and should be discouraged.

Another version of the moral argument against swearing (and probably a much more common accusation) rests on the premise that it is offensive. Our cussing may not directly insult or ridicule another, or damage someone's self-esteem, but it may offend, and this should count from the moral point of view. One of O'Connor's "top ten reasons to stop" is to "avoid offending others," and he says that cussing is bad for society because it "makes others uncomfortable."[43] There are two responses to the argument from offensiveness, one obvious and one requiring more thought.

First, it is clear that in many situations, cussing does not offend anyone. For example, whether in sports or outside of the sports world, various uses may rarely offend anyone (for example, solitary cathartic cussing and commendatory, lubricating, and some comedic cussing), and in virtually any instance it will depend on the context. To the extent that cussing is prevalent in sports, its customary acceptance often negates the opposing taboos that function in other contexts, the result of which is a diminishing worry about offending anyone.

On the other hand, even in sports someone *may* be offended. How much moral weight should be given to this? It depends. Recall the concept of taboo-loading or the level of offensiveness customarily associated with certain cuss words. *Damn, hell, crap, ass*, and *fart* hardly register a blip on our moral radar screen (consider, for example, *The Best Damn Sports Show Period*). Recall Wajnryb's "Dirty Dozen" and "Big Six." *Bastard, bitch, piss*, and *shit* are relatively tame, although we must begin to be more careful when it comes to excreta. At the other end of the scale, the *F* word and the *C* word are most offensive. Wajnryb claims that the *C* word is "easily the most offensive" of our four-letter words (although in my experience this word is rarely heard in sports).[44] When it comes to the possibility of offending someone, the devil is in the details. Even Bobby Knight seems sometimes to err on the side of caution. He cussed in the presence of the president of Indiana University, but he "curbed his language" in the presence of women. O'Connor suggests that we should "imagine Grandma or the kids are listening" as an exercise for "exorcising offensive language," yet as a matter of fact, we know they are usually not around when we cuss, and we should imagine them present only if the other arguments against cussing outweigh this one.[45] (I am assuming there are positive reasons for cussing, embodied in the various usages I have described.)

Cuss words may sometimes not offend, and a kind of moral perception or vision is often required in order to apprehend whether they do offend. Even if they do offend, however, it is still not clear that appeals to offensiveness would always trump other relevant values involved. Despite the fact that appeals to "being offended" and "not to offend" are so common, the role of such appeals in moral argument is far from evident. The experience of being offended involves not only certain kinds of negative feelings but also judgment, as the important work on the emotions by philosophers and psychologists over the past thirty years has shown. The fact that a person may experience some negative feeling should be morally relevant for me, especially if I somehow cause it, but it need not be decisive for my moral deliberations if it is essentially related to judgments I need not respect (as is shown by the racist who is offended by the interracial couple holding hands, the homophobe offended by the same-sex couple walking arm in arm, or the philistine who slashes the painting of the nude in the art museum). An appeal to offensiveness is the beginning of a moral argument that seeks the reasons for being offended, not the terminus. When the appeal is made that we ought to be sensitive to others' feelings, it may omit the notion that the feelings are part of an emotion that includes a judgment that may be incorrect, implausible, culturally narrow, religiously bigoted, provincial, unsophisticated, or the result of irrational taboos. Furthermore, my willingness to offend may be the result of a judgment that more important values (political, moral, aesthetic, educational, or even personal) may override the fact that some may be offended by what I say or do. Appeals to a principle of offensiveness do not resolve the moral messiness involved; they accentuate it.

D. *Social Arguments*

There are various forms of the social argument. Calling it social does not preclude the notion that it is supposed to have some moral weight. In fact, one might construe the argument in broadly utilitarian or consequentialist terms.[46] O'Connor says that an important reason to stop swearing is to "contribute to a better society." According to O'Connor, swearing "contributes to the decline of civility," and the "widespread use of profanity and vulgarity is a factor in the deterioration of civility, good manners, the English language, morality, and decency."[47] If our lives are better lived in terms of social interactions characterized by politeness, good manners, courtesy, graciousness, or a kind of overall agreeableness, then ceteris paribus, good will be maximized if such deleterious consequences of cussing are avoided. For example, persons' reactions to cussing may not rise to the level of being harmed or offended, but it still may seem impolite, bad manners, or just plain annoying when someone cusses in certain contexts.

Although I do not dismiss such concerns, it is not obvious that so much emphasis should be placed on the role of cussing in contributing to the supposed decline of the "English language, morality, and decency." Is cussing a cause of this supposed decline (whatever is meant by the claim) or merely symptomatic of larger social and cultural changes that have complex causes? How would one show this? Moreover, the hardened vulgarian may not park in the disabled parking space, cut in line at the movies, talk loudly on her cell phone, choose the empty express lane for her full grocery cart, or wave the expressive finger at the driver who cuts her off. She may, in fact, think of her linguistic behavior as a kind of revolt, tweaking respectability with words well chosen and well situated to distance herself from priggish life in the suburbs and from those who want to restrict speech. In any case, I suspect that cussing in sports predated the most recent decline of civility (I am only speculating), and its various manifestations are often socially innocuous. (I, too, am irritated by adolescent and immature bad manners, but a defender of cussing need not defend this.)

*E. Virtue Arguments*

These arguments highlight the role of character traits in the ethical evaluation of cussing. Like social arguments, they may have moral or ethical force, so the category merely accentuates a different type of normative appeal. Rosalind Hursthouse, one of the important contemporary defenders of virtue ethics, begins a recent article on applying virtue ethics to our treatment of animals, in this way: "Applying virtue ethics to moral issues should be straightforward. After all, it basically just amounts to thinking about what to do using the virtue and vice terms. 'I mustn't pull the cat's tail because it's cruel,' I might say to myself, and surely that's simple enough." Echoing Hursthouse, O'Connor says, "It all boils down to one thing: what kind of person do you want to be?"[48]

According to O'Connor and other critics, cussing is (or, should we say, can be?) hostile, angry, insensitive, rude, ignorant, immature, inconsiderate, uncivilized, childish, lazy, impolite . . . We might extend the list, but you get the point. If we ask, "What kind of person cusses?" or "What character traits are exhibited when a person cusses?" the list may be damning. The conclusion is clear: a virtuous person should abstain from cussing.

No doubt there are instances of cussing that do or might exhibit bad character traits, but they need not. To the extent that questions of virtue are raised, legitimate concerns are involved. Although such concerns are important, virtue considerations accentuate the messiness of these issues; they do not resolve them. There may be character traits—for example, honesty—that can be interpreted as merely the flip side of moral rules, but even in the case of truth telling, the virtuous person, that is, the honest person, is not merely a rule follower. Telling Aunt Alice that her hat is hideous may be honest but insensitive and inconsiderate. Judgment is required. There are numerous virtues, moreover, that do not reduce to rule following and that require the use of a finely tuned apprehension of the details of particular situations. Case-by-case attentiveness is the basis for choosing wisely or appropriately. Cussing may not be incompatible with virtue in particular cases, and habitual cussing need not be contrary to overall virtue. Recall that Feinstein characterizes Bobby Knight as "brilliant," "compassionate," "caring," "sensitive," and "loyal," despite the fact that his cussing is notorious. Knight's cussing is sometimes less than virtuous, but not always, and he exhibits good character traits despite his "bad" language.

Sometimes O'Connor's related worries are put more generally. He says that cussing "discloses a lack of character." He worries that cussing just is not nice. "Why not put some energy into becoming a nice person?"[49] The relation of good character and "niceness" is tenuous at best. One might say, more charitably, that being pleasant or generally socially amiable may be a part of good character, but how big and important a part is not clear. Joel Kupperman argues that character involves "three major areas of life":

> One is that of moral virtue. To have a good character is to be morally virtuous. To have no character is to be morally unreliable. Secondly, there is behavior toward other people whose seriousness does not rise to the level of the moral or immoral. Part of your character is whether you are considerate, or tend to make wounding remarks, or are unreliable in small things. Finally there is the area of life in which some people give up in the face of difficulties, and others exert themselves and keep going. It is often said that encountering and overcoming adversity is good for character, and this means that it strengthens your performance in this area.[50]

Kupperman's comments are particularly interesting in relation to the issues involved here. First, cussing need not have any direct bearing on whether a person is just, honest, courageous, or trustworthy, and the relation to one's benevolence is not even necessary. Second, even Knight, while not "nice," appears to consider his audience when he decides whether cussing would be appropriate. Being considerate, compassionate, or sensitive with respect to one's language depends on the particularities of the context. Third, the final area of life with which character is concerned is especially interesting in relation to sport since it involves facing difficulties and overcoming obstacles. I am sure that many involved in sport have encountered people who were "nice," yet whose strength of character seemed weak in relation to the determination and perseverance required to succeed. Leo Durocher famously said, "Nice guys finish last," which overstates the case but makes the relevant point. This again raises the fascinating issue of the relation between niceness, which "involves a degree of amiability and charm, advanced social skills, and perhaps even some small acts of kindness," and good character. As Kupperman says, it is difficult not to be attracted by niceness, because living and working with nice people is better.[51] Yet we may wonder whether niceness is morally deep.

> Many of those who kept administering what they thought were serious shocks in the Milgrim experiment must have been nice people. Many nice people, in order to avoid trouble, went along with Nazi or Stalinist authorities. Conversely, there have been virtuous people who were not very nice. Take Socrates for example. He does not appear to have been good at meeting people halfway. His pattern of pursuing philosophical arguments offered a major contribution to human life, but it did involve humiliating unwilling participants in public. It would be widely agreed that the greatness of his virtues outweighs these social faults. But that does not make him a nice man.[52]

A final virtue concern raised by O'Connor involves the accusation that cussing exhibits the vice of being lazy—in the use of language.[53] It is hard to know what to make of this charge. In one sense, it seems question begging, since it assumes that we should attempt to control our cussing, construed as impulsive outbursts or bad linguistic habits. The charge does appear to ignore cussing that is the product of reflection and possibly artful. And even critics like O'Connor admit that cussing may sometimes have cathartic and social benefits. If one appeals to an important concern with better, more effective, and even beautiful language, as if we are ignoring the aesthetic possibilities of language, the argument combines virtue with other ideals.

*F. Aesthetic Arguments*

One person with whom I have spoken put aesthetic concerns above all others. Such language is ugly and unattractive. Even if we could adequately pin down the meaning of *ugly* here, the accusation does appear to depend, once again, on taboo-loading, or the level of offensiveness of the word or phrase. If that is the case, it is difficult not to wonder whether aesthetic concepts are disguised references to social concerns; such appeals have the relative strengths and weaknesses we have already examined. If aesthetic appeals are taken literally, then one wonders whether the use of such language necessarily detracts from the aesthetic value of works by Joyce, Hemingway, Lawrence, and countless others. As we have seen before, such appeals may be the beginning of an interesting but complex discussion about language and aesthetic value, not the last word.

## v. Assessing Cussing: Puritans and Vulgarians

We are now in a position to offer some tentative conclusions about our normative assessment of foul language. As we have seen, the ethics of cussing depends on context, the details of the particular situation. Linguist Timothy Jay claims, "Dirty words are influenced by context more than any other type of language in modern English. Regardless of how one attempts to define dirty words, the ultimate decision about the offensiveness of words relies on context."[54] Despite the fact that his first claim may seem prima facie much too strong, Jay's point about the relevance of context may be made independent of the comparative claim. There are three elements of context that are involved: usage, taboo-loading, and social elements.

Although I have attempted to sketch the outlines of various patterns of dirty-word usage, I fear I have only scratched the descriptive surface. Wajnryb's chapters on the history and usage of various words are full of particular examples. She comments on the "versatility" of *shit,* used when you "spill a drink"; experience "pain"; "encounter a beautiful sunset"; feel "dismayed," "shocked," or "regretful"; or are "on the point of orgasm." Not to be outdone, O'Connor lists seventy common uses of this word. Wajnryb lists the variety of "grammatical opportunities" afforded us by using the *F* word in various ways: as a finite verb, gerund, infinitive, negative command, noun, adverb, and exclamation.[55] These facts are evident if we carefully attend to the linguistic phenomena. Two aspects of usage are striking: first, cuss words are quite functional and flexible; second, in many (most?) cases, there is a disparity between the actual uses of these words and their literal or referential meaning. To concentrate on usage focuses our attention on what the speaker is doing or what the speaker intends to convey, and this often has little or nothing to do with the suspected basis for the offensiveness of the words. Vice President Cheney was not irrationally recommending that Senator Leahy engage in an anatomically impossible act, and various uses that involve references to ducks or the "horse you rode in on" are not endorsements or prescriptions involving bestiality. Cheney's language was earthy, direct, expressive, and unrelated to sex. Frankfurt's use of *bullshit* is obviously nonliteral but clear and culturally important. Coach Knight's uses of various forms of the *F* word, as well as basketball coaches' commendatory use of one of its forms, are not references to sex. In such cases, the character traits expressed in usage, or the intentions involved in the underlying maxims, are not necessarily ethically problematic. On the other hand, if the nonliteral usages function consequentially or intentionally as terms of abuse, ethical concerns are raised.

This line of argument might be disputed by those who focus on the actual offensiveness of the words. The second important element of context concerns the level of offensiveness of the words used, the shock value, or what we have called taboo-loading. This element describes the fact that words do offend, even if we are told that they should not offend because of the way they are actually used. But there is a delicate balancing act involved even if we recognize that some people are offended by dirty words. Some words do not, in fact, offend or offend very little in certain contexts. When we reflect on those words that are, descriptively speaking, more offensive to a wider range of people, we are faced with the question we previously sidestepped. Why are such words more offensive (both qualitatively and quantitatively)? Cheney's impolite and non-literal use of the *F* word offends, as do other references to sex and the body—as if we should be ashamed of even mentioning such things, apart from the meaning involved in actual usage. Some religious references offend, apart from the meaning involved in actual usage, because of religious beliefs held by those who are offended. The difficult question is whether culturally forbidden references to sex, the body, or even religious entities or subjects should trump the other functional elements involved in cussing situations.

The final aspect of context is, of course, already involved in the first two. Speakers engaging in meaningful and purposeful speech acts interact with others who interpret meaning in all kinds of physical locations and contexts and who have their own purposes, expectations, and presuppositions. Richard Nixon's foul mouth in the Oval Office was famously captured on tape, yet I doubt that Haldeman and Erlichmann were offended, hurt, shocked, surprised, or dismayed, and Nixon did not use such language in his political speeches. Likewise, the coach speaks differently in the locker room to his players than to the corporate bigwigs at the country club fund-raiser.

Where does this leave us? Let's distinguish two extreme positions on the ethics of cussing. The puritan is one who believes that it is wrong to cuss, that one ought not to cuss, and one should try as hard as one can to refrain from cussing or should attempt to form habits of speech that disallow cussing.[56] The puritan is a moral absolutist whose guiding linguistic rule is, in any context, "It is impermissible to cuss." At the other end of the spectrum is the vulgarian who denies the puritan's rule by rejecting the conventions against using dirty words and who believes that the use of such words in any context might be useful and valuable—and is always permissible.

O'Connor defends a position I will call "moderate puritanism," because he does not defend the total elimination of cussing. Given his numerous reasons not to swear and his practical recommendations for drastically reducing its prevalence in our lives, despite the admitted cathartic and even some social benefits, the ideal he defends seems close to the puritan. As he says, "If this book helps you stop swearing altogether, good for you. The purpose of this book, however, is not to eliminate the use of bad language in our culture, but to help people control when and where they swear."[57] In contrast, the moderate vulgarian admits that she might sometimes have reasons to choose not to cuss, but she also believes that a heavy burden of proof is incurred by those who want to restrict the use of these extremely useful words. In practice her speech behavior will appear to be more like the vulgarian than the puritan or moderate puritan. Perhaps we can think of differentiating positions on the spectrum between the puritan and the vulgarian in terms of actual linguistic behavior, reasons for that behavior across a wide range of situations in life, and basic attitudes. Both the moderate puritan and the moderate vulgarian recognize the importance of context, but the lingering power of the taboos forms the basis for much more restraint on the part of the moderate puritan. The differences between the two moderate positions may not be sharp in certain cases, but the basic attitudes toward the use of dirty language are quite different: one a begrudging and limited acceptance, the other a rejection of the taboos and a begrudging restraint only in limited contexts.

I believe the analysis so far favors the moderate vulgarian. Given the many problems involved in the arguments against cussing, and the failure of the puritan to attend to the details of situations, it is difficult to see how or why linguistic boundaries should be drawn in the way that the puritan requires. O'Connor admits that "emotional release is a worthy argument supporting salty language," that it can be "funny," and that it can be "liberating and candid."[58] The slope is more slippery than he appears to think. He insists that the positives are outweighed by the negatives (recall the arguments against swearing), but the exceptions are widespread. None of the general reasons not to swear lead to anything even close to the puritan position, and O'Connor's reasons for his moderate position fail to recognize many other positive uses. One might be a moderate vulgarian using primarily words with low-level offensiveness as intensifiers in virtually any context and not offend anyone. One might choose to use supposedly more offensive words only in social contexts with those for whom, in your judgment, the words would be lubricating and expressive rather than offensive. One might use more shocking language in contexts in which the subversive and self-definitional elements, in one's judgment, would outweigh the offensiveness—perhaps as a challenge to the political correctness of a certain group or as a rebuff to the staid and stiff-necked true believers that one might confront. And the moderate vulgarian's basic attitudes in and toward life need not be angry, resentful, or hostile, because her language need not be primarily abusive, disparaging, or expressive of negative emotions or bad character traits.[59]

It might be useful to see these issues against the background provided by the lively critical discussions of virtue ethics in contemporary moral theory. If one argues that actions are right in virtue of being the kind performed by virtuous agents, or good if they express virtue, and one insists that choosing well or appropriately requires good judgment rather than strict rule following, then the importance of context is emphasized in the way we have seen. Hursthouse says this: "Of course, virtue ethicists have always shared a form of antiabsolutism with consequentialists, agreeing with them that many act types—lying, killing, meat-eating—are right in some circumstances, wrong in others, adding 'depending on the circumstances' rather than 'on the consequences.'" Given the status of the taboos in question and their contingent link to harm or offensiveness, the rejection of absolutism here appears to be appropriate.[60]

## VI. Conclusion: Sports and Dirty Language

First, let's state the obvious. Sports are played in all sorts of contexts and at a variety of levels. The participants (in a broad sense) include coaches, players, fans, and officials. The contexts in which sports participants might swear are varied and involve a variety of usages. Given the general messiness involved in reflecting on these issues, I believe one should be wary of offering any careless generalizations concerning the ethics of cussing in sport—or outside of sport. A blanket rejection of swearing (or even extreme vulgarian potty mouth) overlooks contextual details that are essential for good judgment. On the other hand, this conclusion may seem too bland and unhelpful. At the risk of throwing judiciousness out the window—and perhaps to provoke more thought—I will attempt to add some ethical pizzazz to the analysis of swearing in sports.

To the extent that cussing is apparently abusive, whether by coaches, players, fans, officials, or anyone involved in sports, there is a heavy burden incurred by the speaker to see or to show whether there could be other factors involved that override the badness of possible psychological harm. This is particularly problematic in a coach-player relationship, given the dynamics involved. Coaches like Knight may think they are only trying properly to motivate an athlete, but the possible damage done by a coach's tirade may still be palpable and unacceptable. I see no reason motivation requires linguistic abuse. The overall assessment of Knight's speech as a moderate vulgarian is difficult because his individualistic, maverick, and even playful tendencies are combined with his abusive and bullying dispositions. A moderate vulgarian need not find the abuse acceptable.

There may be a propensity by some to associate sport swearing with trash talking and taunting. No doubt there are numerous instances of swearing in these contexts, but I think it is a mistake to assume that swearing in sports is wrong simply because it (usually) occurs in the context of trash talking or taunting. I agree with Nicholas Dixon's criticism of trash talking. He rejects such behavior on the grounds that it fails to respect opponents, insofar as it treats them as mere objects to be overcome by using various forms of verbal abuse.[61] What is wrong with trash talking and taunting is that it fails to respect opponents, not that it necessarily involves swearing. It need not. Swearing, qua failing to respect opponents, is wrong. On the other hand, there are plenty of venues apart from contexts in which trash talking occurs in which the moderate-vulgarian sports participant may use such words (for catharsis, lubrication, commending, subversion, intensification, and so on). The moderate vulgarian need not condone the taunting of opponents by fans (when fans use certain vulgar chants), on the basis of the same concern for respecting opponents or officials.[62] (Also, the fans are usually in no position, as a group, to make a good judgment about the level of taboo associated with various fan-atic chants.)

Another context in which swearing may occur is when coaches or players dispute calls by officials. Consider the situation in college basketball. As reported in *USA Today*, for the 2007–8 season the NCAA decided that "referees will start enforcing a bench decorum policy that won't allow coaches to use profanity, abusive language or display annoyance with officials."[63] The article contrasts supporters of the new policy with the defensive and dismissive responses of various coaches, including Duke coach Mike Krzyzewski. "I'm not going to pay any attention to it," he says. "I'll be who

I am, and if I'm doing something wrong, I'll be punished and I'll change." Bobby Knight is quoted as saying, "Referees, on occasion, make terrible calls. And not to get up and remind them that they've made a bad call, I think, is taking something out of the game. . . . I think that's all bull." (Do you think he really said *bull*?)

The moderate vulgarian may offer a nuanced response to the "bench decorum policy." To the extent that it expresses a puritan rejection of swearing, the vulgarian will not agree that good linguistic behavior necessarily requires the rejection of all forms of swearing. On the other hand, the moderate vulgarian may agree with penalizing and attempting to prohibit abusive swearing directed toward officials when coaches (as well as players and fans) dispute calls. Again, communicating with officials and expressing dissatisfaction need not involve abusive cussing, contrary to what Coach Knight seems to think. (Coach K's response is also interesting because he appears to interpret his vulgarian coaching behavior as self-definitional.) It is also interesting to note that one should not assume that rules about decorum and linguistic propriety would naturally be more loose at the professional levels of sport. The article reports, "NBA coaches have long adhered to a stricter bench decorum code than college coaches, 'without question,' says Colorado coach Jeff Bzdelik, who coached the NBA's Denver Nuggets from 2002 to 2004."

Codes of sportsmanship for younger participants in sports (high school, middle school, Little League, youth sports, and the like) often include absolute prohibitions on swearing. If such prohibitions are promulgated on the basis of a puritan belief that it is always intrinsically unsportsmanlike to use such words, then a moderate vulgarian will reject the rationale. Such a rationale for a policy prohibiting cussing seems unreflectively to reinforce puritan taboos or assume that swearing is always correlated with other unsportsmanlike behaviors such as trash talking or taunting. The moderate vulgarian may still support such a policy, however. She emphasizes the role of judgment in the uses of swear words. This may mean that promoting "proper" linguistic habits in younger sports participants enables them to appreciate the taboos that are, in fact, widely accepted, so they someday will be in a better position to perceive the relevant details of various situations in which they must make good judgments about their linguistic behavior.

Prohibitions on swearing might also be related to the development of other virtues in sports, especially for younger participants. Cathartic cussing seems relatively innocuous even to a moderate puritan like O'Connor, but it might seem less innocuous to a coach who stresses the importance of self-control to his players. Here, however, the stress would be on the goodness of self-control in the face of failure in sport, and the coach's apparent focus on linguistic propriety would be misleading. The euphemistic "Fudge!" or "Godzilla!" after a strikeout would be as problematic, from the standpoint of emotional self-control and competitive even-temperedness, as using more offensive terms. Finally, at virtually any level of sport, even the moderate-vulgarian coach may be reminded that Grandma and the kindergarten kids are right behind the bench, and that might require that the coach's intensifiers are lower on the scale of taboo-loading.

It is noteworthy that the more extreme positions agree on the descriptive power of the words, or at least agree that the words cannot function appropriately if they lose their power to shock or offend. When these words are no longer symbols of the forbidden, as children are taught, when they are overused and underappreciated, they become uninteresting verbal flotsam floating in a culture that has lost its historical sense of the battles fought for the use of these words in art, literature, and everyday life. The danger for the vulgarian is that in constantly thumbing one's nose at the taboos, the words become no more than the verbal tics of the immature or unreflective. The *F* word then has no more significance than the *likes* and *you knows* in today's common youthful speech. The moderate vulgarian insists that cussing must be done well, in order to function usefully as contrarian challenges to the community's insistence on niceness and decorum in mentioning words related to sex, the body, and other supposedly potentially offensive areas of human experience. Forbidden words may be signs of rebellion, identity, connectedness, expressiveness, and keen judgment, but they may also be signs of immaturity, disrespect, and inarticulate boorishness.

We began with the suggestion that a focus on cussing might be especially interesting in relation to sport. Because of its prevalence in sport, if we judged that there are good reasons to stop swearing, in general, then our normative assessment would be especially telling on coaches, players, and fans. We are left with vulgarian messiness, however. The moderate vulgarian in sport might resist the puritan's prohibition in one other respect. Because there is a high degree of conventional acceptance of dirty language in sport, the words function as reinforcements of the distance between ordinary decorum and the more primitive and base world of pursuing physical excellence. Ruth Wajnryb describes the function of dirty talk in the locker room and suggests that "such venues also signal a symbolic escape from the constraints of those who criticize, condemn, or control such language."[64] Perhaps vulgarian coaches like Bobby Knight are reminding us that in their world, the world of sports, the norms are different, and in expressing themselves as vulgarians do, they are asserting their candid rootedness in that world.

Consider the epigraphs at the beginning of the chapter. Kofi Annan's intentions and Pete Rose's joy could not be expressed more clearly or emphatically, and the puritan's rejection of such language seems timid and thin-skinned. In the end, our own language and our reactions to the speech of Dick Cheney and Bobby Knight should be occasions for reflection, not immediate condemnation. Is our vice president a vulgarian? Should we be bothered or offended by his vulgar speech? I, for one, am much more likely to be offended by his politics than by his language. But that is another story.[65]

# Part Two.
## *Sport and Ethical Guidance*

# 6 Celebrated Athletes and Role Models

Are famous athletes role models? Do celebrated athletes have special responsibilities to be good role models? Should we look to such public figures for examples of how to live or for advice about what to do, what to seek, or what kind of person we should be? For me, at least, a long-standing but dormant interest in such questions has been reactivated by reading a thought-provoking discussion of these issues. I had thought the answers to such questions were rather obvious, perhaps not even terribly important. However, I was awakened from my dogmatic slumber by Christopher Wellman's imagined dialogue between Charles Barkley and Karl Malone, famous NBA basketball players. According to Wellman, the dispute between Barkley's position, which I will call "skepticism," and Malone's position, which I will call "exemplarism," is "a deceptively complex matter."[1] According to many with whom I have discussed these issues, Wellman's defense of exemplarism not only wins the argument but does so in a way that underscores the importance of the issues. Sports have enormous influence in our culture, and many think that celebrated athletes can really make a moral difference in the lives of some people, especially children. Even coaches at the high school and collegiate levels recognize the fact that celebrated athletes are role models, and coaches sometimes insist that their athletes participate in programs that can positively influence others. Barkley's skepticism in the imagined dialogue is apparently defeated; his individualism and voluntarism ("I never agreed to be a role model") appear to be self-centered and socially irresponsible. For those interested in the moral possibilities of sports participation and appreciation, such reminders are serious and significant.

In relation to Wellman and probably many others in the sports world, my own views are contrarian. I have been convinced, however, that the issues involved are more complex and important than I had thought, because they involve: the question of special obligations (duties) or responsibilities (these questions involve an athlete's understanding of his role responsibilities and his moral identity); our attitudes toward celebrated athletes (such questions relate to some central issues in virtue ethics, including the significance of moral exemplars in our lives); and what might be called the "ontology of the celebrated athlete" (in particular, questions are raised about the nature of sport, how we imaginatively construct the meaning of our heroes, and the role of sport in society).

First, I offer some useful distinctions that will be important in evaluating the case for exemplarism. Next, I reconstruct the argument for the position that celebrated athletes have special responsibilities to be good role models, and I offer a series of criticisms of exemplarism. Finally, I suggest an alternative way of conceiving of the status of celebrated athletes, one that stresses the role of imagination in our construction of the moral meaning of sports heroes, and one that has certain practical consequences.

## 1. What Does It Mean to Be a Role Model?

First, it is helpful to distinguish the narrow and broad senses of the meaning of *role model*. To be a role model in a narrow sense is limited to a particular context in which some person or persons would attempt to imitate the behavior of the role model. In this sense, the emphasis is on the particular *role* or station in which the supposed role model is involved, whether it is as a teacher, lawyer, or baseball player. For example, in athletics the more experienced members of a team are often called upon to be good "role models" for younger members of the team, in order to show what the coach expects when preparing for games or practicing and playing the game: "be on time," "play hard," "share the ball," "do the little things," and so on. Younger team members imitate experienced teammates. In the narrow sense, to "be like Mike" is to play *basketball* like Michael Jordan. For our main purposes, in the narrow sense a celebrated athlete is a role model qua athlete.

In the broad sense, a role model is significant not simply for how she typically acts in a particular role she plays in life. In a broader sense, a role model shows us how to navigate our way through life in all sorts of situations. Broadly speaking, a role model is an object of imitation when we reflect on the larger ethical questions: How should I live? What kind of person should I be? In this sense, the significance of "be like Mike" transcends basketball and extends to nonathletic areas of life.

If we take this distinction seriously, we might remove part of the ambiguity of speaking of "role models" by distinguishing role models and moral exemplars, where the latter term refers to role models in the broader sense. It is a curiosity associated with the use of *role model*, especially in the context of the debate concerning celebrated athletes, that the behaviors at issue are not simply limited to the person's particular role or station in life qua athlete. If we kept this distinction in mind, it might be better to ask: Are celebrated athletes moral exemplars? Or, do celebrated athletes have special responsibilities to be moral exemplars? And it is clear that the sense in which it would be plausible to speak of athletes as role models is the narrow sense, because there is no reason to think that a role model in the narrow sense is a role model in the broader sense. There is no reason to think that role models are necessarily moral exemplars, or persons whose life as a whole is worthy of imitation, whether we are speaking of Socrates, Confucius, Buddha,

Jesus, or your grandmother. A celebrated athlete may, in fact, be worthy of imitation in the broader sense, but that will be a contingent fact that must be discovered, not assumed (more on this later).

Some will think that I have naively overlooked something that exemplarism should emphasize. Celebrated athletes do have a heightened influence on the conduct of others, don't they? Celebrated athletes *are*, in fact, role models, aren't they? In one sense, perhaps, but it is important to make another distinction. We should distinguish being a role model in a descriptive sense and being a role model in a normative sense. A role model in a descriptive sense is one whose conduct (or life) is actually the object of imitation, or is at least believed to be worthy of imitation. A role model in a normative sense is one whose conduct or life is *worthy* of being imitated or worthy of being some kind of exemplar. Is a celebrated athlete a role model? Yes, apparently, in a descriptive sense, but not necessarily in the normative sense. Even in the descriptive sense, we might be somewhat skeptical of celebrated athletes' supposed influence on the behavior of others. It is an empirical question simply assumed by exemplarism, and however plausible it might appear, we would still need the relevant evidence. Even if we assume this is true, it does not follow that celebrated athletes are worthy of imitation in the broader sense, that they are, in the normative sense, moral exemplars.

There are two facts that are relevant in this dispute, and these facts must be kept in mind when evaluating the following arguments: celebrated athletes have a heightened influence on the conduct of others, especially children, and there is nothing intrinsic to being a celebrated athlete that merits the status of being a moral exemplar.

The conclusions we reach about the special responsibilities of celebrated athletes or our attitudes toward such athletes should be consistent with these two sets of facts. If celebrated athletes do, in fact, have a magnified influence on others, while acknowledging that they might not *be* normative role models or moral exemplars, how should they respond? How should fans respond?

## 11. The Case for Exemplarism

Christopher Wellman's interesting discussion of these issues is especially useful because he attempts to articulate precisely the sense in which celebrated athletes have special responsibilities to be good role models. His insistence that the issue is "a deceptively complex matter" is initially shown by the arguments against Barkley's skeptical voluntarism. Many moral duties, even special duties like the one made famous in Singer's paper on famine (Wellman mentions rescuing a child drowning in a shallow pond), are based not on consent, but on certain contingent facts that are the basis for such responsibilities. Simply saying that one did not agree to do *X* does not mean that one has no responsibility to do *X*. What if someone falls in love with me? Must I marry her? I have no special responsibility to marry. "Whereas marriage is intimate and requires agreement, we *all* have a responsibility to encourage virtue and discourage vice."[2] For Barkley's imagined character, this point simply reinforces his belief in individual responsibility and his insistence that parents are primarily responsible for the moral education of their children. According to Barkley, it is silly to think that celebrated athletes have any special responsibilities in this regard.

At this point, Wellman (Malone) begins to develop his central argument for exemplarism.[3] Whereas parents are supposed to be the central moral influence on their children's lives, they are certainly not the only influence. If we all have a responsibility to encourage virtue and discourage vice, we all have a responsibility to help counteract the corrupting influences on children. In this sense, according to Wellman/Malone, we all have a duty to be good role models. It is obvious, however, that some persons have more influence on people than others, and those who do have such influence have special responsibilities. Here is the sense in which celebrated athletes have such responsibilities. Speaking for Malone,

Wellman writes, "First, I agree that it falls upon all of us to serve as appropriate role models, and so when I speak of celebrated athletes having a special responsibility, I mean only that we have *additional* moral reasons to act virtuously. Thus, I do not claim that we must necessarily behave *better* than others. In short, everyone has moral reasons to encourage virtue and discourage vice, but celebrated athletes have additional moral reasons to behave well."[4]

Although Wellman/Malone admits that politicians, preachers, and ethics professors are more suited to be good role models since they chose roles that do seem to involve the explicit responsibility to exert ethical influence on others, we should not confuse the descriptive and normative senses of influence. In other words, do not "confuse those who *should* have influence with those who *do*." As a matter of fact, celebrated athletes do have influence, so they have "extra moral reasons to behave well" that even those who are "better suited for the job" do not.[5]

We are now in a position to formulate what I will call the Special Responsibilities Argument:

1. If a person has a heightened influence on the conduct of others, then she should be sensitive to this fact.
2. If a person should be sensitive to this fact, then she should admit that she has additional moral reasons to behave well (to act virtuously), beyond the reasons that everyone has to encourage virtue and discourage vice.
3. Celebrated athletes have a heightened influence on the conduct of others (especially children).
4. Therefore, celebrated athletes have special responsibilities to be good role models.

In holding that celebrated athletes have additional reasons to behave well but not moral requirements to behave better than others, Wellman insists that he has carefully chosen to speak of "responsibilities" rather than duties, in order to suggest a kinship with virtue ethics. He says: "I am alleging no more than that a virtuous person in this position would be sensitive to the additional moral reasons to behave well and that anyone indifferent to this magnified influence would be exhibiting a moral vice." Celebrated athletes may not have "duties" in the strict sense, but they would be "blameworthy" if they failed to "own up" to "the magnified part" they "play in the moral education of others."[6]

Two more important points remain in Wellman's defense of exemplarism. First, he admits, as I have previously asserted, that there is nothing intrinsic to athletic participation that makes celebrated athletes more suited for being good role models. The mere fact that famous athletes have such influence is the basis for the special responsibility. Second, Wellman admits, rather curiously, that since athletes are not necessarily well suited for being good role models, "All of us have a responsibility to try to reshape our culture so that when children look for *moral exemplars* they choose people better suited for the job."[7] Now we are in a position to respond critically to Wellman's case for exemplarism.

### III. Criticisms of Exemplarism

If we recall the previous distinctions, it seems clear that for Wellman's exemplarism, celebrated athletes are role models not only in the narrow sense, that is, qua athletes, but also in the broader sense. Celebrated athletes have responsibilities to be moral exemplars, because of the "magnified part" they "play in the moral education of others."[8] It is also evident that he thinks celebrated athletes are moral exemplars only in the descriptive sense, because all of us, including athletes, have a responsibility to teach children that we are misguided to think that celebrated athletes are necessarily well suited for this cultural moral status. However, it is a descriptive cultural fact that we do take our sports heroes as moral exemplars, and that is the basis for thinking they have additional moral reasons to behave well. What should we say about Wellman's case for exemplarism?

First, it is worth asking what it means to have additional moral reasons for doing something. For Wellman, all of us have moral reasons to act virtuously, but celebrated athletes have additional moral reasons to act well. However, if someone has a moral reason to do *X*, it seems superfluous or redundant to say she has an additional moral reason to do *X*. Or, to put it in the language of virtue, if someone has a good reason to be a virtuous moral agent (overall), it seems superfluous to say the agent has an additional moral reason to be virtuous. Wellman insists that having additional moral reasons to act virtuously does not mean that celebrated athletes "must necessarily behave *better* than others," so what are the practical consequences of having such special responsibilities? None, so far as I can tell. If a famous athlete has a moral reason not to fight in a bar with someone who picks a fight with him (to use Wellman's example), insofar as the athlete is a virtuous agent, what difference does it make if he has an additional reason not to fight? Perhaps such reasons are stronger, or provide stronger moral motivations in certain circumstances. Perhaps such additional moral reasons are the basis for performing supererogatory acts, going the extra moral mile, so to speak. But Wellman's exemplarism denies this, because athletes are not required to act better than nonathletes. Hence, at the least, it is not clear what the practical difference amounts to when asserting that celebrated athletes have additional moral reasons to behave well. This appears to be a distinction without a moral difference. However, the problems with exemplarism are deeper.

Because Malone's exemplarism admits, in the end, that celebrated athletes *are not* necessarily moral exemplars in the normative sense, although they are taken to be exemplars by people in our culture, especially children, there may be something dishonest or deceptive at the heart of the position. On the one hand, the celebrated athlete is supposed to act as if she is a moral exemplar, that is, as a person who is worthy of being imitated. But she also affirms that she is not morally special simply because she is taken to be special on the basis of her celebrated status as an athlete. Thus, the celebrated athlete is required to be dishonest; she is required to exhibit a moral vice. She may, in fact, be worthy of having her life imitated because she is a virtuous person. In this case, she will not have to be dishonest about her character. (Of course, for many celebrated athletes, their lives may not be worthy of imitation, so their dishonesty is about who they are.) But she will have to be dishonest about the reasons for her status. She is taken to be a moral exemplar because of her celebrated status as an athlete, but she must also maintain that there is nothing intrinsic to athletic participation that merits her moral status. So in acting as if she *is* a moral exemplar, she promotes the false belief that celebrated athletes are well suited for their cultural status as moral exemplars. If an athlete attempts to become a better person because others take her to be a moral exemplar, this might mitigate the charge of dishonesty, but unless she moves in a public way toward Barkley's skepticism, there is still some deception involved in her behavior. Such deception promotes confusion about the difference between role models and moral exemplars.

Suppose you come to me for moral advice. You may think that I am a wise person, well suited to give you moral advice. In fact, I may believe I am not morally wise and have no good advice to give you in the situation. Do I have the responsibility to try to give you moral advice because you mistakenly think I am wise? No, I do not. I may believe that what is most important is for you to find someone better suited for the role of moral adviser, so my responsibility in this situation is to be honest, proclaim that I am not wise, and suggest that you look elsewhere for someone with good moral judgment.

Or, suppose I live next door to an impressionable teenager who, I find out, has been much influenced by my life and conduct. It seems that he has decided not to study science in college as a prelude to applying for medical school. His parents find that all he wants to do is read philosophy, smoke cigarettes, hang out at the local coffeehouse, and argue about the existence of God with his friends. His parents and friends note that he has become rather cynical and now thinks that life is meaningless. (It seems that he recently read and misinterpreted my celebrated paper on "the absurd.") In this situation, he has taken me as a role model—actually, a moral exemplar. Do I have a special responsibility to him? Should I change my life because of his imitation of me? Should I control my cynical wit, give up my tennis lessons with the local pro so I have more time to help the homeless, and even give up my devotion to good wine? Should I retract my views on the absurdity of life? Suppose I am rather disenchanted with my life because of my sense that the pursuit of a philosophical life has left me skeptical and cynical, clever but not wise. I may be living the kind of life that I would not recommend to my young friend. Because he takes me to be an exemplar does not mean that I am worthy of being imitated. Moreover, because he imitates my life does not entail that I should change it or act as if he is right in choosing me to be his exemplar. Better to be honest than attempt to make my life mirror his misperceptions.

The situation here is rather confusing. In fact, if you take me as a moral exemplar, I can influence you. But if I believe I am not worthy of being imitated, I must also attempt to convince you to look elsewhere for better objects of imitation. You might be disposed to believe me because you do take me to be a moral exemplar, but now I am trying to convince you that I am not a moral exemplar, which seems to undermine the original belief. Dishonesty may require that I live and act according to your misperceptions of me, but honesty requires that I attempt to convince you to give up your misperceptions. The dilemma for exemplarism is that is requires either dishonesty or the denial of itself. Barkley's skepticism is morally preferable.

Exemplarism also appears to promote the false belief that being good at a practice entails being good overall, or living a life whose perceived unity is worthy of being imitated. Yet there is a deeper reason that there is nothing intrinsic to being an athlete that merits special moral status. Recall MacIntyre's view in *After Virtue* that an analysis of the virtues limited to their function internal to practices is incomplete. The athlete whose justice, courage, and honesty in his sport have helped him become a celebrated athlete may be someone whose life as a whole is defective because it is marred by conflict and arbitrariness. "The claims of one practice may be incompatible with another in such a way that one may find oneself oscillating in an arbitrary way, rather than making rational choices."[9] The Gauguin problem inevitably reappears in the lives of celebrated athletes and leaves us with a more plausible and limited context of imitation that stresses excellence within a practice rather than the excellence of a life as a whole.

So far I have argued that exemplarism is both redundant and dishonest. There are also legitimate consequentialist concerns involved in exemplarism's attempt to stress two facts: that celebrated athletes' special responsibilities are based on the notion that acting well causes others to act well and the fact that athletes have responsibilities "to reshape our culture so that when children look for moral exemplars they choose people better suited for the job." It would be more honest to deny that celebrated athletes are moral exemplars in the normative sense. In addition, since we all have a responsibility to reshape our culture so children look for moral exemplars in better places, or choose people better suited for such roles, our society might be better off if we all actively discouraged the notion that athletes have this special responsibility. Since the behavior of celebrated athletes is assumed to have such an influence over others, it is plausible to believe that the best consequences overall, in the long run, would be achieved by celebrated athletes actively and vigorously promoting the notion that they are not moral exemplars and that people should look elsewhere for their moral models. In other words, celebrated athletes should assert that their special (descriptive) moral status is in part based on morally irrelevant features of their lives—for example, being good at a sport, being famous, making a lot of money—and they should recognize that they could do more for the moral education of children by actively discouraging the notion that they are moral exemplars.

This consequentialist argument is reinforced by considering another result of exemplarism. Athletes supposedly are required to act virtuously, or behave well, even if they are not virtuous agents. Since there is nothing intrinsic to participation in athletics that merits their special moral status, we would expect that celebrated athletes, as a group, are not better as moral agents than a group of carpenters or insurance agents. (There may actually be reasons to believe that; given the way they develop and are treated, celebrated athletes may be more prone to certain vices than ordinary people, or even less celebrated athletes.) We would expect that celebrated athletes' major moral failings, because such people are relatively famous, would be quite public and more widely known than the failings of less famous people. What is the likely result of the knowledge that celebrated athletes participate in murders, rapes, assaults, spousal abuse, drug use, and alcohol abuse at rates that are similar to less celebrated athletes or nonathletes? When we find out that they lie, cheat, and abuse others, or that they are sometimes selfish, insensitive, or ignorant, the consequences of our inevitable disappointment with our sports heroes may be a kind of cynicism that tends to undermine our trust in general in others' moral character. There is always the possibility that the famous athlete you invite to the local school to promote the values of education will show up on the evening news after he is arrested. Even the good works of the virtuous athlete may end up being interpreted like the politician kissing a baby, as conduct good for his public image, where our shared moral life is interpreted as mere appearance. Or, if we want to retain our faith in the essential moral goodness of people, we are reduced to the banal judgment that sometimes people just make "bad choices," in order to explain why the celebrated athlete hired a contract killer or raped the nanny.

The final problem that plagues exemplarism involves an epistemological issue that has been raised against virtue ethics. To see this, it will be helpful to explain the structure presupposed by those who take exemplarism seriously, not as objects of imitation but as imitators. If celebrated athletes do have such influence on the moral conduct of others, especially on the moral education of our youth, there must be people who either explicitly or implicitly think in the following way.[10]

1. An act is right, that is, worthy of imitation, if and only if it is typically done by a role model (virtuous agent).
2. A role model (virtuous agent) is one who has and exercises admirable character traits (the virtues).
3. Jones, a celebrated athlete, is a role model.
4. Jones does act *A*, or lives like *A*, or says one ought to do *A*.
5. Therefore, we should act or live like Jones, or do what Jones says we ought to do—that is, we should do *A*.

The Imitation Argument is plagued by the third premise. First, the sense in which the premise may be obviously true or plausibly believed to be true is to assert that Jones is a role model in the descriptive sense. But the sense in which an act is right or is worthy of imitation is if Jones is a role model in the moral sense, that is, if Jones is a moral exemplar, worthy of imitation. So the argument equivocates on the meaning of *role model*. However, it is certainly possible that Jones *is* a moral exemplar and is, therefore, worthy of imitation. But how do we know this? In most cases, we know about celebrated athletes' exemplary conduct in sport, and there is nothing intrinsic to athletic participation that merits the status of being a moral exemplar. Most of us know very little about the athletes whose exploits we admire, and to the extent that we become acquainted with their extra-athletic behavior, we still have the problem that we are supposedly evaluating persons, not simply actions. Robert Louden has argued that this is a major problem for virtue ethics. "There is also an epistemological issue which becomes troublesome when one focuses on qualities of persons rather than on qualities of acts. Baldly put, the difficulty is that we do not seem to be able to know with any degree of certainty who is really virtuous and who is vicious." Since the qualities essential for being a virtuous person are, in part, internal, and we have no epistemic access to such qualities, we must "try to infer character by observing conduct," as Louden says, and there are obvious reasons for being skeptical about such an inference.[11] Since we usually know so little about the qualities of our heroes outside the sports world, the skepticism here is even more pronounced.

Louden's skepticism is extreme, but even if we say that it is sometimes reasonable (not certain) to infer the inner from the outer, when is it reasonable to treat someone as a moral exemplar? Generally (although some may find this unhelpful), it would be reasonable to treat someone as a moral exemplar when we have *good reasons* to think she has a certain kind of character, and we come to have such evidence (although it is certainly not infallible) when we get to know a person well, across a wide range of experiences, or when a person's life as a whole has been well documented. On the other hand, a person may legitimately be a role model for us, in the narrow sense, when we become well acquainted with that person's conduct and character qua role or station in life. In most cases, on epistemological grounds alone we should resist the tendency to treat celebrated athletes as moral exemplars.

I conclude that exemplarism is redundant, possibly dishonest, deceptive, may contribute to bad moral consequences (including cynicism), and is plagued by a central epistemological problem. I turn now to some matters that reinforce the skeptical view of athletes as moral exemplars, but take seriously the view that athletes may be, and should be, role models.

## iv. Role Models, the Imagination, and Lusory Objects

Perhaps the tone so far has seemed too negative. It is natural for a skepticism about the status of celebrated athletes as moral exemplars to refer to widely publicized examples that appear repeatedly in the sports pages and even on the front pages of our newspapers.

Cynicism and irreverence are the inevitable result. But my purpose is not to remind people of such obvious counterexamples to exemplarism. In fact, I am less interested in a debunking operation and more interested in one that salvages important meanings. Cynicism is the inevitable result of exemplarism, not skepticism, and a properly understood skepticism about athletes as moral exemplars is compatible with a view that wishes to retain the magical and mythical status of our sports heroes. Exemplarism leads to cynicism because of its overreaching insistence that celebrated athletes are worthy of imitation as persons whose lives as a whole, including their "real" lives outside of sports, are exemplary. In doing this, exemplarism misunderstands the proper object of imitation. I wish to preserve the symbolic value of heroes by limiting the arena appropriate for their influence, in a way that seems to me to be obvious but is either ignored or denied by defenders of exemplarism. Let's take a brief detour through broader concerns and then return to the question of role models.

It is important to remember the significance of certain categories associated with the concept of play when we think about experiences related to sports participation and appreciation. Although we need not thoroughly rehash the details of Huizinga's phenomenology of play or the way his followers have made rich use of his influential analysis, recall some of the relevant highlights.[12] We play our games because we want to engage in such activities, not because we are forced to play. Unlike "real" or "ordinary" life, playful activities are freely chosen, with no end or purpose other than engaging in the activities in question. Thus, play is somehow set apart from ordinary reality, and it is typically ordered by its own set of rules and conventions, arbitrarily created in order to make these autotelic activities possible. Games are played out within their own self-imposed constraints, trivial activities when compared to the values and demands of everyday life. Shooting and kicking and hitting balls have meaning only within the context of a play world. Special meanings and values arise internal to this world. Spatial and temporal limitations and the intrinsic ends defined by the rules and conventions of this alternative world constitute a distinctively ordered experience, but the internal purposes of the play world are relatively pointless in relation to "real" life. Hence, there is a quality of "unreality" or illusion associated with the world of play. It is, as it were, conventional all the way down, and it exists only to the extent that its participants accept its conventions. It is simply not like ordinary life in certain important respects. The world of play is not "serious," when we contrast its values and activities to work, war, disease, and human suffering. We are constantly reminded that it is important to keep the playing of games "in perspective," as if life is more than fun and games or the overcoming of artificial obstacles. On the other hand, participants often play with utmost seriousness, and the internal goods of the play world are made possible only by being serious about "nonseriousness."

Insofar as sports involve playing games, there are a number of categories that appropriately stress the way the world of play is different from ordinary or real life: "illusion," "being set apart," "self-enclosed," "self-contained," "living as if," "representation." This set of categories also occasions reflection on the relation between sport and art, or at least some artistic forms and categories, like "drama" or "narrative," because stories, and movies, and novels are not real life, but are representations whose meaning and value depend on accepting the relevant conventions. Questions about sport and art put us in a neighborhood that helps us understand the issues that are central to this chapter.

Consider David Best's attempt to distinguish sport and art.[13] In the context of his claim that, unlike sport, the conventions of art allow for "the possibility of the expression of a conception of life situation," Best argues that objects in art are fictional. We must be careful when applying certain aesthetic categories to sport, like the "dramatic" or the "tragic," because the "tragedy" that occurs in drama is quite unlike the way in which "tragedy" might be predicated of an athlete. Real people are injured in sport. Although Gloucester's eyes are put out, the actor playing the character in *King Lear* will still see his friends after the play is over. Best says, "To put the point roughly, it is a central convention of art, in contrast to sport, that the object of one's attention is an *imagined* object."[14] Supposedly, the objects of attention in sport are real in a way that is quite unlike the imaginative constitution of artistic or fictional objects.

I agree with the suggestion that Best's general view of art is too intellectualist, and his specific notion of the proper object of attention in art may be problematic.[15] It is not clear that Best is successful in attempting to distinguish sport and art in terms of an imaginative construction that can comment on life. The position cannot account for how we appreciate nonrepresentational arts like abstract painting, music, architecture, or some forms of dance. In these cases, the notion of an "imagined object" as the intentional object of aesthetic attention is more puzzling. On the other hand, if we sufficiently broaden our notion of the way the imagination can constitute a meaningful intentional object when we attend to such nonrepresentational artistic forms, it becomes plausible to think that the imagination can be put into play when we attend to sports. Consider the competitive aspect of sports and the set of categories appropriate for appreciating this: agon, struggle, contest, victory, failure, triumph, even fate. In this world set apart from real wars, tragedy, and death, such mythic themes are played out and represented to our imaginative appreciation. Christopher Cordner offers the following comments:

> This implies that the meaning and value of sports can be characterized only by reference to our imaginative engagement with it. We see in athletics a suspended "as if" enactment of the "agon" or struggle of war, with a patterning out of these capacities and qualities engaged in that agon, but which can here be appreciated and savored in the bracketing context of sport. . . . [O]f course in one sense the game of football is a struggle, but it is also a game, and appreciating the struggle as engaged in the play of the game is an achievement of imagination.[16]

Cordner's stress on the possibility of an imaginative engagement with sport is echoed in the writings of Michael Novak, A. Bartlett Giamatti, and Christopher Lasch.[17] At least in the case of Novak and Giamatti, their reflections occur as expressions of their love for sports, attempts to articulate their deep attraction for sports, or, as Novak says, the project of "faith seeking understanding." They trace a path that leads inevitably to conceptualize their love in terms of categories that stress the dramatic and imaginative possibilities embedded in sports. Novak's encomium is aptly titled *The Joy of Sports*. In the following he chides those who seek to reduce sports to mere entertainment. Perhaps there is some irony here: "Believers in sport do not go to sports to be entertained; to plays and dramas, maybe, but not to sports. Sports are far more serious than the dramatic arts, much closer to primal symbols, metaphors, and arts, much more ancient and frightening. Sports are mysteries of youth and aging, perfect action and decay, fortune and misfortune, strategy and contingency. Sports are rituals concerning human survival on this planet: liturgical enactments of animal perfection and the struggles of the human spirit to prevail."[18]

Giamatti, the professor of Renaissance literature turned commissioner of Major League Baseball, celebrates sport, especially his beloved baseball, as a form of "Aristotelian leisure," as "the daily re-creation of the impulse of pure play, a reiteration of the hunger for paradise—for a freedom untrammeled." Yet sport lives in the social world; it aspires to paradise, yet it lives in the city. "Sports are conventional, and are self-contained systems of convention." Sports are so "rule bound and internally complete" that they can have "the character of *cults*, those closed-off, self-contained cultures that demand one's total being, one's total assent." The mythic qualities of Novak's Theology of Sport resonate in Giamatti's stress on the cultlike nature of sport, yet the special world that Giamatti describes is wholly conventional, hence "completely artificial." Giamatti speaks metaphorically of the sports venue as a little city:

The little city is special in various ways: If outdoors, it may be completely enclosed, or may not be, but in either case, the spectator is surrounded, if not completely in structure, certainly in crowd, and in expectation. The spectator and participant accept the convention, as one does in a theater, that the life about to be displayed is not real (as distinct from a house of worship, where the claim is that life is more real, the reality of our essence or ultimate end), but different, an enhanced life, not a final one, a life in costume. Uniforms may be *uniform* and thus useful in telling apart the sides, that is, in distinguishing the two parties to this mock dispute that is about to be settled, but uniforms are also costumes, important for identity, colorful, designed to enhance ease of performance—a life strenuously lived *as if.*[19]

In the midst of this cultlike artificial world, this "mock dispute" set apart from the ordinary world, self-contained yet radiant with transparent meanings and efficacious action, actors (players) face freely chosen arbitrary constraints and obstacles. It is within this world that they are called upon to display courage and boldness as they pursue the noble internal purposes shared by teammates, coaches, and fans.

Consider the language Bernard Suits used in his attempt to define games in terms of prelusory goals, lusory means, and the lusory attitude.[20] I would like to borrow this language and speak of "lusory objects." A lusory object is an object whose meaning or significance cannot be understood independent of the way in which the game is defined and interpreted in terms of its lusory means and lusory goals, that is, its rules and conventions. Consider baseball, for example. A piece of wood, a horsehide sphere, and a configuration of stitched leather are transformed into meaningful lusory objects when taken to the field and used on game day: a baseball bat, a baseball, and a catcher's mitt. The player who says good-bye to his wife and children and drives to the stadium becomes a lusory object when the game begins. The person who is a husband and father becomes a "center fielder," "clean-up hitter," and a "clutch player" who often hits home runs of "Ruthian proportion" in the Little

City where his extraordinary achievements are cheered and admired. It is a failure of our language, or rather our linguistic sensitivities, that we refer to the person qua father and husband, with the same name as the lusory object whose athletic deeds, at times, seem to be almost superhuman because they have so far outdistanced the performances of most other players, both past and present. When we refer to our favorite sports hero, a name refers to a lusory object whose heroic performances occasion reflection on the natural, the gifted, and the gritty, the challenges of aging, fierce competition, and moments of enormous pressure. We are projected into their stories, and we make them our own. Michael Jordan is universally acclaimed as the greatest professional basketball player of all time. (Ignore for the moment whether such judgments are appropriate or meaningful.) Michael Jordan, qua sports hero, celebrated athlete, and role model *for basketball players* who seek to perform at the highest levels and for fans who appreciate the ideal of athletic excellence, is not the person inhabiting other roles, or whose life as a whole is taken to be exemplary—Michael Jordan as husband, father, gambler, or whose astounding pettiness was put on display in a Hall of Fame induction speech. The meaning of "Michael Jordan" as a lusory object is quite distinctive and extraordinary. The other Michael Jordan, the "real" Jordan, is irrelevant when it comes to our (the fans' or spectators') relation to the lusory object.

Our sports heroes should be thought of more as imagined objects or fictional characters in a drama, whose characters and exploits we admire within this illusory domain, rather than persons whose lives outside of sports are either exemplary, noteworthy, or even interesting. Again, to use examples from the object of Giamatti's love, it is less misleading to speak of "Charley Hustle," "the 'Say Hey' Kid," or "the Babe" rather than Pete Rose, Willie Mays, or George Herman Ruth, when referring to our baseball heroes. To speak of the "Rocket" conjures up images of a larger-than-life center of athletic intensity, commitment, and record-breaking pitching achievements. "The Georgia Peach." "Hammerin Hank." "Big

Unit." We need know nothing of their lives outside baseball to appreciate their play or encourage young players to learn from them and imitate their conduct within the world of baseball. (Sadly, in some cases it is better to know nothing about their lives as a whole.)

Michael Novak wonderfully describes the "Homeric deeds" of an aging professional football player, George Blanda, many years ago. He captures well our imaginative engagement with the representation of athletic heroism that I have called a lusory object:

> The situations in which destiny places him soon become more trying, more impossible. Struggle is the classic form of human life: the voyages of Ulysses. The trials of Hercules, the great deeds of defenders and attackers at the siege of Troy. . . . The hero is placed in a situation foredooming him to failure, and just as he succeeds new obstacles arise. The hero's enemies determine to defeat him. His friends may, or may not, fail him. His body is afflicted. . . . Against the odds, the hero concentrates. He seeks the single open pathway through the maze. Thus the exaltation, when out of the labyrinth of failure a man suddenly breaks clear, "runs for daylight" as the cliché puts it, scores a sudden touchdown. It is a victory of light over darkness. An almost Persian imagination of reality.[21]

Now we are in a position to offer some conclusions about the status of celebrated athletes as role models.

### v. Applications and Conclusions

Celebrated athletes are role models, not moral exemplars. They are lusory objects whose meaning and significance are internal to the world of the sport within which they excel. The major error of exemplarism is a confusion about the proper meaning of our sports heroes as lusory objects, inhabitants of a world set apart from the ordinary world by virtue of the conventions without which their heroic efforts would have no meaning or significance.

To conceive of role models as lusory objects solves the two major problems that plague exemplarism. First, the epistemological problem arises because we simply do not know enough about our sport heroes in order to believe that they are moral exemplars whose lives or conduct in general is worthy of imitation. If we conceive of the meaning of our sports heroes as lusory objects, we know who is exemplary as well as we could expect in any part of our lives. Within the world of sports, there are standards of excellence against which we measure and evaluate performance. It is reasonable to assume that athletic conduct expresses the inner qualities that are an essential aspect of the virtuous athlete: dedication, commitment, the will to win, the love and respect for the game, and so forth. Our sports heroes deserve to be imitated, qua athletes, because of what they have done in the public arena of athletic competition, filtered through our imagination and reconstituted in light of these categories.

Second, exemplarism is plagued by an is-ought dilemma that leads to the central moral criticisms leveled against it. In my view, celebrated athletes are role models in both the descriptive and the normative senses, since they are believed to be worthy of imitation and are, in fact, worthy of imitation insofar as their conduct has expressed their heroic virtues. They also have a deeper responsibility to show how the game ought to be played, not only in terms of the standards of excellence that measure their exemplary athletic performance, but also in terms of ideals of sportsmanship that arise from a proper understanding of the nature of sport and the meaning of their admirable athletic conduct. Since exemplarism wants celebrated athletes to recognize their moral influence on others, it cannot object to the notion that celebrated athletes have a special influence on how others, especially young athletes, understand the ethical aspects of sports participation. To stress the notion that celebrated athletes are not moral exemplars is not to deny that they have heightened responsibilities to exhibit good sportsmanship—however that is understood. It is ironic that Karl Malone, whose comments have been taken to be the paradigmatic expression of moral exemplarism, had the reputation of being a dirty basketball player. He should have been more concerned with whether his behavior in *basketball* was a model of Thuggery, rather than the notion that his life outside of basketball has, or ought to have, any influence on impressionable young persons. It is ironic that the area of his life in which he *ought* to have the most influence is the one in which his conduct is sometimes less than exemplary.

Although my approach may seem rather abstract, I would like to offer some brief suggestions about how my view of celebrated athletes as role models, as lusory objects, might be applied.

First, there is compelling evidence that Pete Rose bet on professional baseball when he was the manager of the Cincinnati Reds. For this he was banned from baseball for gambling on the game, and he is ineligible for being inducted into the Hall of Fame, despite the fact that he was one of the greatest players ever to play Major League Baseball. Should Pete Rose be in the Hall of Fame? In my view, "Charley Hustle" should be inducted into the Hall of Fame and take his deserved place among the collection of the greatest players who have ever played baseball. Who can remember Pete Rose, qua baseball player, without conjuring up images of his incredible enthusiasm and effort? A man who lacked outstanding athletic abilities, in some sense, became the player who recorded more base hits than any other player in the history of the game. On the other hand, by all reports he was not only a compulsive gambler who destroyed the illusion of the magical world by his betting but also less than admirable in other respects as a human being. (We now also know that he lied for years about his behavior.) Ban Pete Rose from ever playing an active part in the game, but admit "Charley Hustle" to the Hall of Fame, along with great ball players who were racists, alcoholics, adulterers, anti-Semites, homophobes, wife abusers, and drug users. "Charley Hustle" is a hero; Pete Rose is not.

Second, many college athletics programs require their athletes to go out into the community and do good works. From soup kitchens to the public schools, athletes are sometimes apparently coerced into performing supposedly virtuous deeds, undoubtedly documented by the sports information people in releases to local news outlets. If these programs are motivated by the notion that college athletes, because of their public status in their communities, should recognize their special responsibilities to be moral exemplars, then such programs are misguided, for the same reasons that I have given to criticize exemplarism. They promote the idea that celebrated athletes are morally special, in both the descriptive and the normative senses, and they are not, or they should not be. If we want to encourage at-risk students to be serious about their educations, better to send the honors physics students than the guys with the big necks or the really tall girls who recently won the championship.

Third, in a newspaper column, here is how a sportswriter posed the issue.

> Two weeks ago, while chatting on the phone one afternoon with my brother, I caught a glimpse of Court TV and the coverage of Kobe Bryant's arraignment on sexual assault charges.
>
> When I mentioned that Bryant had entered a not guilty plea, my brother sighed.
>
> "Geesh," Jack said. "How do I explain that to my boys? They're starting to get interested in sports and they think Kobe Bryant is some kind of hero. What do I tell them?"[22]

I am not sure why this father found the situation so difficult, nor why the sportswriter's column was titled "Qualifications to Be a 'Hero' Hard to Explain." I suspect the father's puzzlement was related to the is-ought problem, but the answer seems to me to be obvious and straightforward. Kobe Bryant is a great basketball player, not necessarily a great human being. The father had a valuable opportunity to make a significant point related to sports and moral education. Admire the athlete as a player, but withhold judgment and the disposition to imitate the player when he leaves the arena. On the court, Kobe's feats are filtered through the imagination and merit our admiration; in the courtroom, Kobe is just a guy.

# 7 Coach as Sage

*So I withdrew and thought to myself: "I am wiser than this man;* ✱
*it is likely that neither of us knows anything worthwhile, but he
thinks he knows something when he does not, whereas when I do
not know, neither do I think I know; so I am likely to be wiser
than he to this small extent, that I do not think I know what I do
not know."*

Socrates, *Apology*

*But, gentlemen of the jury, the good craftsmen seemed to me to
have the same fault as the poets; each of them, because of his success
at his craft, thought himself very wise in other important pursuits,
and this error of theirs overshadowed the wisdom they had, so that
I asked myself, on behalf of the oracle, whether I should prefer to
be as I am, with neither their wisdom nor their ignorance, or to
have both. The answer I gave myself and the oracle was that it was
to my advantage to be as I am.*

Socrates, *Apology*

*I hear coaches say (they're) in the business of making men in the
future. No. You're not. You're in the business of coaching. I'm in the
business of raising my son.*

Gary Danielson, CBS commentator, *Sports Illustrated*

The argument for the view that sports heroes are role models insists that celebrated athletes have a heightened influence on the conduct of others, especially children, yet there is nothing intrinsic to being a celebrated athlete that merits the status of being a moral exemplar, that is, a person whose life as a whole is worthy of being imitated. There has been considerable discussion about sports heroes as role models—often in relation to repeated and highly publicized apparent moral failures of sports celebrities—yet much less discussion has occurred, if any, about a related issue concerning famous sports figures and ethical guidance. Some look to celebrated athletes as role models. Others apparently look to famous coaches for inspiration and wisdom, not merely about the spread offense, the pick and roll, or the importance of pitching and defense, but about how to live, what to pursue, and what kind of person to be. Many coaches are keen to oblige our desire for ethical wisdom. Some give speeches and even write books in which they attempt to provide sage advice about life, rather than giving explicit instruction about how to attain athletic excellence or how to become good at winning athletic games. Whereas the role-model argument for celebrated athletes focuses on the mere fact of celebrity as the basis for heightened influence on others and special responsibilities to "model" good ethical conduct, the coach who thinks she is in a good position to teacher others—especially young athletes—how to live must conceive of her role responsibilities in such a way that the experience of coaching provides unique opportunities to be a moral educator. How that should be done is an important question.

In the following I discuss the curious phenomenon of what I call the Coach as Sage, not to be confused with other roles that coaches take on: coach as teacher, parent, manager, nanny, and so on. I raise the issue of the fittingness of coaches taking on the role of one who attempts to impart much-needed wisdom to players and to those who buy their books. I am especially interested in the coach who takes on this role in the context of institutions of higher education.

I focus on a recent book by one of the most successful coaches in big-time American college football, Jim Tressel, former head coach at the Ohio State University. I shall attempt to show that we should be wary of the Coach as Sage despite common praise for coaches who say they are most interested in educating athletes for their whole lives, not merely as instruments for winning games. Although my remarks will be critical, I end with more positive comments about the complexities associated with the role of the coach as ethical guide.

## 1. A Coach Book

Peruse the shelves in the sport section at your local bookstore, and you will see numerous books written by coaches. I will refer to them as "coach books." The approach in coach books is diverse: instructional manuals, autobiographies, memoirs, leadership and management guides, and monographs that offer advice for life. Although many coach books are hybrids, combining accounts of practice and game-management strategies, anecdotes from the locker room or playing field, autobiographical descriptions of backgrounds and influences, and advice that might be helpful outside of sports, there is another type of coach book whose pretensions are rather breathtaking. This is the kind of book in which sport seemingly takes a backseat to life. Here the goal is not so much to help us become acquainted with a successful life in sports, or to contribute to our voyeuristic obsession with celebrity. The goal is to show us how to live, to impart much-needed wisdom concerning a central question in the history of ethical thinking: what does it mean to live a good human life? We may be surprised to learn that a successful coach is in a position to advance our understanding in this area, but there is little doubt that some coaches are eager and quite sincere in their attempt to contribute to this monumental task. To whom do we look for wisdom in contemporary popular culture, for advice about how to live? A short list of Characters whose books are found in the self-help section of the bookstore might include: the Preacher, the Successful Businessman, the Therapist–Counselor–Life Coach, the Artist, the Politician, and the Old Wise One. To this list we must now add the Coach as Sage.[1]

It would take considerable time and effort to canvass adequately the array of coach books whose intention is to impart ethical wisdom, in the broad sense of offering instruction in how to live. For our purposes I will initially concentrate on *The Winners Manual for the Game of Life*, by Jim Tressel.[2] I do this for reasons of content and context. First, it is a quintessential example of a coach book whose pretensions are immoderate. It is a pure example of the kind of book in which I am interested. As Tressel says, "This is not a book about football as much as it is about life" (xviii). I realize that one must be quite careful in generalizing based only on a specific case. I do not claim that my discussion of Tressel's book will constitute a decisive response to all coach books of this type. I do think that the discussion will be relevant for critically examining other books of this type, because my arguments appeal to principles and evaluative factors that extend beyond a single text. I raise questions that are more broadly applicable, but I leave it to others to connect the dots. Tressel's book is the best example I could find (at least from more recent publications) whose author takes on the role of a person whose goal is to provide wise counsel for young athletes.

For me, context is as important as content—perhaps more so—because Tressel's pupils are first of all the college football players on his teams at Ohio State, not the readers of his book who made it a *New York Times* best seller (whatever that means), as it claims on its cover. The primary readers of the larger version of *The Winners Manual* are students attending one of the great public universities in America. It is one thing for the company to pay thousands of dollars to a successful coach in order to give a motivational speech to the employees or for the manager to distribute a coach book to the sales representatives to enhance the sale of widgets. It is quite another thing to decide, as a coach, to be concerned to "develop a whole person" (xix) in one's players by offering explicit ethical instruction about how to live and to require players to spend considerable time, outside of the playing field, attempting to implement the coach's vision of the good life. In the context of higher education, the important question is not simply about the supposed wisdom being imparted; it is as much about whether the methods of teaching are compatible with the values of the academy and whether the notion of the Coach as Sage is an appropriate role for a coach to embrace.

The published version of *The Winners Manual* is a distillation of a larger version that was given each year to Jim Tressel's football players at the Ohio State University. The larger version contained predictable team-specific elements such as schedules, team rules, and the like, as well as a mission statement and parts that apparently were included to reinforce patriotism: the Pledge of Allegiance, the Gettysburg Address, and "a section on the importance of the American flag" (xiv). The *New York Times* best seller explains the nuts and bolts of "the game plan" in part 1 and "the Big Ten Fundamentals" in part 2, "a step-by-step process of personal assessment and goal setting that players find helpful. We take each player on a journey of success" (xiv). The book is full of pithy slogans (sayings, quotations—Tressel usually refers to them as "quotes") that are supposed to capture the point of the moment or occasion deep thinking. The sources range from numerous Bible verses ("Humility precedes honor") to Charles DeGaulle ("Graveyards are full of irreplaceable men"), from Thoreau and Voltaire to Liberace and LL Cool J. In the chapter on "faith and belief" (one of the "Big Ten Fundamentals" that are essential for becoming a "winner"), Tressel quotes noted theologian Louis L'Amour: "To disbelieve is easy; to scoff is simple; to have faith is harder." Each year Tressel collected new sayings that he had come across or that he had been given and revised the manual that he gave to his players. How he found these quotations is not made explicit. It is not at all clear that he actually read Thoreau, Voltaire, Goethe, Confucius, Seneca, or others whom he cites, since the quotations simply appear as sidebars, never in the context of a substantive discussion of the ideas and arguments offered by these thinkers and writers. He never explains how he acquired the insights of Bette Davis or Irving Berlin (not Isaiah Berlin). It *is* clear that Coach Tressel believes these sayings have an important educational and moral role to play in what he is trying to accomplish in using the manual. They appear in each chapter devoted to a "Big Ten Fundamental"—for example, "attitude" and "discipline"—and are presumably the object of reflection during what Tressel calls "Quiet Time." During Quiet Times (parts of team meetings), a section from the *Winners Manual* might be assigned reading, and players quietly jot down a few thoughts as they reflect and are "able to use the next eight to twelve minutes of quiet to help them develop their inner person" (xx).

Tressel begins and ends the manual by telling us that a simple question he heard as a teenager at a Fellowship of Christian Athletes football camp profoundly affected his life: "If the game of life ended tonight, would you be a winner?" He says the question intrigued and motivated him throughout his life and defined his life "as a son, a husband, a father, and a coach" (xiii). So the book is his attempt to answer that simple, vitally important question—hence, the "winners manual."

I do not want to appear to be too uncharitable to Coach Tressel, and as we will see, there are probably unexceptional aspects of his ethical instruction, but even at the beginning of his book we might wonder about his response to the question. He often exhorts his players to "think," yet it never seems to occur to him to wonder whether it makes sense to speak of being a winner "in life" or whether the notion is a useful or insightful metaphor for living well. Taken literally, the question makes little sense. In sports there are winners and losers, rules that create artificial obstacles, and the freedom to pursue the goals of the play world. If I win a competition with you, then you lose. If I live a good life, however that is understood, if I live the best life I am capable of or if I flourish as a human being, does that mean that others must "lose" or live less well? Perhaps there are pockets of competitive structures in life, but life as a whole is not like that. There are important questions about whether it makes any sense to say of a life that it is a winning one, or how we should construe such a claim. We should be perplexed by those who claim that sports can teach us how to be winners in *life*, or that a losing high school coach should be fired because he is teaching his players how to be "losers" (a real-life example).[3]

To be a winner, to "progress" in life, we need to think that "success is a journey we all take" (3). The first chapter, "The Journey of Success," offers us key insights as we begin our "journey." (He talks as if this tired metaphor is a novel insight.) Tressel learned from the great basketball coach John Wooden that "success is found in 'peace of mind.' That was a revolutionary thought to me" (5). It is puzzling why such a commonplace assertion could be a "revolutionary thought," but that is one of the insights at the heart of the book. Tressel adds a communal component: "Success is the inner satisfaction and peace of mind that come from knowing I did the best I was capable of doing *for the group*" (5). Individualism is problematic in sports and society. *The* group? What is success? It is feeling good about doing your best for whatever group you are a part of or with which you identify. Such a claim immediately occasions for me questions about the sorts of groups with which one might identify. Don't we need to do some sorting here? There are obviously groups with whom my participation would be morally problematic. Tressel seems to think that social life is all about being a member of teams or groups, yet his "definition" appears to be limited by his moral imagination, as if he needs to be reminded of the "moral history of the Twentieth Century," as Jonathan Glover describes the sorry events associated with Stalinism, Nazism, the Khmer Rouge, and other "groups."[4] It is also obvious that we need not be required to look to world-historical events for our counterexamples, since contemporary social life is littered with the detritus of morally reprehensible social groups. Tressel thinks that adding the group requirement is essential. "It forces us to define success in terms of what the group needs, what our team needs, or what our society or country needs" (5). The simple-mindedness of these claims is breathtaking. Even at this point in reading the manual, I wondered about the reactions of at least some of Tressel's players who were pursuing a broad liberal arts education and were being challenged in their classes to think about fundamental issues in ways that expose the shallowness of Tressel's blueprint for the good life.

If success as peace of mind is taken to be one of the central insights expressed in the manual, another is the distinction between one's purpose and one's goals. Tressel has discovered that many are simply confused about who they *are*, and what they do, that is, their purpose and their goals. What we do in life must spring from what we are in order to be a winner. "The problem for many people today is that they've mixed up their purpose with their goals" (25). Tressel conveys these claims in an oracular tone. "Our task as coaches is to get our players interested in *being* first and letting what they *do* flow out of that" (26). One's purpose comes first, then one's goals. Tressel explains the distinction in terms of what he calls "The Block O of Life." Imagine an octagonal *O* with three sides in the upper half of the diagram, *Ohio State* printed in the middle to divide the two halves and extending past the two longer sides of the *O*, and three sides in the bottom part of the *O*. The upper half represents one's purpose; the bottom half represents one's goals. The categories of purpose are "constant," as he says, whereas the part representing goals is specific to individual lives and can be "customized." Our task is to find our purpose, understood in terms of the central categories that Tressel offers. The purpose component of the "Block O" includes "Personal/Family," "Spiritual/Moral," and "Caring/Giving." We are all part of a family, we have spiritual needs, and we find ourselves living in communities. Tressel thinks these categories define who we are in some deep sense and generate specific goals that we should strive for, but how this works is initially perplexing. He says that some of his players "tend to get stuck on the Purpose section. They don't have any idea what their purpose is" (25). I sympathize with Tressel's players. I have no idea what my purpose is, or whether I have one. I do think that I have moral responsibilities because of family membership or the fact that I live in a community with others whose lives I should respect or whose ends should be morally relevant when I act. Claims about moral responsibilities are not simply reducible to claims about an individual's "purposes," as Tressel thinks. Why does Tressel insist that the key to being a "winner" on the "journey of success" is to find one's purpose?

The answer is not hard to find. Despite the fact that Tressel sometimes says that he is not trying to force his Christian worldview on his players, and that they are free to follow their own spiritual path, his view is unmistakable. "We were created not just to exist, not just to pass through this world and be *about* something, but to live with *purpose*" (7). Whose purpose? God's purpose. "God has plans for all of us that are good plans, not plans for disaster; and as long as we search for that rewarding life and carry that hope with us, we have a chance to end up leading winning lives" (238). "Purpose is a gift from God. Without him, I would still be searching for purpose in my life. Lasting goals are also from God. . . . And every component of the Block O of Life can be traced back to principles discussed and fleshed out in the Bible" (262). Despite Tressel's protests to the contrary, it is apparent where he thinks this journey is headed. Quiet Times, infused with encouragements that these young adult athletes should seek to discover their purpose, beyond mere football, could scarcely get off the ground without certain assumptions. The most obvious ones are the central tenets of Tressel's religious commitments: that Christian theism is true and that the key to a good human life is discovering what God intends for us. Worldly purposes are ultimately expressions of Divine Purpose. References to secular purposes are disguised appeals to Tressel's God, and his statements about religious diversity are disingenuous. "Faith is who you are" (106). "As a Christian I never want to set myself above another person or infer that I *know and you don't*. I *get it and you don't*" (116). Of course he does, and that is why at every team meeting players see the Block O of Life staring at them from the front wall and why they are given a "wallet-size card with the same information" to carry with them (33). "Far be it from me to suggest that my way is the only way" (28). Yet Tressel's way *is* the only way for his players to start their journey to being a winner.

The Spiritual/Moral category assumes the centrality of religion in Tressel's life, therefore in all lives. He calls this the "faith aspect of a person's life" (114). It is difficult to understand what he means by "faith." Is it trust? Confidence? Does it refer to religious experience? Does faith involve or entail propositional belief? How is faith related to reason? I have no idea what he means, since Tressel seems incapable of anything other than slogans. "Faith is the bedrock of a winner" (114). "Boiled down, faith is who we are on the inside" (116). He also says some peculiar things. "Faith is who you are. Belief is what you do with your faith" (106). "Belief is centered more in the individual, and it represents a strong internal feeling that suggests, 'I can do this'" (110). He quotes Augustine, "Faith is believing what we do not see. The reward of faith is to see what we believe" (110), but seems to ignore the way Augustine understands the important concepts in the quotation. Also, the reference to "moral" in this category of purpose is unexplained. Perhaps he thinks that one's moral identity is essentially related to one's spiritual or religious commitments. That need not be the case, as is shown theoretically in the history of moral philosophy and practically by the moral lives of religious skeptics.

The goal components of the Block O assume that college football players are the intended audience, so the important categories are "Football/Family," "Strength/Fitness," and "Academics/Career." "When I talk about goals, I always emphasize that they must be *measurable*. You need to be able to quantify what you want to accomplish" (22). I assume this means that a player must specify, for example, that he wants to make an A in a philosophy course, or have a 3.0 GPA in the fall semester, rather than express a desire to understand better various arguments or gain wisdom from reading Plato.

The second part of the book runs for more than two hundred pages and consists of ten chapters on "the Big Ten Fundamentals." These include "Attitude," "Discipline," "Excellence," "Faith and Belief," "Work," "Handling Adversity and Success," "Love," "Responsibility," "Team," and "Hope." "Each of the Big Ten Fundamentals is designed to drive you toward either your purpose or your goals" (29). So, for example, the chapter on attitude is both an exercise in positive thinking (Tressel mentions that he is a fan of Norman Vincent Peale)[5] and an appeal to the importance of some specific attitudes: gratitude, humility, and enthusiasm. During daily Quiet Time players are asked to write down something for which they are grateful. Tressel believes that he must instill in his players the notion that a good life is a "grateful life" (49). For Tressel, worldly gratitude is importantly related to Cosmic Gratitude. The behavior of the slacker at work shows a lack of gratitude for her job. The next sentence connects this with God: "We've neglected our relationship with God. That comes directly from a lack of gratitude" (49). The essence of humility is explained by referring to a biblical passage. (One might compare Tressel's account of humility with Iris Murdoch's discussion of the selfless seeing of the way things are.)[6] Even enthusiasm is given a theistic twist. Its Greek roots mean "full of spirit, full of God." "It's our hope that every team member will catch that vision and live, practice, and play in a way that's full of spirit and full of God" (60).

The remaining discussion of the Big Ten Fundamentals consists of a series of truisms that are neither esoteric nor remarkable. They may appear to be exceptional only when they are given Tressel's Christian interpretation. "Work hard" is conjoined with "Work is really a gift from God" (129), and hoping to win the big game when things look bad (trailing in the fourth quarter against Michigan) is followed by "hope puts faith to work" (230). (Claims about the centrality and meaning of "faith and belief" are neither truistic, transparent, nor supported.) What does Tressel recommend? However you live, you should have a positive attitude, be disciplined and attend carefully to what you are doing (focus on the moment— very Buddhist), do your best, work hard, be persistent and tough, learn to handle success and adversity, love your neighbor, be responsible, not swear, make your interests subservient to team interests and put team first, and be hopeful. Who could object to such platitudes?

Tressel ends his winners manual with some discussion of "heroes and winners" (including a heartfelt description of his father) and an epilogue that returns to the central question, "If the game of life ended tonight, would you be a winner?" He makes explicit what he calls "God's Fundamentals: Know Him, Love Him, Serve Him" (265–68). He still insists that his religious worldview is not oppressive. "I've never had a player tell me he felt uncomfortable with my approach or that I jammed religion down his throat. I respect our players too much to do anything like that" (262). It is interesting that Coach Tressel raises the issue of respect for his players in his closing remarks. Perhaps he is aware that this is a significant issue.

## 11. College Athletics, Authority, and Wisdom

As I suggested earlier, an appropriate response to a book like this might raise questions of both content and context. Questions about content concern both style and substance, tone or voice, and the specific instructions offered by the author. Questions concerning context raise larger issues that are not specific to Tressel's book. Questions of content concern the details of this particular book, whereas questions of context raise issues concerning books of this type. Methodological issues bridge the gap between the two. I am most interested in the broader issue, but the details are relevant.

I found this book to be drab, dull, and uninspiring. I have no doubt that Coach Tressel is a decent man, yet the book drips with sincerity. (I could not help but think of Sartre's "champion of sincerity" when reading the manual.)[7] From the concern for the "whole person" to the goal of developing the "inner person," its aspirations are wildly at odds with its style. The writing at times has a sort of "gee-whiz" quality, where humdrum commonplaces are put forward as original and profound insights. (We are going on a "journey of success." Success is "peace of mind.") The tone combines the stern and caring authority of Ward Cleaver with the gentle suggestions of Mr. Rogers prodding reflections during "Quiet Times." Perhaps the third part of this tonal triad includes Billy Graham or a fatherly Sunday-school teacher leading adolescents in thoughtful reflection on Bible verses. The book is an expression of a mind devoid of detachment, healthy skepticism, irony, or critical reflection. Everything is in its place, tidy, as it should be. Its very innocence and naïveté are oddly disturbing. Perhaps that is one of the reasons I found the book so depressing. Tressel seems to have a hatred of complexity. He says the Block O of Life is a "simple illustration" (26) that "does make life more *observable*" (18). No. It reduces life to the level of the playbook, with pat categories and insipid instructions. If this play is to be successful, we just need to block that outside linebacker. If your life is to be successful, you just need to find your purpose—by being positive, working hard, and being satisfied with your station in life. The possibility of political protest is never mentioned. The vocabulary of justice is absent. The tragic dimension of life is transformed into "handling adversity and success" on your "journey of success." Metaphysical puzzlement is replaced by assurances that the Big Coach in the Sky has a plan for you, all of this expressed in the charming straightforwardness of the picture books we read to our children.

When we move more explicitly to content, the issues are not so much about what Tressel includes in his bromidic proclamations but what he leaves out. I have already suggested that the central question that unifies the book is either incoherent, misleading, or opaque. I have also suggested that the book is full of uncontroversial platitudes that often leave us nodding affirmatively. "Well, of course. Thanks, Coach, for reminding me of that." At other times, we want something deeper than "try hard," "be tough," or "work on your faith plan." The list of the "Big Ten Fundamentals" raises all sorts of questions that are left hanging. Why just these personal qualities? Compare Tressel's list with Aristotle's list, Ben Franklin's, or Nietzsche's. What is left out? Given the interest in a good life, why no discussion of wisdom, courage, justice, autonomy, creativity, self-expression, curiosity, reasonableness, beauty, or play? Play? After all, this is a book by a coach, for players. There is no serious discussion of the nature of sport nor the meaning and importance of sportsmanship. There does appear to be the assumption that sport is instrumental, not intrinsically valuable, and the Coach as Sage has the task of finding the proper means to the important end of being a winner in life. This is a winner's manual for the *game of life*. Am I misguided to expect some insightful discussion of the relation between sport and life? Tressel sees nothing problematic in what he is doing because he raises no questions, as if he is unable to step back from his project and critically reflect on other possibilities and responses. When he moves from the pedestrian to something more controversial—for example, his three-sentence rejection of "the problem of individualism in sports as well as in society" (6)—he is content with hand-waving. You should block the safety on this play. You should reject individualism. It is in the playbook. It is right there in the blueprint for the play—and the game of life. Self-expression? Is there a unique self in Tressel's world? We do not know. Questions. Questions. Questions.

Such questions raise broader issues concerning Tressel's methods in wanting "to be able to articulate wisdom and life principles . . . and pass them along to the players" (17). I do not think it is an error to place this book in the context of the long-standing attempt in Western and non-Western philosophy (and literature) to reflect on perhaps the central ethical question. As Socrates says in the *Republic*, we are, after all talking about how to live.[8] This is no ordinary issue. It was a central question for Socrates, Plato, Aristotle, the Stoics, the Epicureans, Augustine, Aquinas, Kant, Mill, Schopenhauer, Nietzsche, Camus, Sartre, James, Dewey, Rawls, and a host of others who have carried on the tradition of ethical reflection in the history of Western moral philosophy. (Obviously, I do not exclude Buddhist reflections, Chinese philosophy, or other non-Western contributions to the vast literature in ethics.) Tressel's book shares the concerns of serious books in ethics, but shares neither the complexity nor the methods of these thinkers. What is the basis for the "wisdom and life principles" that Tressel shares with (forces upon?) his players? As far as I can tell, the book constitutes an extended appeal to authority. He appeals to the authority of the many (what we all know) and the authority of slogan (offered without support or explanation), but ultimately the appeal is to *his* authority, Coach as Sage, and God's authority mediated by Tressel's chosen scripture and the sage's understanding. The role of the coach has been transformed from a repository of technical expertise about his craft (sport) to a source of moral wisdom, with nary a skeptical question to inhibit the intended transfiguration.

In the tradition of ethical thinking it has been common, and it continues to be common in some persons' attempt to provide a general theory of ethical life, to ground rightness or goodness in the authority of God, as if what is right or good is simply a function of what God commands or wills. For our purposes, we need not rehearse the standard objections to the divine command theory of morality. What is important is to see that appeals to authority are groundless. Peter French puts this nicely in a book on ethics and college sports. "The idea that morality emanates from authority is, of course, a very old one, but the authority figures then were not college football and basketball coaches. Indeed, they were not human beings at all. The notion that authority is a font of moral wisdom and moral principle has clearly morphed from a divine command theory to the idea that anyone in a position of authority in any human endeavor by virtue of that authority has superior moral authority over those not in the position of authority."[9]

Some, like Tressel, are apparently ignorant of the attempts to provide a rational account of moral life. The history of moral philosophy consists of attempts to provide reasons for various kinds of ethical prescriptions. French comments on the rejection of moral authority: "Most of the history of ethics has been an attempt to purge such a notion from the way we think about ethics, to find in reason and argument rather than appeals to authority the foundations of our moral beliefs and principles. Nonetheless, the appeal to authority continues to be attractive, especially to those who by virtue of signing a contract with a university to coach one of its athletic teams gain authority over those students who would seek to participate on the team and play the game."[10] There are two disturbing consequences of Tressel's extended appeal to authority. First, the manual's central metaphysical and ethical claims are not addressed to players' reason. The assertions simply emanate from authority. He does not ask, what are your critical reactions to the claim that each human being has a purpose? He asserts it. He does not ask, can we know whether God exists? He claims that we must have faith and then talks as if we do know that God exists; God has a purpose for us, and we can know this. He does not ask, if God has a purpose, why should we live according to such a purpose? (It is God's purpose, not mine. Wouldn't that reduce me to an object whose purpose is bestowed on it by some external authority? Would that give *my* life meaning?) Insofar as Tressel's book is bereft of arguments, forcing his players to mold their lives in light of his worldview is a failure to respect his players as rational human beings. It is a denial of their intellectual autonomy unless questions are raised, arguments are offered, objections are considered, and conclusions are presented with a tentativeness commensurate with the relevant arguments.

The denial of intellectual autonomy is especially problematic because we are talking about *student* athletes, the cliché used to refer to Tressel's clientele. The second disturbing consequence involves the educational context within which his instruction takes place. Tressel's players are students in an institution of higher learning, whose central intellectual or academic ideal is the notion of reasoned inquiry.[11] Reasoned inquiry, the cornerstone of the pursuit of knowledge in the academy, includes questioning, generating hypotheses, appeals to whatever evidence or reasons are appropriate to the kind of inquiry involved, a skepticism that grounds expectations concerning the burden of proof, and a community of inquirers committed to ideals such as the rejection of dogma and prejudice.[12] The role of Coach as Sage is particularly troublesome in the context of higher education. Tressel's book is motivated by the pretentious desire to impart "wisdom," yet its methods are inappropriate to such a context, and his knowledge of the tradition and complexities of ethical reflection is absurdly incongruent with his desires. Despite Tressel's protests, his book is an expression of a significant lack of humility—intellectual humility. Tressel is a contemporary Euthyphro, apparently not having to be bothered by the pesky questions of a person like Socrates.

Let me be clear that these arguments are not necessarily related to the particular content of Tressel's proselytizing. The issue is not simply the Christian form it takes, although it is noteworthy that public reaction to his concern for the "whole person" might be quite different if he were a Muslim, a Buddhist, or an outspoken proponent of evolutionary biology. Imagine what would happen if the coach assigned readings from one of the "new atheists" (Dennett, Harris, Dawkins, Hitchens) during Quiet Times. Any form of proselytizing, whether implicit or explicit, is a problem in the context of a commitment to the academic values associated with critical inquiry, assuming that the purported process of conversion uses nonrational modes of persuasion. (I am not claiming that such proselytizing takes place in no other parts of the university besides team meetings in the new multimillion-dollar athletic complex.)

"Knowledge" does not appear on the list of "Big Ten Fundamentals"; "faith" does appear. The language associated with appeals to faith is quite distinct from claims about justified true belief, yet Tressel continually muddles the two. As I have suggested, it is disingenuous to repeatedly stress the importance of "faith" yet go on and on as if the claims that are expressions of faith are true and we know them to be true. We do not.

These criticisms are primarily related to the context within which Tressel offers his manual of instruction for the game of life. Of course, he has every right to present his wisdom to the world in the form of a book that so many have purchased. This leads to the question of why anyone besides his players, who were forced to read the manual, would want to read this book. Why would anyone be impressed by his endeavor? In part, I believe it is a function of an audience (and an author) that does not know the difference between good and bad writing and thinking about such issues, or are unacquainted with deeper and more sophisticated forms of ethical reflection found in philosophy and literature. Claims about the illiteracy of the audience sound snooty, yet one of the goals of a liberal arts education is to broaden one's perspective in a way that Tressel's book is incapable of doing. There is, however, a somewhat more charitable way of approaching these questions, and it involves difficult questions about the very nature and meaning of human wisdom and our desire to be wise in how to live.

The Coach as Sage does want to teach us how to live wisely. Tressel is quite candid about his intention to show us how to be "winners" in the game of life. What is wisdom? Tressel never explicitly raises this question. Is it theoretical knowledge? Is it a kind of practical know-how? Does it involve understanding? How is it related to action? Is it simply a matter of making good judgments about the relation of means to ends? Doesn't it require judgments about ends, about what is really valuable or important or significant in life? Can wisdom be disconnected from metaphysical commitments? How is wisdom related to other virtues? These questions are formidable and enigmatic. Although ordinary people may not raise these issues precisely in the ways that philosophers have, they certainly have a sense that it is important to distinguish the wise from the foolish and to seek advice from those who might be considered wise for various reasons. (Because they are winning football coaches?)

As a first approximation, one might begin by recalling Socrates's famous description of his wisdom, which consisted in acknowledging his own ignorance. He did not claim to know what he did not in fact know. The famous Socratic description of wisdom as ignorance, or knowledge of one's epistemic limitations, does not seem to get us very far because it is essentially negative. It has no positive content. On the other hand, Tressel fails this minimal Socratic test of wisdom in certain respects because he does claim to know a great many things about how the universe is constituted, such that his prescriptions concerning how to act, what to pursue, and how to live depend on knowing what he does not know.

If we move from the Socratic notion of wisdom to some notion that might generate positive content, a very rough method of sorting approaches might be to distinguish an esoteric approach to wisdom and one that emphasizes the truistic character of such insights. The esoteric approach insists that wisdom is hidden, rare, and largely unavailable to the ordinary person. Things are not as they seem, so one needs to find someone (a sage or a mystic) who has plumbed the depths of existence and has seen what we have not seen. At the other extreme is the view that wisdom consists largely of universal truths that we all know but we tend to ignore because our lives are full of distractions that lead us to devote ourselves to triviality and insignificant ends.[13] The truistic approach generates a different model of the sage and might very well naturally connect age and wisdom, where the accumulation of experience has shown that it is foolish to ignore some universal elements of human existence. The perspective generated by age and experience reminds us of important, obvious, yet often ignored bits of wisdom. For example: All persons must die. Material things will not make you happy. Make your happiness depend on those things you can control, so do not make yourself unhappy by wishing things to be other than they are. Do not worry about insignificant things. Do what you love to do. Your life is unimportant in the grand scheme of things. Friendship is important. And on and on.

Here is how Stanley Godlovitch explains the truistic approach to wisdom:

> Those who see in wisdom a variety of knowledge may quite pertinently say that the general truisms of the wise take on an entirely different tinge when cast in the perspective of the ways men are prone to regard their existence. It may just be a fact of our existence that we live and think of our lives as though such universal truths had no substance. We may indeed bathe in the illusions of arrogant omniscience, or immortality, and fashion our activities as though these were genuinely to be counted on. The wisdom of the Stoic, for example, cuts deeply into our expectations and deceptions, and persists in the reminder that our individual affairs are not quite nearly so magnificent in their triumph or grief as we care to imagine them. What the wise have is not a secret repository of knowledge unavailable to the masses, but rather the good sense to take seriously the unquestionable truth of the truism.[14]

At this point my more charitable hypothesis concerning Tressel's readers is simple. To the extent that wisdom has a truistic content and to the extent that reminders are sometimes needed in order "to take seriously the unquestionable truth of the truism," readers who share Tressel's worldview, admire his success as a football coach, are willing to be interested in and influenced by celebrity, and can recognize in Tressel's book a combination of questionable metaphysical claims that they endorse and unexceptional truisms that they recognize will purchase the book, read it, and be favorably impressed. The problem, however, is that both the author and the positive reader will be impressed only by the fact that the truistic part consists of claims we cannot deny, and they will be unable to note the distance between the pedestrian and the profound because of what is left out in the truistic account of wisdom. Some things are missing. When wisdom is reduced to a collection of truisms combined even with the sense of taking them seriously, we are still left with the question of how these truisms are related to other matters that are not truistic, and for that we need critical reflection. Godlovitch's truistic account cannot really respond to the criticism he raises against this very account. About such claims he says this:

> They are so broad as to be platitudinous, at least as truths about the human condition. After all, how seriously could a man resist the imputation that he will never know everything, and why indeed should he? Such claims which dodge the fallibility of the empirical, claims about the limitations of the individual or those hazy truths like "this too will pass," are not in themselves deeply profound because they fail almost stunningly to tell us anything about ourselves which we might possibly have missed. Their cosmic generality is won only through their seemingly banal immunity from question. Though they are not formally empty as are tautologies, they are, as truths, just as hollow. The flight to the pure, eternal, and unchangeable seems scheduled to land at the mundane and mouldy. Wisdom still awaits clearance.[15]

Tressel thinks he has found wisdom. He wants to impart such wisdom to his players—and to those who read his book. Yet wisdom is not simply the reminder to take seriously the truth of truisms. Work hard. At what? Your life is only important in relation to the "team." Which team? Be hopeful. For what? Aren't some hopes unrealistic or absurd? Aren't some desires futile? When truisms have some relatively specific content (for example, all persons die), we still wonder what it would mean to live wisely in light of such truisms. When they are more general ("Consistency is the hallmark of excellence"), they are hollow, as Godlovitch says. And surely, parts of wisdom, or aspects of living wisely, cannot be reduced to such platitudes, because we are, after all, talking about what it means to live well. This involves substantive discussion about elements of good lives.

In her discussion of wisdom Phillipa Foot says that a part of wisdom involves the "elusive" idea that "some pursuits are more worthwhile than others, and some matters trivial and some important in human life." Because people often waste parts of their lives attending to triviality, "it is not possible to explain the important and the trivial in terms of the amount of attention given to different subjects by the average man." Such comments might be particularly interesting for those whose lives are devoted to winning games, but it is difficult to explain the distinction between the important and the trivial. Foot continues, "But I have never seen, or been able to think out, a true account of this matter, and I believe that a complete account of wisdom, and of certain other virtues and vices, must wait until this gap can be filled."[16] I agree. Foot's intellectual humility strikingly contrasts with Tressel's lack of this virtue. Nevertheless, we can ask, what would be required for us to develop an understanding of the difference between the important and the trivial?

Richard White's insightful discussion of wisdom, which he calls a "radical virtue," attempts to generate aspects of wisdom by a negative route. He considers famous literary examples of folly and asks what is lacking in such characters. His examples are King Lear, a foolish old man; Ivan Ilyich, Tolstoy's paradigm unreflective functionary; and Don Quixote. From these fictional characters he extracts "three basic aspects that should form the core of any more sustained account of wisdom: reflection, integration, and the thoughtful awareness of others."[17] For our purposes, White's account of the role of reflection is especially important.

For White, reflection "implies the ability and the readiness to stand back or stand apart from what is given to consider its value, its ultimate significance, as well as its strengths and weakness." White mentions the importance of self-knowledge, "know thyself," "which, as Socrates shows, means know your limitations and mortality." Tressel, unlike Ivan Ilyich, does not lack this quality because he has failed to take stock of his life in a way that Ivan's imminent death forces upon him. Tressel seems incapable of seeing himself from an external perspective, with the warts and imperfections that are characteristic when we face our limitations. As White says, "Reflection implies detachment or the ability to take a distance from things, including one's self." Detachment generates the ability to see the conventional as conventional, to see ways of thinking and living against a wider array of possibilities, and grounds the potential for breaking away from routine modes of thinking. This means that reflection, as a core aspect of wisdom, is importantly related to autonomy, the ability to think for oneself, control one's own life, be independent, and determine for oneself how to live. Two of the most inspiring figures in the history of philosophy, Socrates and Nietzsche, teach us even now the importance of critical distance from the ordinary and the power of radical reflection. Jean Kazez argues persuasively in her reflection on the good life that personal autonomy is an essential aspect of good lives.[18] If it is, then both the content and the method of Tressel's book are seriously flawed. It is neither a compendium of wisdom nor a call to think seriously about life. It describes the life of the functionary, the organization man, the comfortable believer, das Man, the herd. Like others in sport, he seems to be wary of eccentricity. The fact that Tressel forces his players to read his manual is an affront to higher education. Better that he uses his authority to force his players to attend university lectures, poetry readings, art exhibits, documentaries, or noncommercial films of note. Better that he sends them to Quiet Times to read Kafka or Kerouac, Borges or Berlin (Isaiah, not Irving), Epictetus or Epicurus. Better yet—that he organizes Socratic discussions of fundamental questions. Better to reflect on these comments by Peter French on what he calls the "character education myth" sometimes used to defend big-time college sports:

> Of all the students on a university campus, none are afforded less freedom to explore their moral development and autonomy than those

participating in intercollegiate athletics. Their lives are the most regulated and supervised on campus. What are they not allowed to do that other students do? They are required to allow their university to periodically and randomly test them for drug use. When they are deciding on attending a specific university, they must limit their expense-paid visit to that institution to forty-eight hours. Perhaps more important, to remain on the team, intercollegiate athletes typically have to practice daily at odd hours, attend tutorial sessions, work out in weight rooms, eat at training tables, attend special study halls, travel to and from practice, watch game films, and engage in "team-bonding" experiences. They are expected to attend unscheduled, volunteer practices that are "suggested" by coaches.[19]

I would add that their classroom behavior and performance are closely monitored by academic counselors. University and college teachers are required to give special attention to them by filling out forms for athletic department scrutiny. Now we should add that football players at a major university were required to attend closely, during meetings and Quiet Times, to their coach's vision of the good life. Such is required to conform to Tressel's innocent and supposedly praiseworthy interest in the player's "whole person."

### III. An Alternative Model of Coaching and Ethics

So far my remarks have been critical, for the most part, yet I remain hopeful that coaches may have some significant role to play as ethical guides in the lives of young athletes. I have been a college coach as well as an academic egghead. I have coauthored, along with another philosopher-coach, a book-length practical guide about "coaching for character," so these issues are not, for me, merely abstract and academic. Nor do I think that all coach books are shallow and uninteresting. In fact, some important conclusions might be generated by contrasting Tressel's approach in *The Winners Manual* with a book written by Dean Smith, one of the most successful and respected college basketball coaches in history.

Smith's memoir, *A Coach's Life*, was written after he retired as basketball coach at the University of North Carolina.[20] I want to make a number of points about the contrast.

First, throughout his book, Smith stresses the importance of the context of his role as a *college* coach. Early on he says, "I love the college atmosphere, the studious pace of life, the sense of intellectual hunger in the air." Intellectual hunger? For Tressel, this involves collecting aphorisms in a box. Smith mentions reading Buber, Kierkegaard, and Victor Frankl in his own search for meaning. He describes attending a lecture by Paul Tillich. He repeatedly mentions the quality of education provided by the University of North Carolina and the importance of keeping a proper perspective on athletics in this context. "But more important, in those years at Carolina we gained a clear and vital understanding of the place of collegiate athletics on a campus. The team was a small part of a university community in which people argued politics, passed and failed classes, followed changing fashions, attended church, and lived their lives."[21]

Second, Smith describes the turbulent times of the sixties on a college campus and what he learned. (Was Tressel on campus in the sixties?) For Tressel, concern with the "whole person" generates his goal of teaching his players how to be winners in life by offering them explicit moral instruction. Smith's approach to the "whole person" in the context of higher education is more nuanced. "I think we're human beings first, coaches and players second, and in the '60s we had to strike an extremely delicate balance between the two. Sometimes there was a dichotomy at work. But I was aiming to show our players that there was nothing wrong with that because complexity is a part of life." Once he allowed a player to miss practice in order to speak at a political rally. Smith says, "It was difficult for me to tell a student not to be politically active on his campus when I felt the chief reason they were there was to ask questions and develop their own convictions." Tressel's football players have the opportunity to develop their inner person in eight to twelve minutes of Quiet Time; Smith's players go to political rallies. Tressel's players have life mapped out in the "Block O of Life," life according to the Coach as Sage. Smith comments, "I wanted our players to be involved in the issues of the day and feel they could talk freely about them to me. I was eager to know their opinions, so I often mentioned current events in individual meetings. In a one-on-one meeting with a player, I would ask his opinion on a current event. I rarely gave my opinion. I would try (to get him) to talk so they [*sic*] would feel he had the same freedom of expression as other students."[22] Smith views his athletes as inquirers, appreciates the complexity of integrating athletics into the lives of students, and respects their autonomy.

Third, Smith's insistence on keeping a proper perspective on athletics in the context of a university community also suggests that he is very much aware of the importance of critical reflection and a certain degree of detachment, not only with respect to his role as a coach but also in relation to his religious views. Like Tressel, Smith is a committed Christian, yet the tone of the chapter on "some of my beliefs and understandings about faith, God, and life" is cautious. The chapter is titled "I May Be Wrong, But!" He seems almost apologetic about offering such remarks. In interviews he resisted the attempt to focus on his personal beliefs. "I just wasn't comfortable using the podium provided me as head basketball coach at North Carolina to talk about myself, and I certainly had no desire or hidden agenda to tell others how to live their lives, how to behave, or what to believe." Smith's intellectual and moral humility strikingly contrasts with Tressel's goal in the manual. Smith says, "I do not pretend to have the 'right' answers for everyone, so if you disagree with what I have come to believe, I certainly honor your right to do so."[23] We believe him. Tressel's humble pronouncements ring hollow, given the nature of his project. In fact, given Smith's disclaimers, he is not so much interested in "taking" each player on a "journey of success." Rather, he is there to assist them in their own searches, more like Socrates goading them to examine themselves than a sage delivering pronouncements from on high.

Fourth, Tressel seems to think he has figured things out. He is in the wisdom business, don't you know. After all, he is giving his players a manual of instruction about life, not football. If Smith's approach seems more Socratic, then there is considerable irony in the notion that the Socratic approach to coaching, teaching, and living in the shadow of a university seems much wiser, despite the fact the he is hesitant to take on the role of providing a certain kind of explicit ethical instruction. And the role he exemplifies is the Aristotelian one, a person of practical wisdom who may be consulted for advice because of his ability to make sound judgments. There is considerable evidence that Smith's former players often seek out his advice on practical matters. Coaches do have special relationships with players, as teachers, not quite parents, and friends of a sort. Players may appropriately turn to coaches for advice about matters outside of the coach's craft, not because of the coach's ability to master $X$'s and $O$'s or consistently win championships, but because the coach is trusted on the basis of just the kinds of factors that lead people outside of sports to seek advice from wise persons with good judgment. There is nothing inappropriate about this, as long as the advice is sought and received in an atmosphere of critical dialogue rather than authority and obedience.

Finally, although Smith eschews the role of Coach as Sage, there is little doubt that he exerted a major influence on his players because of his demanding standards *as a coach*. There is another important Aristotelian theme here. Aristotle insisted that moral virtues arise from habituation, not instruction. One becomes just by performing just actions, courageous by performing actions that require courage, and so forth. Participation in a practice like football or basketball provides opportunities to become excellent in the relevant sport. Sport participation also provides opportunities to engage in actions that promote virtues that arise internal to sports (courage, perseverance, justice, respect for others) but also may promote character traits that are important outside of sports. At the heart of the character-education defense of sports is the Aristotelian insistence that good habits may be formed by showing up on time; working hard; being responsible for one's actions; not making excuses; confronting failure; respecting opponents, officials, coaches, and teammates as necessary and valuable elements in the attempt to achieve athletic excellence; submerging one's self-interests in larger concerns; and a host of other ethical possibilities embedded in sports participation. The Coach as Sage, at least as it appears to be exemplified by Jim Tressel, is mistaken about the appropriate methods of ethical instruction, not necessarily the content. There is another irony here. Virtue may be developed, and an interest in the "whole person" reinforced, by rejecting the classroom "Quiet Time" model of ethical instruction. The coach should simply be a coach and not pretend to be a sage. The coach's ethical task is to reinforce the values that arise internal to sports participation with the hope that the ethical habits that are developed will extend to life outside of sports. Although it may be an oversimplification, thinking about the distinction between the internal and the external may do some work here. Coaches may appropriately insist on behavior that arises from an understanding of the nature of sport and the goals of sport participation. It is not the job of the coach to foist her own religious, political, metaphysical, or narrowly moral beliefs on players. And in the context of college athletics, the coach must respect and reinforce the values of the academy.

## IV. Conclusion: Coaches and Entitlement

Important questions occasioned by Tressel's book are not merely the ones raised by the content of *The Winners Manual*. For various reasons I have given, I found the book to be shallow and uninteresting. The larger issue concerns the appropriateness of the very project that he attempts in the context of higher education. It is common for celebrated athletes to be criticized for a sense of entitlement that leads to egotistical and boorish behavior. It is less common, however, for anyone to criticize coaches for their sense of being entitled to wield their authority to promote their vision of "success" in life. Why do coaches believe that they are entitled to be sages? When did this become a part of their job description? It is clear that there is nothing intrinsic to being a celebrated athlete that merits the status of being a moral exemplar. Likewise, it is evident that being a successful coach does not, in itself, qualify one to give sage advice about how to live. In fact, it is exceedingly strange to think that being a successful coach would, in itself, allow one to be wise about how to live, yet this strangeness does not seem to be noticed by many people. It is not that being a coach disqualifies one from sagehood. There is a contingent relation that might ground an initial skepticism about the relationship between one's role and the possibility of human wisdom. Such wisdom about life depends on a variety of factors, none of which are directly related to helping others achieve athletic excellence or the ability to win games. In the context of higher education, intellectual standards associated with serious ethical reflection are largely absent in Tressel's manual for the game of life. The story I have told about his book is a cautionary tale. The narrow conclusion is that Tressel's attempt to impart wisdom in his "step-by-step process developing the inner person" is unfitting in the context in which he does this because his methods are inappropriate—not merely that his insights are hollow. It may be fitting for him to do this if he were coaching a middle school–level church team where parents share his worldview and have no problem with their children being indoctrinated. It is neither appropriate nor praiseworthy in the context of coaching college football players in a state university.

The broader conclusion applies to other books of this type. Unless authority is filtered through the kinds of intellectual ideals we find in university and college classrooms, we should question the appropriateness of this kind of entitlement found in college athletics. Unless the coach's authority is infused with broad learning rather than religious zeal, we should be skeptical about commitments to athletes' "whole lives." We should not expect celebrated athletes to be moral exemplars. We should not expect famous coaches to be wise, nor should we praise them for the purity of their religious commitments or the breadth of their concerns. We should criticize them for the misuse of their authority. It is fine for them to sell their books if they can find an interested readership. It is not fine for them to force their players to embody their worldview.

Recall Tressel's claim: "My job as a coach is to do more than just teach the *X*'s and *O*'s of the gridiron" (19). Gary Danielson responds: "I hear coaches say (they're) in the business of making men in the future. No. You're not. You're in the business of coaching. I am in the business of raising my son." (See epigraph.) I agree with Danielson. I have tried to offer an extended discussion that explains and defends this viewpoint.

# Part Three.
## *Sport and Meaning*

# 8 Sport and the Question of the Meaning of Life

## 1. The Attraction of Sports

Two stories, noteworthy for these reflections, were narrated in the daily sports pages to which I am devoted. One was a national story, all the rage on every sports-talk radio show in the country, the other a sad local account of a fallen young sports hero. These stories came together to once again raise an issue I have been thinking about for many years. The great football player Brett Favre decides to call it quits and wait for the Hall of Fame to call. But he could not stay retired; he could not give up the game and retire "gracefully," as many said. Why does he come back? What does he have to prove? Is he addicted to the competition? Maybe it is just the money. So he returns, not quite his former self, but surely more capable of performing in his later years than other aging athletes, such as Willie Mays, stumbling around in center field for the Mets in 1973 at the age of forty-two, or even Michael Jordan, unable to will the Washington Wizards to the playoffs in his final year. Why can't they give up these games? What is the attraction?

The much sadder story is about a young man, merely twenty-five years old, high school football star, Division I running back who played in one of the BCS conferences, leading his team in rushing for four consecutive years, with dreams of playing in the NFL or at least in the Canadian Football League. It was not to be. "A nice young man," everyone said. He graduated from his university, had no apparent history of drug problems nor mental health concerns, but . . . what to do after football? You might guess where the story is going. He seemed lost without his sport, frustrated, so . . . he apparently threw himself from a bridge, dying of head injuries suffered in the fifty-seven-foot fall.

Favre could not give up the game he loves so much; our young football player was forced to give up football, contrary to his deep desire to continue playing. How might we explain their attraction to their sport? At the level of sports talk, the incessant focus on competition and competitive desires seems thin. Maybe there are more great Santini-like athletes than I think, but for me the competitive aspect of sports was more like a necessary evil than the essence of the activity, more an aspect that provided the condition for seeking to become good and for the moral test of sustaining a cooperative relationship with opponents. At a somewhat deeper level, reference to the way an athlete's identity and self-esteem are fixed in relation to his participation in sports is undoubtedly important, yet when the newspaper reporters asked the experts in sports psychology to comment on the young man's suicide, their responses seemed prosaic. Tell me something I don't know. Help me understand on a deeper level, or . . . perhaps there is nothing deeper going on. About Favre, many said he had nothing left to prove. But why think that such a claim pinpoints the fundamental motivation of a high-level athlete? Favre talked about enjoyment, not "proving" something.

Such questions about the attraction of sports have always been deeply personal for me, because I have wanted to understand the role and importance of sport in my own life (while being attuned to difficult questions about the relation between a sports phenomenology that focuses on first-person experience and attempts to generalize about "sport" and the possible experiences of others). For me, the attraction of sport is better understood in the neighborhood of play, freedom, narrative, and self-knowledge.[1] Yet there may be more to say; there may be other—undoubtedly there are many other—themes upon which it is interesting and appropriate to reflect concerning the attraction of sports.

I start with a simple thought, occasioned more by the events from the life of the young football player, yet surely related to Favre's situation and the situation of many athletes who have had to retire, quit, finally place their athletic pursuits in the past, or attempt to pick up new ones not requiring a more youthful body. Here is the thought: sport is a fertile ground for meaning in life. Our young football hero may have come to experience his life as meaningless because the central source of meaning in his life had evaporated. It might be interesting to consider seriously the attraction of sport in the context of questions about the meaning of life or meaningful lives. (As we will see, the distinction may be very important.)

Some, perhaps lovers of sport, may find my initial suggestion to be rather obvious, as prosaic as pop psychology–sounding claims about self-esteem and identity. Of course people find meaning in sports, many might say. Others, however, will be unimpressed and will take my thought to be an instance of preaching to the choir. (Religious metaphors may be apt here.) They will find the connection between sport and the meaning of life to be not only counterintuitive but absurdly implausible—at best, a provocation to reflect on the capacity of rational human beings to engage in self-deception and mass delusion. One hundred million people watch the Super Bowl, many of whom care who wins. An overwhelming number of Americans believe in God, souls, heaven and hell, angels, and other bits of metaphysical legerdemain. We are supposed to be surprised that people find "meaning" in attending to sports? People also worship nonexistent gods.

One group of skeptics about sport and meaning includes those who not only see sports as worthless; they see such activities as downright dangerous and even despicable. For these people, sports are neither harmlessly benign nor innocently trivial. As one critic put it, "What is truly chilling is that there are a lot of smart people interested in sports. That just gives you no hope at all for the human race."[2] Certain critics are disturbed by the moral atmosphere of sports and the way they encourage the inevitable side effects of competition: aggression, violence, alienation, and a lack of civility. As highly commercialized competitive activities, sports often highlight greed, crass materialism, egotism, and, at least every four years, jingoistic nationalism. If meaningful lives and meaningful activities are somehow connected to morality and important social values, then the connection between sport and meaning would be perceived to be tenuous at best.

A somewhat different group, including some contemporary scholars of sport, has variously described these activities as trivial, pointless, futile, illusory, and artificial—even absurd![3] It is striking that these concepts regularly pop up in discussions of the meaning of life, or meaningful lives, or meaningful(less) activities. If meaningful lives must be full of meaningful activities, and such activities must not be characterized as worthless, pointless, trivial, or futile, then the original thought about the connection between sport and meaning might appear to some to be questionable. How could something as trivial or even socially damaging be a significant contributor to meaning in life? No doubt many people *treat* sport as supremely significant or the source of "meaning" (whatever that means), but they may be deluded. The young suicidal athlete may be merely an extreme instance of a type who needs therapy to escape false consciousness, who should direct his attention toward true or genuine sources of meaning in life.

With respect to more exalted sources of meaning in life, we should not ignore those who treat the question of the meaning of life more metaphysically or religiously, as if the necessary and sufficient condition of a meaningful life is that there is a meaning *of* life, in some transcendent or cosmological sense. For those who believe we are doomed to meaninglessness unless we suppose that some version of supernaturalism is true and naturalism is false, or who believe that some grand religious narrative is a correct account of the nature of things, claims about sport and meaning will be too mundane to salvage a meaningful existence. If God does not exist, life is meaningless. According to this view, the meaning of life is found outside of life, not *in* life and surely not in trivial, impermanent, bodily activities.

A final source of unease about my suggestion might be found in those who think that the ultimate justification of sports, especially in educational institutions, must be moral. If sport is valuable, it must serve some moral ends, since athletic achievements, associated with the quest for excellence in sports, are useless or pointless. If sport provides a source of meaning rather than being an instrument for moral education, the justification of sports must be broadened. Some might resist this move.

In the following pages I propose to place sport in the context of contemporary discussions of the meaning of life. I will spend considerable time engaging various attempts to provide general accounts of the meaning of life. It is one thing to assert that some life or project is meaningful or meaningless; it is another to attempt to understand what kind of claim is being made, what that claim amounts to, and whether it is reasonable. I will attempt to provide a kind of road map through the twists and turns of representative aspects of discussions of the meaning of life, primarily in recent analytic philosophy. I will be forced to say much more, at times, about general accounts of the meaning of life than about sport itself. At every point, however, it is important to keep the question of *sport* and meaning on the horizon. Despite this, in some sense I am as interested in the general question of the meaning of life as the specific question of how sports might fit into a broader picture.

I will approach these discussions with a high degree of intellectual humility. I am not sure that the point of reflecting on the meaning of life is to seek argumentative finality. Given the disparate uses of the concepts associated with discussions and judgments about the meaning of life, perhaps the best we can do is to appreciate complexity, as Socrates might have recommended, or to embrace a sort of Wittgensteinian sensitivity to the kind of work done by various concepts in our reflections about the meaning of life. My tentative conclusion will involve the attempt to defend a deflationary attitude toward the question of the meaning of life, because of the meaning of meaning in judgments about meaningfulness. There are numerous sources of meaning in life, so there is nothing very mysterious about meanings in life. Given this deflationary attitude, it is not surprising that sport can take its place as an important and accessible "space of meaning" in life.[4]

## II. The Question of the Meaning of Life

The question of the meaning of life is persistent, yet puzzling, fascinating but frustrating. Inside of philosophy, its reputation, once thoroughly tarnished, has been revived, but suspicions remain. Outside of philosophy, the question needs no contemporary New Age resuscitation. It appears to live not only in the self-help sections of bookstores, but also in the natural reflective responses of ordinary people (nonacademic philosophers) to real concerns in life. People unapologetically wonder about the point of it all in the face of evil, disease, death, and unhappiness, while others, at some moments, feel the need to take stock of their lives and search for something more "meaningful" to pursue or with which to deeply engage themselves. For many, the notion of the meaning of life, or rather, a meaningful life, is a significant evaluative category—indeed, enormously so.

I would also like to take stock—not of life, but of the question of the meaning of life, some relatively recent attempts to engage the issues associated with asking, "What is the meaning of life?" and how sport might fit into such discussions. Philosophical thinking about the meaning of life is not new. One might extract insights about life's meaning from a variety of historical sources: Aristotelian arguments about the end of man, Kantian judgments about the intrinsic worth of the goodwill, aphoristic comments about power and creativity scattered throughout Nietzsche's corpus, Taoist sentiments about the inscrutable character of the Path or the Way. Often, however, the supposed connections between these claims and questions about the meaning of life are indirect or are assumed as the result of an interpreter's judgment about what is going on when one raises the question.

More recently, at least since Kurt Baier's seminal 1957 lecture "The Meaning of Life," and especially in the past two or three decades, there has been a growing literature in analytic philosophy, not merely in the central texts of European existentialism, that explicitly examines the meaning of life.[5] To study this material is exciting and at times even uplifting—yet can also be exasperating and disappointing. For those whose sympathies—with existentialist concerns about meaning and with ordinary folks' reflective yearnings for meaningful lives—have not been extinguished by positivistic skepticism about whether the question makes any sense or by condescending suspicions about continental philosophy's obscure language and opaque texts, the more recent literature is both interesting and promising. On the other hand, I hope to show why initial suspicions about the perplexing character of the question and various responses to it are not unfounded. We might initially approach the question of the meaning of life by wondering how important it is to raise such issues and to employ the evaluative apparatus associated with judgments about the meaning of life or meaningful lives. As I have suggested, my own views are what I now call deflationary, a notion I hope to clarify and defend. My thesis is that the question of the meaning of life is not as important as many people think, and it is surely not a question that we should worry about, especially to the point of causing some psychological distress. In my view, the central question is, "what are the conditions of meaningful activities?"; the answer to this query is neither esoteric, mysterious, nor transcendent. The question of the meaning of life is not at all *the* fundamental philosophical question, because it is not about whether life is worth living or whether we have reasons to live. The central interest is to specify the conditions under which lives or activities are meaningful. If this is the case, it is not prima facie implausible to raise the question about the contribution of sports to meaningful lives, as it would be if we insisted that the primary perplexity raises cosmological concerns. Probably because of well-known suspicions about the meaning of the question of life's meaning, many philosophers in the analytic tradition assure us that wondering about the meaning of life is vitally important, as Robert Nozick asserts at the beginning of his discussion in *Philosophical Explanations*: "So heavily is it laden with our emotion and aspiration that we camouflage our vulnerability with jokes about seeking for the meaning or purpose of life."[6] Nozick's initial inflationary sensibilities frame amusing stories about the seeker and the sage as just so many self-deceptive attempts to deflect our insecurities about what it is to live an all-too-human life. The worries are real, so we transform our vulnerabilities into jokes. So, life is not a fountain? Yet Nozick is also aware that there is an obvious deflationary interpretation of the seeker and the sage, or, I should say, various interpretations that would deflate the importance of the seeker's journey. The question is confusing and not at all clear. What is the seeker looking for? Does he want a nice, tidy answer to his query about the meaning of life? Here are some possible confusions. The seeker has a craving for generality, as Wittgenstein might have said. The seeker may be mistaken in looking for a formula. Since the seeker journeyed so far (why is the sage typically described as meditating in the mountains?), the answer must be esoteric, not the kind of thing that one could learn from a kindergarten teacher, Morrie, or the latest self-help best seller. Since the meaning of life is esoteric, it must be transcendent or hidden in some essential way, not obvious to normal persons in everyday life. The comedy may arise because of the absurd gap between such expectations—wanting a formula, assuming the answer is esoteric, thinking it must be transcendent—and legitimate answers that are neither formulaic, esoteric, nor transcendent.

For some, to avoid raising the question of the meaning of life is evasive. Given the normal course of a life involving failure, disappointment, suffering, disease, and death, how could one fail to raise the question of what it is all about?[7] For others, to reflect on the meaning of life is a matter of "growing up," becoming mature enough to confront life's limitations head-on.[8] The question also appears to connect deeply with our religious sensibilities, our cosmic aspirations. As we will see, the theistic model of meaningfulness is a powerful and appealing structure for many, so doesn't the question of the meaning of life lead naturally to questions about God?[9] When one's theistic aspirations are disappointed, one arrives at Camus's hyperbolic and inflationary claim about the question of the meaning of life at the beginning of *The Myth of Sisyphus*. "There is but one truly serious philosophical problem, and that is suicide. Judging whether life is or is not worth living amounts to answering the fundamental question of philosophy."[10]

There is another way of looking at such matters, one that is rather different from the usual method of sorting the proposed approaches and answers: theistic versus nontheistic; supernaturalism versus naturalism; subjectivism, objectivism, and nihilism; God centered and soul centered; and so forth.[11] In one respect, my approach reflects the important distinction between attempts to provide a first-order account of the meaning of life as opposed to a second-order theory that attempts to make sense of the meaning of meaning in the question. Once this second-order view is clear, then something follows about the supposed importance of the question. My approach is a heuristic device, helping us to understand the structure of the debate and where it ultimately leads. Compare the question of the meaning of life and the question of whether God exists (or, more narrowly, whether theism is true).[12] Many simply assume that the question of whether God exists—and whether we believe that God exists—is decisively important, for various reasons. I do not think this is the case, but it is a substantive philosophical issue that needs to be supported, or at least mulled over.

Likewise, the standard view is that the question of the meaning of life is extremely important. In part, my interests are therapeutic. Some worries should be dissolved or calmed. It is a question of the weightiness of the question.

### III. Examples and Intuitions

Before considering central responses to the question of the meaning of life, one other aspect of the contemporary debate should be mentioned. It is important both methodologically and as a background for those who believe the question has ultimate weight. In the attempt to clarify the notion of a meaningful life, it is hard to wrap our arms around this slippery notion, so some take the negative route, exploring images of meaninglessness in the hope of finding what is missing in these disturbing pictures. Richard Taylor admits that the "idea of meaningfulness is difficult to grasp," yet "the idea of meaninglessness is perhaps less so." So what we need is a "clear image of meaningless existence." "A perfect image of meaninglessness, of the kind we are seeking, is found in the ancient myth of Sisyphus."[13] Susan Wolf's procedure is similar: "It may be easier to make progress by focusing on what we want to avoid. In that spirit, let me offer some paradigms, not of meaning-*ful* lives, but meaning*less* lives."[14] For Wolf, the paradigmatic image of a meaningless life is "The Blob," whose life is lived in "hazy passivity," spending day and night drinking beer in front of the television set. (For our purposes, perhaps he is addicted to ESPN.) A picture holds us captive. Our lives are haunted by the possibility that they may be too much like the form of Sisyphus's pointless rock rolling or the "hazy passivity" of The Blob to escape the important corrective of a critical reflection that raises the question of meaningfulness. What is missing in such lives? Sisyphus's rock rolling has no point. The problem with The Blob's life is that it lacks active engagement in projects. We are able to generate plausible conditions of a meaningful life by reflecting on the examples. The images guide the arguments, which assume that our intuitions are spot-on when we think about these pathetic lives. Would that our lives escape these worrisome forms.

Consider some images we meet in the literature or in reflecting on the notion of meaningless lives.[15] For now, I will simply mention the names. Their significance as embodiments of meaninglessness is in some cases self-explanatory. We will return to some of them later. They generate categories or notions that are relevant in judgments of meaningfulness. Are any of these characters analogous to athletes or certain types of sport participants? Fans? Spectators? How about "Softball Guy," a ridiculous character obsessed by success in the slow-pitch "beer league"?

Here are some characters of meaninglessness: the Existentialist Hero, the Pig Farmer (who buys more land to grow more corn to feed more pigs to buy more land to grow more corn to feed more pigs . . . ), the Lint Collector (seeking to accumulate the biggest ball of lint), the Great Astrologer (seeking to be the most excellent astrologer), the Plant Communicator (seeking to communicate with asparagus plants), the Tasty Cutlet (a person whose purpose is to be the main course for the aliens' dinner), the Evangelical Christian or Missionary Atheist (in a Godless or theistic universe, respectively), the Unhappy Moral Saint (Mother Teresa?), the Happy Nazi, the Obsessed Shopper, the Bored Cancer Researcher, the Failed Scientist, the Deceived Businessman (whose happy life is the result of the delusion that he is loved and respected by family, friends, and colleagues), and more. If our lives or significant parts of our lives come to resemble any of these characters, such lives may be characterized by ultimate insignificance, uselessness, pointlessness, worthlessness, futility, failure, triviality, lack of autonomy, boredom, alienation, or delusion. If this is the case, then the threats seem real, and the question of the meaning of life is weighty indeed. Of course, to the extent that these characters misrepresent normal life, are overly simplified and misleading portrayals of our lives, are not remotely similar to sports participants, or are evaluated on the basis of intuitions we come to reject, their philosophical status will be undermined and their relevance for sport and meaning nonexistent.

## iv. Theism

John Kekes provides one helpful but not wholly satisfactory way to sort the possible answers to the meaning of life. He distinguishes the religious answer, which asserts that "there is some sort of cosmic order in reality," and the moral approach to the meaning of life, which holds that "what gives meaning to life is the pursuit of good projects."[16] The reference to "cosmic order" is somewhat misleading, and because references to a moral approach might be taken in either a narrow sense (having to do with right action, duty, obligation) or a much broader sense (relating to the good, or how one ought to live, without assuming one is talking about "morality" proper), a more useful way to organize typical approaches is to distinguish a metaphysical-teleological interpretation of the meaning of life and an axiological approach.[17] Cosmic order may or may not be purposive (Spinoza's God does not direct the universe toward some final end—Nietzsche's concept of eternal recurrence negates a teleological view of the universe), and it would be odd to claim that the meaning of life is to be part of a causal process necessarily unfolding or repeating itself but going nowhere. (Wouldn't that mean that life has no meaning?) Let's take the theistic approach to be a paradigm example of a certain kind of metaphysical-teleological answer.

According to William Lane Craig, life is absurd without God (and immortality).[18] A Godless universe would lack an "ultimate" context of meaning, purpose, and value, so life in general and each individual person's life would be "without ultimate significance." Craig does not clearly explain the difference between claims about "ultimate significance" and "ultimate purpose," but they seem to amount to pretty much the same thing. If there is no God, then the meaninglessness of life seems essentially related to the fact that the universe is just here, utterly contingent, with no reason for being, no purpose that invests things with some ultimate end. If theism is true (and in particular, for Craig, if biblical Christianity is true), then there is some larger context of purpose within which to understand why there is something rather than nothing, why it is that whatever exists has the characteristics it has, and why individuals come to exist in such a universe. According to this view, the whole has an explanation in terms of Divine Purpose, and the meaning of each individual's life is to contribute to the larger cosmic purpose, either generically, relative to other individuals, or in particular ways assigned by God. (We might all have the purpose of being morally good, but particular assigned roles, like being an athlete instead of an artist, might be quite diverse.) The meaning of the world transcends the world. Without transcendent meaning, there is no meaning.

In Craig's account in "The Absurdity of Life without God," he specifically mentions, among others, Sartre and Camus, as if the theist's primary adversary is the Existentialist Hero who creates his own meaning in an objectively meaningless—that is, Godless—universe. According to Craig, the condition for happiness is a sense of meaning, value, and purpose grounded in God, so if our Godless hero is to be consistent, he must be unhappy. Craig seems to admonish the atheist: how dare you pretend to be happy![19]

As I have mentioned, this model of meaningfulness is powerful, insofar as it shows us a central way to understand meaning. Meaning is understood as "being a part of," "being related to," or "being connected with," in such a way that a reference is made to some larger context of purpose that makes certain facts intelligible and supposedly grounds value. The world is God's world. The specific reference to the agency of an Infinite Person to account for the meaning of life is plagued by certain problems, yet these problems may lead in certain fruitful philosophical directions.

There are numerous questions associated with appeals to God's purpose to answer the question of the meaning of life. Some are particularly troublesome (notwithstanding the issue of whether theism is true). First, how can we know what are God's purposes? (This is a part of the larger problem of knowing what God is, or whether God is.) The narratives offered by the various world religions are diverse, the gap between finite and infinite agency is enormous, the problem of evil is formidable, and for many God is hidden.[20]

Second, even if we believe that we do know God's purposes, for the universe and for us individually, such purposes are God's, not ours. If we have been assigned a purpose by God, then wouldn't we be treated as objects or artifacts, not fully autonomous persons? If we found out that the human race was placed here as a laboratory experiment for an extremely intelligent race of aliens, then we would know our purpose, but would that give our lives meaning? Worth? For some, simply being assigned a purpose is not sufficient for a meaningful life.

Third, the alien example suggests that being assigned a purpose by an external agency not only may violate our autonomy but also leaves open the question of whether the purpose in question is worthwhile. If we found out that our ultimate destiny is to be transported and resurrected, as in *Star Trek*, then used as tasty cutlets for aliens, or to be put in extraterrestrial zoos with other lower-level life forms in the universe, we would not judge such purposes to be worthy or worthwhile.[21] Such examples also show that judgments about purpose may be distinct from judgments about worthwhileness. Put differently, judgments about meaningfulness may seem to be more about justification than explanation, more about values than factual claims.

Fourth, it is implausible to claim that ultimate contingency renders meaningless the lives of at least exceptional individuals like Einstein, Picasso, Gandhi, Tiger Woods, or Michael Jordan. (Choose your own exemplar of excellence.) Why is "ultimate" purpose or "ultimate" significance required for individual lives to be meaningful or for various kinds of achievements to be worthwhile, including athletic achievements? Baier's distinction in his seminal paper has become something of a truism for some. Just because there is no Cosmic Purpose or Transcendent Purpose *of* life does not entail that there can be no worthwhile purposes *in* life.[22] The focus on divine agency points squarely to the importance of the relation between appeals to purpose and judgments of meaningfulness, but the problems with the theistic answer point in the direction of a naturalistic and finite teleological account, as well as an approach that distinguishes between the meaning of life (in general—overall—why is there something rather than nothing?) and the question of the conditions under which a particular life is meaningful. We should ask, "What is a meaningful life?" rather than "What is the meaning of life?"

The upshot of Craig's approach is paradoxical. The reference to divine agency suggests that meaning is either having a purpose (as God does) or serving a purpose (as a person would). But it is clear that insofar as persons have purposes, their activities can be meaningful, in a sense analogous to the activities of an Infinite Agent. The reference to God is unneeded. Moreover, if the appeal to a transcendent context of purpose assumes that such purposes are worthwhile, then surely it is possible for similar finite purposes to be worthwhile, unless purposes must be eternally significant. (For example, both finite agents and an Infinite Person could have moral purposes—or aesthetic purposes.) Why would a purpose have to be embodied in an infinite context of agency in order to be "meaningful"? Since the reference to an external purpose also raises the question of whether a person must identify with some imposed purpose, the subjective contribution to meaningfulness is left unclear.

For many, these arguments transform the debate concerning the meaning of life. As a reflective agent, I want to know whether and how *my* life could be meaningful. It seems clear that a life may or may not be meaningful independent of any reference to facts about God's existence, nature, or purposes. If God sentenced me, for no reason, on a whim, to a Sisyphus-like existence, *my* life would not thereby be meaningful. And if God assigned me the purpose of being a cancer researcher, my life would be meaningful, not because God assigned me some purpose but because of the nature of the project. (This relates, of course, to the Euthyphro dilemma.) The reference to God is superfluous, as is the reference to the supposed purpose of everything, life as such—the whole works. Judgments about the meaningfulness or meaninglessness of specific lives or activities need not be delayed until we resolve the question of God's existence, nor should people despair about the meaning of their lives as a result of a creeping religious skepticism.

Before we turn to naturalism, there is one other theistic worry expressed by Craig but put famously and poignantly much earlier. Poor Tolstoy. He had it all, but it was not enough—fame, fortune, family. He tells us in *My Confession* that he was plagued by questions about the meaning of life despite living a life that most would judge to be objectively good or worthwhile—even great. It was as if Tiger Woods or Michael Jordan began to be bothered by the question of the meaning of life. (Is the comparison appropriate? We will see.) What was the source of what I call "Tolstoyan anxieties"? It is obvious that Tolstoy was bothered by a number of things, not the least of which were the possibility of an infinite regress of reasons when asking why he should do specific things or anything at all and that scientific naturalism provided no teleological account of the order of things.[23] For Tolstoy, the gravest threat to a meaningful life is death. Like Craig's claim that immortality is essential in order to escape contingency and ultimate meaninglessness, Tolstoy was disturbed by the possibility of being annihilated.[24] "I could not ascribe any sensible meaning to a single act, or to my whole life. I was only surprised that I had not understood that from the start. All that had long ago been known to everybody. Sooner or later there would come diseases and death (they had come already) to my dear ones and to me, and there would be nothing left but stench and worms. All my affairs, no matter what they might be, would sooner or later be forgotten, and I myself should not exist. So why should I worry about all these things?"[25]

Much has been written in response to the death argument and the apparent assumption that a meaningful life or meaningful activities in life must somehow last, escape impermanence, transcend forgottenness, and so on.[26] Most add up to some central intuitions. It is not clear why either having significant purposes or engaging in worthwhile activities must have anything to do with lastingness, permanence, being remembered, or being immortal. Whether we are immortal or we will be annihilated, whether theism is true or false, life can include worthwhile activities, as is clearly shown by the lives of Einstein, Picasso, Gandhi, and Willie Mays.[27] With regard to famous athletes, it might seem that being famous and being remembered sustains or even grounds claims about the meaning of sporting activities or significant athletic achievements. At some point, however, our collective memories fade, yet why should we think that either the relatively brief period of athletic achievement or the finitude of human memory would rob these activities of meaning? There is no obvious relationship between being remembered (or lastingness) and the meaning or value of achievements, athletic or otherwise. We should seek the explanation of meaning or value elsewhere. Here we have mentioned instances of extraordinary people. Perhaps less exceptional, more ordinary lives are problematic, more like Sisyphus than an übermensch or a sports hero.

To sum up: The central error of Craig's theistic approach to the meaning of life is to insist that a necessary condition of a meaningful life is that there is a meaning *of* life, in a transcendent sense. (Ignore the specific cosmic narratives associated with different religions.) Even if there is no cosmic point of everything, specific lives may be meaningful. The existence of God does not necessarily matter when making judgments about meaningful lives, including the lives of athletes or sports participants. But more needs to be said about what does matter for meaning. We need to offer some explanation for claims about meaningful lives or meaningful activities in a world that may or may not be "meaningful" in a cosmic sense.

## v. Subjectivism

The locus classicus for a subjectivist account of meaningfulness is Richard Taylor's captivating interpretation of the myth of Sisyphus, condemned by the gods to an eternity of endlessly rolling a rock to the top of a hill, only to see it roll back down, to be retrieved at the bottom by Sisyphus in order to roll it again to the top, and so on, endlessly—endless, pointless repetition.[28] The commentary on Taylor's commentary, though not endless, has been a recurring aspect of contemporary discussions of the meaning of life, because his approach makes such a plausible and compelling case for the notion that the meaning we are searching for is a wholly subjective notion. Unfortunately, his argument for subjectivism is flawed, and the position itself is problematic.

Taylor's argument is straightforward. Sisyphus's toil is meaningless because it is pointless; it accomplishes nothing. As he says, "Nothing ever comes of what he is doing, except simply, more of the same."[29] The image would be significantly altered if we imagined that Sisyphus's trips up the hill resulted in a collection of stones being used for building a "beautiful and enduring temple." Then his rock rolling would have a purpose. "Meaningfulness would at least have made an appearance, and we would see what it was." The problem here is that even an "enduring" temple would not last. Whatever goals that Sisyphus might have, in an altered image, would be of "transitory significance," his achievements mere "bubbles," and "those that do last, like the sandswept pyramids, soon become mere curiosities while around them the rest of mankind continues its perpetual toting of rocks, only to see them roll down." And if Sisyphus were to succeed in constructing a temple after eons of toil, his fundamental project would be complete, yet now his existence would be plagued by "infinite boredom."[30] The kind of meaning that is absent in the original image of Sisyphus would not really be helpful. Even activities or projects that have a point would be undermined by impermanence and eventual boredom when fundamental desires are satisfied.

It is clear that sporting situations do have a point, internally at least. In this sense, as well as others, sports seem quite unlike Sisyphean struggle. Taylor's worries about the transitory significance of certain kinds of goals, however, are relevant. There may be no "enduring temples" when it comes to sports—unless we think of records in terms of this metaphor—but victories and championships seem to fit Taylor's account of the way achievements may be mere "bubbles." If his more general account of goals and achievements is at all plausible, it might be particularly worrisome for the reflective athlete bothered by the impermanence of whatever internal goals she may have—athletic excellence, enjoyment, victory—and she might come to think that such impermanence would undermine the meaningfulness of sports activities. We play our games, win, then . . . poof. Next game? You win the championship, then retire. Now what? Boredom?

Taylor suggests that another alteration in the original image is more promising: "Let us suppose that the Gods, while condemning Sisyphus to the fate just described, at the same time, as an afterthought, waxed perversely merciful by implanting in him a strange and irrational impulse; namely a compulsive impulse to roll stones." Now his toil would be radically transformed—or, rather, his view of his life would be radically altered, because his fundamental desire would be fulfilled, endlessly. The boredom occasioned by rolling rocks would be transformed into bliss. An "objectively meaningless" life could be converted into one that is meaningful to Sisyphus by a change of perspective, one that is available to anyone, not because of an injection, but by changing one's "state of mind and feeling" toward one's activities. Even if our lives are like Sisyphus's, they can still be meaningful to the extent that we shape our wills by taking a "deep interest in what we find ourselves doing. . . . The strange meaningfulness they possess is that of the inner compulsion to be doing just what we were put here to do, and to go on doing it forever." Despite the fact that "each man's life thus resembles one of Sisyphus' climbs to the summit of his hill, and each day of it one of his steps," we can bestow meaning on our lives, supposedly, by an act of subjective identification. A life may have no overall point, and purposive activities and achievements may fade, but Taylor's optimism is undefeated. "The meaning of life is from within us, it is not bestowed from without, and it far exceeds in both its beauty and permanence any heaven of which men have ever dreamed or yearned for."[31] On this account, the meaning that sports provides is subjective. Regardless of how we evaluate the worth of the activities or their impermanence, the participant's deep interest (passion) is enough to explain the constitution of (subjective) meaning.

What do we say about this moving hymn to our wills, a song sung to overcome the despair caused by an intuition that our lives are really quite like Sisyphus: repetitive everydayness, no overall point, and no lasting repository for our accomplishments? Like the theist, Taylor situates the initial intuition of meaningfulness in a context of purpose, a claim generated by a negative path. Since Sisyphus's labors have no point, they are meaningless. Initially, Taylor insists that it is not the eternal nature of rock rolling that is so problematic; it is the pointlessness. "Again, it is not the fact that the labors of Sisyphus continue forever that deprives them of meaning. It is, rather, the implication of this: that they come to nothing."[32] If that is the case, the notion of meaningfulness is relatively clear. It is activity that has some point or purpose. Build temples, write books, raise families, develop friendships, help the homeless, sell cars, fix the plumbing, play games, and more. Meaning is everywhere. Note that there is a possible equivocation on "pointlessness." There may be a variety of reasons for engaging in certain activities. Some may be engaged in for their own sake; others may be performed for the sake of other ends. Sports have internal goals, such as becoming good at the sport, winning, enjoyment, and so on. They may or may not serve other ends, like moral education, honor, prestige, wealth, and self-esteem. In both instances, whether they are motivated by intrinsic or extrinsic reasons, they are not pointless. And even if we deny that sports are useful or serve any external ends, they are certainly purposive activities. So, they are quite unlike Sisyphus's rock rolling. Playing sports may "come to nothing" in one sense, but not in another sense. By their very nature they come to something, since they are rule-governed activities that have a means-end structure, the end being winning, the means including whatever it takes, within the rules, to bring about this purpose, for its own sake or for the sake of making the activity possible.

Taylor's next move is wrongheaded. Reflecting on Sisyphus's plight, Taylor says, "Meaninglessness is essentially endless pointlessness, and meaningfulness is therefore the opposite." Why does he insert the qualifying notion of "endless" here? Why should an end have to be lasting? "Activity, and even long, drawn out and repetitive activity, has a meaning if it has some significant culmination, some more or less lasting end that can be considered to have been the direction and purpose of the activity."[33] But that conclusion does not follow from the original image, as Taylor himself insists. Some meaningful activities may have more lasting ends than others, but purposiveness need not be dependent on lastingness. Meaning does not depend on permanence. The problem is not *endless* pointlessness; the problem is pointlessness. In this sense our lives are quite unlike Sisyphus's repetitive rock rolling, because they are full of activities, both ordinary and extraordinary (including sports), that do have a point, regardless of relatively lasting culminations.

Taylor's argument also shares the theist's concern that if life in general, or any particular life, has no overall point or purpose (some end toward which it is aimed), then a particular life (any life) is objectively meaningless. Of course, the theist asserts that life does have some overall purpose. Yet Taylor's subjectivism is fueled by the notion that each person's life does resemble "one of Sisyphus' climbs to the summit of his hills"; hence, life is "objectively meaningless," that is, pointless. But even if this is true, even if there is

no cosmic purpose of life in general, particular lives may be meaningful, insofar as they contain activities that do have a point. Taylor's worries and his move to subjectivism are plagued by the error
that infects Craig's theism. A meaningful life is not dependent on
the notion that there is an overall meaning of life or that a particular life must have some end. Again, life may be full of worthwhile activities in the absence of God or a cosmic order.

Apart from Taylor's argument for subjectivism, what should we
say about the notion that the necessary and sufficient condition of
a meaningful life is that such a life must be meaningful to the person whose life is being judged, that the person must identify with
or be deeply interested in or enjoy the activities that make up her
life? John Kekes defines such subjectivism as "agents' thinking that
their lives have meaning is the necessary and sufficient condition
for their lives having meaning."[34] Although it may be important to
pin down precisely the subjective conditions that constitute meaningfulness ("deep interest," identification, belief, satisfaction, happiness), none of them will be necessary or sufficient if we accept
Taylor's starting point: pointless activities are meaningless, and
meaningful activities are the opposite. Activities may have a purpose
or point, lives may be goal directed in a variety of ways, yet the
subjective conditions that accompany such activities are contingent.
J. S. Mill famously tells us in chapter 5 of his *Autobiography* that he
lost his interest in being a utilitarian reformer; he ceased to have
the requisite feelings that would make him a happy moral warrior.
It may be correct to say that seeking the general good was no longer
"meaningful" for him, in the sense that he lost his motivation to
pursue his utilitarian goals. But indifference, boredom, and alienation are irrelevant in judging whether the possible courses of conduct a utilitarian agent might pursue, for example, are morally
worthwhile. That is, they have a point and a worthwhile purpose,
qua maximizing utility. Mill says, "I was thus left stranded . . . without any desire for the ends which I had been so carefully fitted out
to work for: no delight in virtue, or the general good, but also in

anything else." However we put it, we may find ourselves no longer caring about specific things, or certain things may no longer matter to us. But the caring and the mattering to us are independent, in principle, from judgments about the point and worthwhileness of activities themselves. We may no longer take delight in moral virtue, or take joy in being an excellent architect, teacher, physician, scientist, Walmart greeter, or athlete. But our interests and enjoyments are separate matters—buildings still need to be designed, students need to be taught, the well-being of people is a good to be valued, and so forth, regardless of the psychological variables involved. Perhaps good lives are subjectively happy, or the best lives are satisfied lives, but these are separate matters. A meaningful life, a life full of meaningful activities, may or may not be maximally satisfying to the agent. The example of J. S. Mill's arrest, like Tolstoy's anxieties, shows what is obvious: that it is better to care about our activities and projects; that it is better for our activities to matter to us and for us to identify deeply with them. This may be the reason for evaluative language suggesting that we sometimes take meaningfulness or meaninglessness to admit of degrees, as if we might come to experience a part of our life as more or less meaningful. On the other hand, meaningful activities, in the sense suggested by Taylor's attempt to undermine so-called objective meaningfulness, are unproblematically independent of positive attitudes toward them, and they are pervasive in life. Yet there is an additional worry about the worth of certain purposive activities or the value of the ends we seek. For some, this may be particularly troublesome when we consider the worth of the ends we seek in sports.

What if one does believe one's life is meaningful or does take a "deep interest" in one's activities, or deeply wants to be doing precisely what one finds oneself doing? Is that sufficient for meaningfulness? Are there constraints on meaningful identifications? There are at least four worries associated with the notion that some subjective condition is sufficient to make a life meaningful. The meaningfulness of one's activities, and thus one's life, may be threatened by triviality, coercion, immorality, or futility. Thus, to be meaningful, one may think that our lives must be full of or dominated by or include worthwhile activities or projects; these activities must be the result of autonomous choice, they must pass the test of morality, and the goals we pursue must at least be possible, in some important sense. We will take up each of these concerns in the following sections. Some will require more discussion than others.

## VI. Worthwhileness and Objectivism

The paradigm examples of meaningful lives—Gandhi, Einstein, Picasso, Jefferson—show us that it is possible to find or achieve meaning in life. (As before, I would add examples of great athletes here, but I admit that such intuitions remain to be explained and defended.) Perhaps our intuitions about such lives form the basis for our pretheoretical judgments about meaningfulness: that some lives are more meaningful than others, that ordinary people do desire meaningfulness, that people are inclined to evaluate their lives in terms of these normative categories (meaningful, meaningless), and that individuals may come to judge their own lives as more or less meaningful.[35] The problem, however, is that while extraordinary moral, scientific, aesthetic, and even athletic achievements are meaningful, the tendency is to use such lives to establish standards for more ordinary lives. Is it a danger to assume that because there are paradigm examples of meaningful lives, we will be forced to establish a kind of scale of meaningfulness, with extraordinary lives at the top, ordinary lives falling somewhat short with regard to worthwhileness, and pathetic lives full of triviality consigned to meaningless worthlessness? An added issue is that this procedure seems to reduce judgments of meaningfulness to judgments about worthwhileness or worthwhile purposes. Lives of great accomplishment show that meaningfulness does not depend on cosmic purpose or on various psychological contingencies. According to the objectivist, such lives depend on the fact that some activities and projects really are more worthwhile than others.

Whereas the main player in Taylor's drama is Sisyphus, Susan Wolf's objectivism is developed on the basis of intuitions about other characters: The Blob, The Useless (the idle rich, the corporate-executive workaholic seeking only to accumulate wealth, the pig farmer who buys more land to grow more corn, etc.), and The Bankrupt (the businessman whose company fails after a life of work, the scientist whose lifelong research is rendered useless by some other breakthrough). Such images lead to the central position: "Roughly, I would say that meaningful lives are lives of active engagement in projects of worth." She reduces her thesis to a slogan. "Meaning arises when subjective attraction meets objective attractiveness." The Blob is characterized by "hazy passivity," so he is actively engaged in nothing. "A person is actively engaged if she is gripped, excited, involved by it."[36] But such involvement, in which one feels "especially alive," is analogous to Taylor's notion that taking a deep interest in one's activities is vitally important (necessary?) for meaningfulness. Our lives are better if we are neither bored nor alienated, but meaningfulness is not dependent on heightened feelings of engagement. Ordinary yearnings for meaningfulness may sometimes express our hankering for more excitement, more pizzazz in our life. The job may become boring, and one may become tired of changing diapers or lubricating family relationships. Such activities may be meaningful nevertheless, that is, purposive and worthwhile.

The other condition is more interesting, simply because it may seem to be a truism: a meaningful life must involve "projects of worth."[37] Wolf admits that her claim is controversial because it seems committed to the notion of objective value, and her theory of meaningfulness, she says, is conceptually related to this commitment. "Indeed, it is this linkage that I want to defend, for I have neither a philosophical theory of what objective value is nor a substantive theory about what has this sort of value. What is clear to me is that there can be no sense to the idea of meaningfulness without a distinction between more or less worthwhile ways to spend one's time, where the test of worth is at least partly independent of a subject's ungrounded preferences or enjoyment."[38] Although some might challenge her theory of meaningfulness on the basis of its reliance on the notion of objective value, I am willing to admit that judgments of value might be objective. The problem is the supposed conceptual link between meaningfulness and objective worthwhileness.

I believe it is a mistake to claim that meaningful activities must be (relatively) worthwhile, because judgments of meaning are, in principle, independent from judgments of worth, and this independence need not be based on the subjectivist notion that meaningfulness is simply a function of an activity or project being meaningful because some agent enjoys it, takes some deep interest in it, or believes that it is meaningful. Wolf's own examples show the tenuousness of the link she wants to support. To show what it means to be actively engaged in activities, to feel "especially alive," she mentions climbing a mountain and training for a marathon. Although these activities or projects may require quite admirable character traits and the achievements may involve standards of excellence, the goals themselves are relatively trivial. One well-known account of sport, conceived as game playing, describes it in a pithy phrase: "the voluntary attempt to overcome unnecessary obstacles."[39] Describe some goal that may be achieved apart from the sporting activity in question: getting to the top of the mountain, arriving at some place twenty-six miles from your current location, putting a little white ball in a cup (golf), throwing a ball through a hoop, and so on. Now establish rules requiring that the specified goal can be brought about only in certain highly restricted and inefficient ways: you must climb to the top rather than take a helicopter; you must run to a spot some twenty-six miles hence, and you may not take a bicycle, car, or any kind of shortcut; after placing the cup many yards away, you must hit the ball into the cup, using only a long metal club, and you may not simply walk toward the cup and place it there with your hand. The goals themselves are rather trivial, and because the required methods to bring about the ends are inefficient, the activities are quite absurd, at least from the point of view of everyday life, where efficiency is often related to rationality. Such activities are trivial when we compare them to great intellectual, moral, or aesthetic achievements. Yet athletes and even everyday participants in sports find these relatively trivial activities highly meaningful, because they do have a point, a purpose, a context for intelligible goals. They represent the attempt to overcome some (artificial) difficulty, yet when successful, such overcoming constitutes real achievement. Sporting activities take place in a context of meaning, a "world," involving clearly delineated goals, standards of excellence, and meaningful ends, internal to the sport. Elsewhere, I have characterized sport as "splendid triviality."[40] Playing and winning games and becoming good in a sport are meaningful activities, yet trivial in an important sense.

Wolf says that "it would be odd, if not bizarre, to think of crossword puzzles, sitcoms, or the kind of computer games to which I am fighting off addiction as providing meaning in our lives," and she also mentions "chocolate and aerobics class" as the sorts of things that are somewhat worthwhile, but "not the sorts of things that make life worth living."[41] First, I do not think it is bizarre to judge that doing crossword puzzles is a meaningful activity—that is, it has a point, can be cognitively and intellectually challenging, and provides some momentary satisfaction. But Wolf is apparently looking for Meaning, not mere meaning, and the Crossword Puzzle Champ, yet another character of meaninglessness, has no categorical desires that would make life worth living. But it is not at all obvious that Wolf's intuitions are right about the example or the question of meaningfulness itself. It is not at all obvious that the question of the conditions of a meaningful life is about what makes life worth living, and even trivial activities, like creating the largest ball of adhesive tape (a real-life example), may be sufficiently gamelike to be meaningful. Why is it that climbing a mountain (and risking death) may involve the kind of value that contributes to meaning but doing crosswords would not? Why not say that both are meaningful, so meaningful activities are not really threatened by (relative) triviality?

It may be that Wolf's paradigm examples, even bizarre ones like collecting rubber bands or memorizing the dictionary (for real-life examples see the *Guinness World Records*), are to be construed not as short-term activities but as projects, which are relatively long-term, require more perseverance and commitment over time, and tend to unify a life because the dominance of the desires that motivate the project may negate other aspects of good lives. Yet lives dominated by bizarre projects may include many other less bizarre but meaningful activities, so even if such lives were judged to be meaningless, qua bizarre dominating triviality, they still might be full of other meaningful activities, and the overall judgment of these lives would be unclear. I see no reason to deny that even a dominating trivial project is meaningful, in the clear sense that it has a point. I am not recommending that people spend their lives devoted to trifling and petty projects or activities. The important issue concerns worthwhileness, not meaningfulness. The important question may involve how to live wisely, not meaningfully. Contrary to Wolf's intuitions and her attempt to take seriously the pretheoretical judgments of ordinary people, meaningfulness is not necessarily threatened by triviality. People do probably yearn for a life full of worthwhile activities and projects, and it is a difficult philosophical task to sort out the significant from the insignificant. But it is unhelpful and misleading to speak of meaningfulness if we are really concerned about worthwhileness. Even if we consider sports to be relatively trivial activities, they may nevertheless be meaningful.

### VII. Autonomy and Morality

Questions concerning autonomy were first raised in relation to the theistic notion that the meaning of life consists in conforming to

God's assigned purposes or to the purposes determined by an external agency. Taylor's subjectivism also seemed problematic because the subjective conditions that are supposedly necessary and sufficient for meaningfulness could be the product of manipulation or coercion. John Kekes argues that the discovery that our desires have been manipulated would constitute a decisive rejection of subjectivism because we would not judge a project to be meaningful if the desire to pursue it was not our own. "If meaning were subjective, if it were created merely by our wants and beliefs, it would make no difference to meaning whether wanting to pursue a project is genuine or manipulated." But it does make a difference, so if subjectivism were true, "it would be inexplicable how the discovery of manipulation could lead us to regard as meaningless a project that we regarded as meaningful before the discovery."[42]

Kekes's argument confuses judgments of meaningfulness and judgments of value. Because we value autonomy, we would be dissatisfied to discover that our desires have been manipulated or our purposes assigned to us. But such discoveries do not undermine meaning, unless meaning is reduced to meaningfulness or worth *for* me, in some subjective sense. Activities can be meaningful whether they are the product of autonomous choice or whether they are generated by desires that have been manipulated. Some person might come to realize that her desire to be an Olympian (lawyer, architect, electrician, physician) has been manipulated, coerced, or determined by her strong-willed parents. (You could substitute the mad scientist as the source of manipulation.) That discovery would not undermine the meaning of a career in medicine, the meaning of the various health-promoting activities of a physician, or the worthwhileness of such physician-related activities or projects. Nor would it undermine the meaningfulness of activities directed toward the goal of becoming an Olympic athlete. Suppose she has had to submerge her athletic desires and finds that she does not really want to become an Olympian. Or suppose she judges correctly that God wants her to be a physician, but she finds in herself competing desires to be an Olympic athlete and then a coach that outweigh these divinely ordained purposes. She may decide to become an athlete and coach, not because she found that her other activities would be meaningless (on the grounds that they would be the product of manipulation), but because she finds that other values involved in being an athlete, like autonomy, bodily excellence, self-expression, self-fulfillment, and even beauty, were more important to her. The issue is not meaningfulness versus meaninglessness; it is about the comparative axiological differences in diverse kinds of meaningful activities. The example shows not that meaningfulness requires autonomy or self-expression, but that an activity involving autonomy, self-expression, and meaningfulness may be more valuable to an agent than an activity characterized by meaningfulness, beneficence, and coercion. The issue is worthwhileness, not whether the activities in question do in fact have a point or purpose—and possibly a quite important point at that. It is misleading for Kekes to claim that discovery of manipulation necessarily undermines meaningfulness.

A related worry associated with subjectivism concerns lives in which a person might be deeply interested in or actively engaged in projects that are "destructive, like having enough drugs to support an addiction," or activities that are paradigmatically immoral. Some may think that morality is an important restraint on judgments of meaningfulness, so a life characterized by morally repugnant acts would be meaningless. (We might wonder about the meaningfulness of being a boxer or engaging in mixed martial arts because of the aggression, violence, and harm involved in these sports.) What do we say about the Happy Nazi, or Heinrich Himmler doing his perceived duty as the Nazi bureaucrat efficiently administering the Final Solution? What about Osama bin Laden? Is morality necessary for meaningfulness? Although I have criticized Wolf and Kekes on other points, on this issue I fully agree with both. For Wolf, projects of worth need not be distinctively moral. She mentions "Gaugin, Wittgenstein, Tchaikovsky—morally unsavory figures all, whose lives nonetheless seem chock full of meaning." Kekes's examples are similar, but more deeply problematic from a moral point of view: "That immoral lives may be meaningful is shown by the countless dedicated Nazi and Communist mass murderers, by those sincerely committed terrorists who aim to destabilize one society or another through committing outrageous crimes against innocent civilians, and by people whose rage, resentment, greed, ambition, selfishness, sense of superiority or inferiority give purpose to their lives and lead them to inflict grievous unjustified harm on others. Such people may be successfully engaged in their projects, derive great satisfaction from them, and find their lives as scourges of their literal or metaphorical gods very meaningful."[43] Likewise, lives devoted to the achievement of various kinds of nonmoral excellence—the athlete, chef, or Scrabble champ—are meaningful, or at least might include meaningful projects, despite the fact that they could devote more time to helping the homeless or reducing world poverty and hunger.[44] I conclude that neither autonomy nor morality constitutes necessary constraints on meaningfulness.

### viii. Futility

So far, we have seen that the question of the meaning of life is most importantly a question of the conditions of a meaningful life, and that issue is usually analyzed in terms of meaningful activities. Meaningless activities are pointless, and various attempts to characterize other constraints on meaningfulness—that such activities require active engagement, that they must be robustly worthwhile, that they must be the product of autonomous choice—have been shown to be unsuccessful. A further worry is not that our activities have no purpose or that the ends we seek are trivial or the product of manipulated desires. The worry is that we seek impossible ends or goals. As Kekes says, "There are also lives directed at goals impossible even of approximation, like communicating with the dead. These lives are futile."[45] In W. D. Joske's astute discussion of meaningful (and thus meaningless) activities, he offers this analysis: "I shall call an activity 'futile' if, although it has a point or needs a point in order to make it fully meaningful, the world prevents the achievement of the required end."[46] There are various ways in which the world might prevent the achievement of the required end. Some ends might be necessarily unobtainable (Joske mentions squaring the circle or solving Euler's puzzle), while in other cases contingent features of the world might make the end futile. (A person decides to retire early, at age sixty-two, in order to pursue his dream of playing in the NBA.)[47] Futile activities are paradigm examples of Nagel's concept of the absurd, which involves "a conspicuous discrepancy between pretension or aspiration and reality."[48] Less absurd examples are prevalent in sports, when outclassed individuals or teams pursue goals that are virtually impossible to achieve or are practically unobtainable, where hopes and dreams clash with athletic limitations.

Futility is a significant constraint on meaningfulness, unlike active engagement, worthwhileness, morality, or coercion, but we must be careful how judgments concerning futile activities relate to judgments about futile "lives," as Kekes says. First, let's distinguish absolute and relative futility. I will refer to absolute futility if the end in question is an all-or-nothing goal that cannot be partially satisfied or achieved, or cannot be tangentially approached. The attempt to communicate with plants and the desire to get to heaven are absolutely futile activities if it is impossible for persons to communicate with plants or if heaven does not exist. Relative futility involves seeking an end that is in fact impossible to achieve fully, but it is one that we can approach, one to which we can come more near or can gain upon. Working to achieve world peace and to rid the world of poverty and hunger are relatively futile, but we can conceive of the way in which progress can be made toward these ends. The attempt to persuade everyone of the truth of one's philosophical beliefs is futile, but one might persuade some people. Relative futility is no threat to meaningfulness, insofar as such activities will have an intermediate partially fulfilled end, even if the world might make impossible the full achievement of the end. On the other hand, an absolutely futile activity or project is meaningless because the end is impossible.

Even lives dominated by or that include absolutely futile projects may include many other accompanying meaningful activities, and some absolutely futile projects may involve typical concomitant activities that are meaningful. An evangelical preacher's project of helping people to achieve salvation through accepting Jesus's message is absolutely futile if a trinitarian theistic God does not exist. Yet her other activities as a pastor, parent, friend, and member of the church bowling team are meaningful. The retiring man's absurd project of pursuing his NBA dream will involve participation in games, intrinsically valued skills development, and attempts to achieve better physical conditioning. It is a mistake to say, as Kekes does, that lives directed at impossible goals are futile, unless we agree with some assumed and unargued claim about the relation between futile activities that may be a significant part of a person's life and a judgment about the overall significance of a life in relation to some of its futile parts.

Goals related to some religious metaphysics are particularly interesting in this regard. Some think that their lives would be meaningless unless the ends associated with their religious beliefs are fulfilled. If those beliefs turn out to be false, then at least some aspects of their lives are futile. Perhaps decisive commitment to a religion involves a greater risk of futility, given the widespread disagreement among diverse religious interpretations of reality. On the other hand, it does not follow that enormous numbers of lives that include or are even dominated by such ends are futile, and therefore meaningless. Given the fact that lives that do include futile projects may include other meaningful activities, and that some futile projects will typically include attendant meaningful activities, the worry concerning futility, though not negated, is surely less weighty than one might initially assume. Worries about futility, which are really worries about meaningless activities, are less important, given the fact that life is full of ample opportunities for other meaningful projects and activities. Also, in some cases we are not in a position to claim to have true beliefs about reality such that we would be assured that our projects are or are not futile. Such factors should make us much less inclined to pronounce judgments about meaningless lives, qua futility, or to believe that the normative category "meaningless life" is very useful in this context. Lives centered on the achievement of extraordinary athletic goals need not be deemed "futile" or meaningless if individuals fail to achieve such goals, despite the fact that such lives are marred by failure.

Having made our way through various attempts to provide a general account of the meaning of life or meaningful lives and activities, we are now in a position to bring together various avenues of criticism in order to provide a more adequate account of meaning. To this we now turn.

# 9 Meaning, Sport, and Deflationary Attitudes

In the following discussion I attempt to place sport in the context of a more general account meaning and a scheme that identifies various areas in life in which people seek and provide meaning in and for their lives. I will end with some comments about the relative importance of raising the question of the meaning of life and how sport might be understood in the context of such reflections.

## 1. Meaning, Transcending, and Connecting

What has been absent in the discussion so far is the articulation of a deeper theory about the basis of diverse and competing claims about meaningfulness and meaninglessness, although at times deeper assumptions have been questioned. Both Craig and Taylor (and Tolstoy) seem to assume that permanence would be required for meaningfulness, yet there is no obvious reason this is the case. Why not think that the preference for permanence is a metaphysical prejudice? Wolf thinks it is just obvious that meaningfulness is a matter of engaging in worthwhile activities, that "there can be no sense to the idea of meaningfulness without a distinction between more or less worthwhile ways to spend one's time," yet trivial pursuits can be meaningful. Kekes asserts that a recognition that our attitudes or desires have been manipulated would result in a judgment that the activities motivated by such desires would be meaningless, yet manipulated activities or projects could be quite meaningful. Futile projects are problematic, yet futility may be only one aspect of lives full of otherwise meaningful activities. (All of these judgments are related to my initial claim about sport as a source of meaning in life.) Why accept these counterexamples? At the least, my intuitions about the purported meaningfulness of desires, activities, projects, and lives are contrary to the intuitions of other philosophers, and this may show the tenuousness of making certain judgments involved in discussions of the meaning of life. Skepticism generated by an awareness of competing "intuitions" may be enough to ground a deflationary resistance to the inclination to judge persons' *lives* as meaningless or meaningful. But we need something more. We need to explain the important intuitions. In offering something more, I endorse the spirit of David Schmidtz's suggestion that seeking knockdown arguments in questions about the meaning of life is probably misguided. He says about his own interesting thoughts in this area, "So, I do not here seek the kind of argumentative closure that we normally think of as the hallmark of success in analytic philosophy. This chapter is simply an invitation to reflect."[1]

Consider again the theistic model of meaningfulness and why so many find it powerful and persuasive. In searching for the meaning of life, we want to place "life," as it were, in some larger context in order to make sense of it, explain it, and perhaps to justify our very existence. Life as such is supposedly meaningful in virtue of its relation to some larger whole, some context of purpose, and the activities of a life are thought to be meaningful in virtue of the way that means are related to some ultimate ends (a proper relation to God, eternally satisfying existence, and so forth). According to this model, a meaningful life is connected to a wider frame of reference, and the attempt to live meaningfully is the desire to live in light of such connections or relations. If theism is true, then a meaningful life connects with Infinite Value, insofar as God is unsurpassably good. But meaningfulness is not reducible to connecting with Infinite Value; it is a function of "being a part of," "being connected to," or "establishing a relation with." The model straightforwardly shows the structure of meaningfulness, and the structure is available even when we move to naturalistic approaches to the meaning of life.

If the myth of Sisyphus is a "perfect image of meaninglessness," as Taylor says, it is because we must agree that pointless drudgery, that is, mind-numbingly repetitive physical toil engaged in for no reason would be unintelligible and unjustifiable. It connects with nothing. We would have no frame of reference within which to understand the activity. It would literally be "meaningless." Yet even here, it is somewhat misleading to characterize Sisyphus's rock rolling in this way, because it is described in terms of a larger context of purpose, significance, or meaning. After all, Sisyphus is being punished. That is the point of rolling rocks up the hill. The punishment is for Sisyphus to be forced to engage in meaningless activity. (There is nothing paradoxical about this if we make the proper distinction.) In this sense, the activity is meaningful because it takes place and can be understood to take place in relation to other factors—the gods' purposes or reasons. Suppose the reasons for the punishment are morally trivial or unjust. That would make the punishment lack justification or moral worth, not meaning.

Notice that activities, projects, individual lives, and life as such may be placed in all sorts of relational contexts. Contexts of significance may include attempts to connect with facts or values. When we consider lives that exemplify great scientific, moral, aesthetic, political, economic, or even athletic achievements, we see the way in which activities and projects are meaningful in virtue of certain kinds of involvements. But even more ordinary or less consequential involvements are meaningful in terms of being framed in a larger relational context or background structure. The craftsman working in his little shop (or studio) making toys or jewelry is as involved in meaningful activity as the Teach for America recruit or the Peace Corps volunteer.[2] The issue of the relative value or merit of such activities is separate. Meaning is relational or arises in relations.

This point is reinforced by a brief consideration of Alasdair MacIntyre's concept of a practice: "By a 'practice' I am going to mean any coherent and complex form of socially established cooperative human activity through which goods internal to that form of activity are realized in the course of trying to achieve those standards of excellence which are appropriate to, and partially definitive of, that form of activity, with the result that human powers to achieve excellence, and human conceptions of the ends and goods involved, are systematically extended."[3] The concept of a practice is broad and extends to a vast array of human activities, such as farming, science, architecture, portrait painting, politics, chess, helping to sustain a family, sports, and so on. (MacIntyre mentions all of these.) To the extent that we have available to us the possibility of participating in such a vast array of "coherent and complex" forms of cooperative human activities, with standards of excellence, internal goods, and practice communities, meaningful activities are ubiquitous. Such involvements situate our lives and activities in essentially relational contexts involving other people and shared concerns, traditions and present realities, regardless of the judgment concerning the relative worth of the internal goods that might be achieved—for example, becoming good in a sport, conceived as splendid (meaningful) triviality, or becoming adept at solving crossword puzzles.

Robert Nozick comes close to the position I am attempting to explain and defend, but his most general and abstract way of referring to meaning, "transcending limits," needs to be qualified somewhat. Nozick's central insight is that individual lives may be more or less limited with regard to the way in which discrete moments of temporally unfolding experience are integrated into some kind of unity. He mentions "the life of the amnesiac who is unable to plan over several days or even moments because he forgets each day (or moment) what came before." Another interesting example is what we sometimes call "psychopaths." Reminiscent of the negative strategy of Taylor and Wolf, Peter Singer uses as his perfect image of meaninglessness the example of a psychopath, "a person who is asocial, impulsive, egocentric, unemotional, lacking in feelings of remorse, shame or guilt, and apparently unable to form deep and enduring personal relationships." Such people "live largely in the present and lack any coherent life plan." According to Singer, their lives are meaningless because "psychopaths are egocentric to an extreme: neither other people, nor worldly success, nor anything else really matters to them."[4]

The example of the psychopath suggests that for most people, having plans or more long-term purposes involves transcending narrowness and achieving some coherence or unity in their lives. Nozick says this: "Attempts to find meaning in life seek to transcend the limits of an individual life. The narrower the limits of a life, the less meaningful it is." The task of integrating a life involves more than summing up the quantity of pleasures achieved, according to Nozick. He comments on the hedonist: "Of such lives we ask, 'but what does that life add up to, what meaning does it have?' For a life to have meaning, it must connect with other things, with some things or values beyond itself. Meaning, and not merely of lives, seems to lie in such connections. To ask something's meaning is to ask how it is connected, perhaps in unspecified ways, to other things. Tracking, either of facts or of value, is a mode of being so connected, as is fitting an external purpose."[5]

If meaning in life essentially involves relational contexts, or "connection to a wider context," it is clear that such a view explains the notion that meanings in life are everywhere, as I have claimed. Connecting or relating to God (if God exists) may be a paradigm case of meaning, but such a relation, even if possible, would not exhaust the sources of meaning in life. Nozick reinforces this pluralism: "The particular things or causes people find make their life

*meaning = transcend limits* [handwritten marginal note]

meaningful all take them beyond their narrow limits and connect them with something else. Children, relationships with other persons, helping others, advancing justice, continuing and transmitting a tradition, pursuing truth, beauty, world betterment—these and the rest link you to something wider than yourself. The more intensely you are involved, the more you transcend your limits."[6]

In my view, Nozick is close to the truth, but the language of "transcending limits" is not the best way (at least in one significant case) to capture the most general account of what is going on when we try to understand meaning as connecting, or, in Nozick's own words, "if meaning itself is not a thing but a relationship." One of the main reasons that Nozick is drawn to the notion of "transcending limits" is that it seems to explain why we tend to think, as Craig, Tolstoy, and others have, that death (annihilation) undermines meaning. "Mortality is a temporal limit and traces are a way of going or seeking beyond that limit. To be puzzled about why death seems to undercut meaning is to fail to see the temporal limit itself as a limit."[7] But one can imagine transcending the limit of mortality and being left with a meaningless existence.[8] Not only may immortality be boring and tedious, but it could be meaningless if such an existence were conceived as eternal isolation, perhaps a disembodied soul living in an eternal now with no memory or imaginative capabilities. (Would merging into the unified Ocean of Being "transcend limits"? Would the negation of individuality make a life "meaningful"?) Transcending limits, of mortality, at least, is not sufficient for meaning. On the other hand, in ordinary life when we make connections, establish relations with wider contexts of facts or values, when we find ourselves involved in larger frames of reference, we are going beyond ourselves. Perhaps the underlying motive is not "mere" transcendence, but the desire to escape metaphysical isolation, that "terrible loneliness" that Russell spoke of as the object of love's overcoming—love, a fundamental mode of human connection.[9] In any case, now we are in a better position to reflect on sport and meaning in life.

## 11. Sport and Spaces of Meaning

Once we have arrived at the notion that meaning comes with relations of all sorts, we have only to make explicit what has been implicit: that sport is a fertile area of meaning in life, notwithstanding the contrary intuitions to which I referred in the beginning. The notion of "transcending limits" may be sufficiently flexible to illuminate numerous possibilities involved in sports participation.

The thin description of transcending limits refers to being interested in sports (or a sport) or becoming involved in developing sporting skills in particular ways. This, in general, is a mode of self-transcendence, going beyond the self-absorption of Singer's psychopath to become related to or connected with a practice and a practice community. To engage in sports is to have purposes, necessitated by the means-end structure of such activities, else the person would not be engaged at all. Certainly, becoming interested in, loving, or respecting the "game" is to be related to something wider than oneself, taking one beyond one's narrow limits, in Nozick's sense. Sport is one among numerous things in life to which one can become connected.

In a thicker sense, sport is a mode of connection that involves individuals in specific modes of self-transcendence or more specific ways in which individuals are called upon to transcend their limits. Sport, construed as the "voluntary attempt to overcome unnecessary obstacles," is by its very nature the attempt to confront difficulty and seek achievements in the process. Sport, as the quest for a certain kind of physical excellence within a complicated web of rules and strategic know-how, challenges persons to come to grips with their limitations, to understand themselves in order to succeed or to become better. Sport requires self-expansion and self-knowledge, insofar as sport participants must acknowledge their limits in order to overcome them and become better or succeed in various ways. Here is how Anthony Skillen characterizes sport:

The rules of sport establish limits within which skills and capacities are pitched against each other. But the relativities of victory and defeat, as of their components in successful or unsuccessful passes, tackles, shots, scores and moves, are against the background of more "absolute" relativities: the limits of even the greatest human skill, strength, wit and endurance. Because it is one of the few domains in which humans are encouraged to stretch to their limits, sport has the potential to teach us to live with such limits. And at the same time, because we have to be "given" a game by the person who beats or is beaten by us, sport has the capacity to teach us to live with the limits of a human fellowship informed by awareness of common frailty. Good sports have generous wisdom in their bones.[10]

I would not say, as Skillen does, that sport is "one of the few domains in which humans are encouraged to stretch to their limits," but it does encourage or demand a relatively distinctive kind of transcendence, involving, as it does, capabilities that have a significant physical or bodily component, and it is highly accessible. Becoming a physicist, poet, ballerina, software programmer, senator, priest, good parent, or moral human being—all involve the demand to stretch personal limits in a variety of ways. Each of these endeavors provides meaningful activities for a person. Skillen also reminds us of the social dimension of sports, connecting us to others in meaningful ways that demand cooperation and trust, as other meaningful activities do. Also, the motivation to transcend our limits forces us to recognize them.

Owen Flanagan provides an insightful way to appreciate the numerous ways in which people seek to find meaning in life, yet he does not mention sport as a basic and distinctive venue of meaning. In the context of reflecting on the contemporary conflict between a scientific view of persons and a religious view of persons and the nature of things, Flanagan attempts to broaden our sense of the variety of "locations" in our world within which differing images of persons and meaning are generated. He calls these "spaces of meaning": art, science, technology, ethics, politics, spirituality. "Each of these six spaces of meaning names, or gestures in the direction of, a large domain of life." Here is how he describes his notion: "The basic idea is that in order to understand how any group or individual self-conceives, what their practices of self-location, self-understanding, and their ideals for human development are, and how they work, one must give concrete values to these six variables." Instead of reducing the central contemporary cultural conflict to a dispute between religion and science about who and what we are and what is our place in the universe, we need to broaden our sense of the ways we interact with other areas of life within which we generate our self-conceptions. Here are other ways he explains the basic idea: "We experience the world in and through these spaces. Regardless of whether a space or an image gets things right, we utilize modes it affords and/or recommends for self-conceiving." "Each member names an abstract scheme, a 'form of life,' or an aspect of a form of life which humans intersect with, participate in, utilize, and deploy in making sense and meaning of things, including themselves." "The central claim is that it is, to some significant degree, by living in these spaces that we make sense of things, orient our lives, find our way, and live meaningfully."[11]

Because of the way that Flanagan explains his notion of "spaces of meaning," and because, as he says, "I don't claim that the list is exhaustive,"[12] it might be useful to wonder whether sport could (or should) be added to Flanagan's list. My only hesitation arises from questions about the relations between the abstract and the concrete in thinking about the sense in which, as he says, "most contemporary people interact with all six of these spaces."[13] It is clear in paradigm cases how these interactions work, whether we are reading or writing poems, listening to music, evaluating Darwin's account of evolution by natural selection, reading or writing about political matters (or voting), thinking about some religious text or engaging in some religious practices, reflecting on the morally correct thing to do or what kind of person to be, or making moral choices. Other activities are more ambiguous: artworks may have political ambitions; biologists or physicists may endorse naturalism, intelligent design, or the Big Bang version of the cosmological argument for God's existence. Sport may be sufficiently complex to occasion competing claims about its relation to other spaces of meaning. For example, some have argued that sport is art. Others have endorsed the notion that it provides aesthetic possibilities for athletes and fans, despite the fact that it is a mistake to call it "art." Sport may involve the political and even the spiritual—the political in ways associated with nationalism, the spiritual in the form of providing experiences of unity and coherence. And sport may involve the development of moral as well as nonmoral goods or excellences, so its relation to the ethical is a common theme in reflections on sport. Should we add it to the list? Sport may engage participants in such a unique way that it is a mistake to reduce it to one of the other spaces of meaning. Conversely, it may make no difference whether we raise it to the status of art, ethics, politics, or spirituality, when we consider sport as a locus of meaning. In raising these issues, we are certainly "gesturing" to a domain of meaning that is central for some and basic for many, at the least related in important ways to Flanagan's list of spaces of meaning.

The discussion of spaces of meaning also fits nicely with the notion of meaning arising in relations or connections, as well as the pluralism that results from this explanation of meaning. If this scheme or something like it is largely correct, then, as Flanagan explains, "there are plural ways of making sense of things and finding meaning. This is because there are in reality a multiplicity of kinds of things . . . and relations. Different spaces are suited to speak most profitably about different relations."[14] There are causal relations, aesthetic relations, logical relations, personal relations, and so forth. Finding meaning and making sense of things, qua engaging in sports, involves the kind of personal involvements we have previously described.

There is another interesting implication of considering the notion that meaning comes with relations of certain kinds and is constituted by transcending the limits of an individual life. Recall Nozick's claim that the "narrower the limits of a life, the less meaningful it is." Although I am suspicious of general claims about the meaninglessness or meaningfulness of lives (because of the vast plurality of ways we can become engaged with ideals, values, people, practices—the world), it does seem to me that judgments about the meaningfulness and meaninglessness of activities, projects, or parts of individual lives do admit of degrees, as Nozick's comment suggests. People do sometimes talk about finding "more meaningful" jobs, careers, relationships, and so on. W. D. Joske's analysis of ways we can criticize an activity for lacking in meaning (worthlessness, pointlessness, triviality, and futility) uses the concept of activity being "fully meaningful": "I shall say that an activity is *fully meaningful* if it suffers from none of these defects, so that it is valuable in itself, directed towards an end which is not trivial, and is not futile."[15] *is something meaningful?*

Although I do not necessarily endorse the concept of "full" meaningfulness (on the grounds of my uncertainty about the necessary and sufficient conditions for this ideal being met), I do endorse the notion that judgments of meaning that are, in fact, made are sometimes matters of more or less, and intuitions related to common usage may include a variety of elements. Instead of speaking of the concept of a "fully meaningful" activity, I prefer to speak in terms of activities being relatively strong or weak in terms of meaning. I am sympathetic to the general line of Joske's analysis. He says, "Many people who seek a short answer to the question 'what is the meaning of life?' are, I suspect, looking for some simple fact or vision which will enable a human being who knows the secret to so organize his life that all of his activities will be fully meaningful."[16] I would say that persons are looking for (strongly) meaningful ways to engage the world. On the other hand, if, as I have argued, meaning is everywhere, the task is neither difficult nor puzzling, in a minimal sense. If we conceive of meaning as coming from relations or meaning as transcending the limits of an individual life, this condition is met in a vast amount of ways throughout virtually every person's life. Psychopaths are rare. This is the basic reason for my deflationary attitude toward the question of the meaning of life, which is really a question about how to live meaningfully. In the course of this discussion we have examined a number of serious attempts by philosophers to provide some general account that overlooks what I (along with Nozick and Flanagan) take to be the basic condition that must be met for an activity or domain of life to be meaningful. I shall call an activity weakly meaningful if this condition is met. A charitable way to interpret the various answers to the question of meaningful lives—Taylor's subjectivism, Wolf's "active engagement in projects of worth," Kekes's stress on autonomy, even intuitions concerning morally correct action or attractive ethical ideals—is to construe them as recommendations for valuable and desired properties that would make activities more strongly meaningful, in senses related to a broader variety of common usages concerning judgments of meaning. Meaning comes from relations, and may "track" either facts or values, so the emphasis on genuine worthwhileness or autonomy will seem to add to an activity's meaning.

Let me be clear here. Futile activities are meaningless because it is impossible to achieve the ends being sought, despite the fact that one may enjoy such activities, choose them, be passionately engaged in them, or believe they are fulfilling. Activities that seek trivial ends are meaningful, but worthless, in a highly restricted sense related only to the value of the end being sought. Weakly meaningful activities *are* meaningful. More strongly meaningful activities are, or are judged to be, more valuable. This accords with some aspects of common usage and some of the central claims made by the philosophers whose views I have examined. As I have said, it is a mistake to conflate judgments of meaning and judgments of value, yet I am willing to retrieve axiological concerns as long as it is clear that such notions really add value to activities, not meaning as relation or connection. Meaning sometimes involves more complex modes of axiological tracking. Weakly meaningful activities—that is, meaningful activities—are everywhere, as are more robustly valuable or worthwhile activities, which we may want to call more strongly meaningful.

Given this attempt to provide an account of our sense that activities can be more or less meaningful, sport holds up rather well as a locus for meaning in life. It is not only weakly meaningful; it may involve active engagement (passion!), enjoyment, self-expression, self-fulfillment, autonomy, physical excellence, beauty, practical intelligence, valuable human relationships, moral character, and more. The main worry may involve the relative value of the ends sought in sport. Like Wolf, I have no theory of objective value, yet it seems clear that sports participants should be modest about the value of the internal goods sought in their sporting activities, in contrast to other intellectual or moral ends we might pursue. Despite this, sports may be strongly meaningful for many.

One final point in relation to Nozick's claim that more narrow lives are less meaningful. Again, I am not sure about overall judgments of lives, but Flanagan's account of "spaces of meaning" provides another way of understanding our sense that the more opportunities we have to interact in significant ways with more of these spaces of meaning, the more possibilities we have to engage in meaningful activities. For most of us, we interact with art, music, politics, religion, technology, and the ethical in various ways. Some  are more passionate about art, politics, or spirituality than others, but, as Flanagan says, "we do not seek to find the main source of fulfillment in any one of these spaces." Some of these spaces do become the object of "single-minded passion," however. "The space of spirituality and religion is designed, it seems, to function comprehensively for those to whom it is designed to appeal—in principle to everyone in the vicinity. Among secular Western liberals, ethics and politics (and law) taken together, do similar work."[17]

We began by considering the sad case of the young football player who committed suicide. The upshot of these reflections is to recognize that sport may be more than simply a space of meaning for people young and old; it may become the object of "single-minded passion." It may function comprehensively as a location for making and finding meaning. The best we can do, especially for young people, is to recognize both that people may need such a special space and that they must also be encouraged to expand their limits by seriously engaging the other spaces. Coaches and parents, especially, should keep this in mind.

### III. Meaning, Values, Motives, and Satisfaction

In my view there are at least three distinct but related matters involved when people raise the question of the meaning of life. Because both philosophers and ordinary people fail to distinguish these issues, the problem of the meaning of life seems confusing, overly complex, and even insurmountable. First, people are worried by the problem of meaning proper, or what I have called meaning as connection or relation. How do I understand my life (or parts of my life, or life in general) as part of something greater, some wider context that makes it intelligible as a relation or in terms of relations, or insofar as it is linked to other facts or values? Second, what is worthwhile to pursue in life? What are the ends that I should seek? Are some activities or projects more worthwhile than others? Third, how can I live in order to be satisfied or fulfilled by the things I choose to do or the kind of person I attempt to be? How can I sustain a level of satisfaction in life in order to be motivated to continue to live as I choose or to continue to live, period?

If questions concerning the meaning of life, or a meaningful life, or meaningful activities or projects, are questions about relations or connections, it is clear that contexts of meaning are everywhere in life, as I have said. If we assume that meaningful lives are full of meaningful activities, as most are—ignoring problems concerned with judgments about the whole in relation to judgments about parts—worries about a meaningful life qua meaningful activities are like worries about whether most lives will involve purposive activities, goal-directed behavior, relationships with other people, asking questions, appreciating sunsets, enjoying good food, and the like. It is difficult to imagine a form of human life that would not contain a vast assortment of meaningful activities. So what is the point of such existential concerns occasioned by reflections about presumed threats to a meaningful life?

If some find this conclusion extraordinarily counterintuitive, it is probably because they interpret the question of the meaning of life as one that raises primarily axiological issues, as if we are really asking: What is worthwhile? Or, what is valuable to pursue? Is life worth living? But it is a mistake to reduce questions of meaning to questions of value. Some important intuitions are explained by this distinction. If the life of a Happy Nazi, gang member, or terrorist is meaningful in virtue of being related to others, unified by shared but abhorrent "values," then meaning involves the connection to others and to shared commitments, regardless of what is "really" valuable or worthwhile. Nozick makes the point clearly (ignore his account of intrinsic value as organic unity): "Value involves something's being integrated within its own boundaries, while meaning involves its having some connection beyond these boundaries." In many cases when we transcend our limits, when we look for meaning, "what we may find is a connection with value," but meaning is found in the relation or "link" to perceived value, not the value itself. "We need not look beyond something to find its (intrinsic) value, whereas we do have to look beyond a thing to discover its meaning."[18]

When asking questions about meaningful lives, if people are worried about what is worthwhile or valuable, it would be less misleading and confusing just to say so, and then we might be less inclined to seek transcendent or esoteric answers. I agree with Kai Nielsen's claim, asserted in an early attempt to clarify the question,

*[margin note, handwritten]* Connection = value / relation = meaning

that "we need not fly to a metaphysical enchanter" in order to answer it. For Nielsen, Baier, Wolf, and others, a "non-obscurantist, non-metaphysical treatment" of the question is appropriate because it involves only axiological worries.[19] I agree that perplexity about what is worthwhile in life is appropriate and crucially important if one wants to live well. It is clear what such befuddlement is about and that it need not be related to transcendent concerns. But perplexity about "meaning" is not reducible to perplexity about value.

A third related issue is exemplified by Tolstoy's account of his "arrest of life" and J. S. Mill's description of his breakdown.[20] In both cases lives that were meaningful, even extraordinary, judged from an external standpoint, were racked by doubts that left these individuals as lifeless shells, lacking motivation to continue to pursue worthwhile ends or the satisfaction associated with the achievement of such ends. No doubt people do fall prey to what Tolstoy calls a "mortal internal disease" characterized by utter indifference to activities and projects and the sense that nothing really matters. Does this mean that such lives, or the activities and projects that are a part of them, are meaningless? Of course not, if we understand meaning in the way I have described. Boredom, alienation, indifference, lack of motivation—these are real problems in life. But they are not problems because of the meaninglessness of lives marred by these psychological fissures that seem to cleave our unhappy, hyperreflective selves from fulfilling involvements. The problem is not the meaningfulness of activities—that's easy. The problem is how to remain motivated and satisfied amid distracting reflections about worthwhileness, mortality, and metaphysical perplexity.

Raymond Martin distinguishes the problem of the meaning of life, which he takes to be the question of whether life is worth living, and the problem of life, "the practical question of how to live our lives so that they are as worth living as they can be." As I have argued, the problem of the meaning of life is not whether life is worth living. That is a question of value, not meaning. A meaningful life may not be worth living. For example, pain from a terminal illness or severe psychological distress might render a great artist's life no longer worth living, not meaningless. The distinction is valuable, however, because there is a difference between the problem of meaning and psychological problems that are an inevitable part of life. Commenting on Tolstoy's anxieties, Martin says, "There's something fishy about existential anguish."[21] Martin wonders about the doubts generated by Tolstoy's philosophical questions—and, I should add, they are doubts generated by notoriously bad arguments. Are such doubts "psychologically genuine"? I do not know how to evaluate whether such doubts are genuine, but Martin's more important point is this: despite the fact that our lives could be going very well, it is hard to remain satisfied. The psychological problem (as Buddhists emphasize) "may simply be that we cannot satisfy ourselves completely for long. That is why even among people whose lives are going quite well, almost every one is chronically unsatisfied." We should not confuse the problem of remaining satisfied and philosophical worries about the meaning of life. Martin recommends that we resist the distraction of such worries and "follow our recipes for happiness: a fast car and a good woman, or whatever you think will do it for you."[22] Fine. I agree with the deflationary sentiments about the question of the meaning of life. Play golf. Shoot hoops. Go bowling. Tennis anyone? Don't worry. But philosophical perplexities about the good life, a life lived well and wisely, surely remain. *life ≠ unified meaning*

## IV. Conclusion: Sport and Meanings in Life

Many important questions remain, but one of them is not, what is the meaning of life? It is a bad question. There is no reason to believe that "life" as such has a unified meaning, and it may cause us to look in the wrong place for meaning(s). Life as such, or my life considered as a whole, may or may not be a part of something broader, some grand cosmic narrative or metaphysical picture that places it in some context. But that does not matter. A meaningful life, or a life full of meaningful activities, is neither difficult to achieve, esoteric, nor mysterious. Futile activities are problematic because attempted connections or relations are impossible. Yet there is much more to life than impossible aspirations. It is important to wonder about the good life and to solve the problem of satisfaction and self-fulfillment, but these are not synonymous with solving the problem of the meaning of life. Better to avoid such worries and attend to the more important axiological and psychological concerns. Better to deflate the importance of the question of the meaning of life and avoid unneeded distress.

Many have what I would call an inflationary view of the question of the meaning of life and a deflationary view of the meaning of sports. The main thrust of my arguments has been the reverse. Is this a paradox? Not really. As soon as we recognize that we need not travel long distances to seek advice about the meaning of life from the sage, or seek our answers outside the world, we should worry less and recognize ubiquitous possibilities. Here is Flanagan again, commenting on why it is a mistake to look for meaning in either a theological or a naturalistic story about origins: "If meaning and worth come with relations of certain sorts, perhaps in the first instance to other selves, but also to nature, to work, to oneself, then perhaps we are wisest to look for grounds of meaning and worth in this life—in relations we can have during this life."[23] I would add that we may look for and find grounds of meaning in our play, and we should recognize that its ultimate attraction may be essentially related to our quest for meanings in life, not competitive dominance or public recognition.[24]

*don't waste time answering the unanswerable you'll miss what makes life worth it*

# Notes

### 1. A Pluralist Conception of Play

1. Johan Huizinga, *Homo Ludens: A Study of the Play-Element in Culture* (Boston: Beacon Press, 1955); Roger Caillois, *Man, Play, and Games*, translated by Meyer Barash (1961; reprint, Urbana: University of Illinois Press, 2001).

2. See Bernard Suits, "Words on Play," in *Philosophic Inquiry in Sport*, edited by William J. Morgan and Klaus V. Meier (Champaign IL: Human Kinetics, 1988), 17–38; *The Grasshopper: Games, Life, and Utopia* (Peterborough, Ontario: Broadview, 2005); "Tricky Triad: Games, Play, and Sport," *Journal of the Philosophy of Sport* 15 (1988): 1–9; and "Venn and the Art of Category Maintenance," *Journal of the Philosophy of Sport* 31, no. 1 (2004): 1–14. "Tricky Triad" also appears in *Philosophy of Sport: Critical Readings, Crucial Issues*, edited by M. Andrew Holowchak (Upper Saddle River NJ: Prentice-Hall, 2002), 29–37. I will refer to "Triad Trickery" as it appears in this anthology.

3. Suits, "Words on Play," 17.

4. Suits, "Words on Play," 19, 20, 22.

5. Suits, "Words on Play," 22.

6. Colin McGinn, *Sport* (Stocksfield UK: Acumen, 2008), 100–102.

7. Diane Ackerman, *Deep Play* (New York: Vintage Books, 1999), 17, 26.

8. Stuart Brown, with Christopher Vaughan, *Play: How It Shapes the Brain, Opens the Imagination, and Invigorates the Soul* (New York: Penguin Group, 2009), 6, 11–12, 201.

9. Ackerman, *Deep Play*, 18; Brown, *Play*, 16–21; McGinn, *Sport*, 100–102.

10. Huizinga, *Homo Ludens*, 13, 26.

11. Brian Sutton-Smith, *The Ambiguity of Play* (Cambridge MA: Harvard University Press, 1997), 3, chap. 1, "Play and Ambiguity," 1–17.

12. Brown, *Play*, 30; Robin Marantz, "Taking Play Seriously," *New York Times Magazine*, Feb. 17, 2008, 3, in the text found at the *New York Times* website.

13. See the discussion as described by Brown, *Play*, 27–29.

14. This is the first property of play mentioned by Brown, *Play*, 17, and also mentioned in Marantz, "Taking Play Seriously," 3.

15. Quoted in Brown, *Play*, 15–16.

16. See Brown's discussion in *Play*, esp. 30–42, chap. 3, "We Are Built for Play," 47–73; and Marantz, "Taking Play Seriously."

17. Brown, *Play*, 15–16.

18. Klaus Meier, "Triad Trickery: Playing with Sport and Games," in *Philosophy of Sport*, edited by Holowchak, 50. The article first appeared in the *Journal of the Philosophy of Sport* 15 (1988): 11–30. I refer to the article as it appeared in *Philosophy of Sport*.

19. Angela J. Schneider, "Fruits, Apples, and Category Mistakes: On Sport, Games, and Play," *Journal of the Philosophy of Sport* 28, no. 2 (2001): 156, 158.

20. Brown, *Play*, 59, 60.

21. Suits, "Venn and the Art of Category Maintenance," 9–10.

22. Suits, "Tricky Triad," 36.

23. Daniel A. Dombrowski offers a similar argument in *Contemporary Athletics and Ancient Greek Ideals* (Chicago: University of Chicago Press, 2009), 26.

Nonetheless, I would like to offer a preliminary example to indicate some of the complex factors involved in judgments regarding amateur and professional. Unlike Socrates (*Apology* 19E), I am a professional philosopher in the sense that I get paid to teach philosophy and to read and write as a philosopher. I do not get paid a great deal, but certainly enough to live well. But at the same time, I am an amateur in the sense that I love what I do and wake up every morning with a Bergsonian élan vital and a bounce in my step as I go to "work." I would philosophize even if I were not paid to do so; indeed, for many years I (along with many others) willingly studied philosophy without pay. Hence, my being a professional philosopher does not strike me as being at odds with philosophizing "for its own sake." It is unclear to me why something analogous could not obtain for paid athletes who love their sport.

24. Huizinga, *Homo Ludens*, 8; Randolph Feezell, *Sport, Play, and Ethical Reflection* (Urbana: University of Illinois Press, 2004). I offer this description at various points in the book. See esp. chap. 4, "Play and the Absurd," and chap. 5, "Sport and the View from Nowhere."

25. Fred Feldman, *Pleasure and the Good Life: Concerning the Nature, Varieties, and Plausibility of Hedonism* (Oxford: Clarendon Press, 2004), 56.

26. Suits, "Tricky Triad," 30; Kenneth Schmitz, "Sport and Play: Suspension of the Ordinary," in *Philosophic Inquiry in Sport*, edited by Morgan and Meier, esp. 30–32; Bernard Suits, "The Elements of Sport," in *Philosophic Inquiry in Sport*, edited by Morgan and Meier, 39.

27. Suits, "The Elements of Sport," 43.

28. Refer to Huizinga's definition previously quoted. See also Caillois, *Man, Play, and Games*, chap. 1.

29. Caillois, *Man, Play, and Games*, 7.

30. See Caillois's analysis of "*paidia*" and "*ludus*" in *Man, Play, and Games*, 13, 27–35.

Rules are inseparable from play as soon as the latter becomes institutionalized. From this moment on they become part of its nature. They transform it into an instrument of fecund and decisive culture. But a basic freedom is central to play in order to stimulate distraction and fantasy. This liberty is its indispensable motive power and is basic to the most complex and carefully organized forms of play. Such a primary power of improvisation and joy, which I call *paidia*, is allied to the taste for gratuitous difficulty that I propose to call *ludus*, in order to encompass the various games to which, without exaggeration, a civilizing quality can be attributed. In fact, they reflect the moral and intellectual values of a culture, as well as contribute to their refinement and development. (27)

31. Suits, "Tricky Triad," 36.
32. Huizinga, *Homo Ludens*, 1, 4. Caillois, *Man, Play, and Games*, 9–10.
33. See Brown, *Play*, 17–18, for the list of properties and any direct quotes.
34. Huizinga, *Homo Ludens*, 10.
35. Hans-Georg Gadamer, *Truth and Method*, 2nd rev. ed., translation revisions by Joel Weinsheimer and Donald D. Marshall (New York: Continuum, 1995), 100.
36. Gadamer, *Truth and Method*, 102, 103, 104–5.
37. Gadamer, *Truth and Method*, 105.
38. See Mikel Dufrenne, *The Phenomenology of Aesthetic Experience*, translated by Edward S. Casey (Evanston IL: Northwestern University Press, 1973), for an account of aesthetic experience that emphasizes the autonomy and demanding character of the aesthetic object, that is, the work of art as perceived. Dufrenne characterizes the being of the aesthetic object as an "in-itself": "it means that the object does not rely upon me in order to exist and that there is a fullness of the object which remains inaccessible to me" (221).
39. Gadamer, *Truth and Method*, 106, 108.
40. Gadamer, *Truth and Method*, 109, 108.
41. See Drew Hyland, *The Question of Play* (Lanham MD: University Press of America, 1984), chap. 5, 79–115, for an informative treatment of a "decentered" approach to play, including a discussion of Gadamer, Fink, Derrida, Foucault, and Nietzsche.

42. Schmitz, "Sport and Play," esp. 32. "The essence of play comes into existence through the decision to play. Such a constitutive decision cannot be compelled and is essentially free. Through it arises the suspension of the ordinary concerns of the everyday world."

43. Alfie Kohn, *No Contest: The Case against Competition*, rev. ed. (Boston: Houghton Mifflin, 1992), 81, 82.

44. Kohn, *No Contest*, 83.

## 2. Sport, Vulnerability, and Unhappiness

1. In the following discussion I will distinguish two broad approaches to achieving happiness: optimizing and adapting. See Steven Luper, *Invulnerability: On Securing Happiness* (Chicago: Open Court, 1996), chap. 3.

2. William B. Irvine, *On Desire: Why We Want What We Want* (New York: Oxford University Press, 2006). See the introduction for an overview of his book.

3. Like Irvine, in *On Desire*, I am interested in the larger strategy as well as the way it is described in the specific traditions.

4. Luper, *Invulnerability*, esp. 44–46.

5. See Joel Kupperman, *Six Myths about the Good Life: Thinking about What Has Value* (Indianapolis: Hackett, 2006), esp. chap. 1, for a clear and insightful discussion of these issues.

6. Luper, *Invulnerability*, 45.

7. For a compendium of recent psychological research on hedonism, especially the phenomenon that researchers call "adaptation," see Daniel Kahneman, Edward Diener, and Norbert Schwarz, eds., *Well-Being: The Foundations of Hedonic Psychology* (New York: Russell Sage Foundation, 1999).

8. Luper, *Invulnerability*, 7. See his definition of competitive desires on 67.

9. Michaelis Michael and Peter Caldwell, "The Consolations of Optimism," in *Life, Death, and Meaning*, edited by David Benatar (Lanham MD: Rowman and Littlefield, 2004), 383.

10. Michael and Caldwell, "The Consolations of Optimism," 388.

11. See Michael Novak, *The Joy of Sports: End Zones, Bases, Baskets, Balls, and the Consecration of the American Spirit* (New York: Basic Books, 1976), x; Michael Mandelbaum, *The Meaning of Sports: Why Americans Watch Baseball, Football, and Basketball and What They See When They Do* (New York: Public Affairs, 2004), xiii–xiv; and Dombrowski, *Contemporary Athletics*, 1.

12. See Feezell, *Sport, Play, and Ethical Reflection*, esp. chaps. 1 and 2.

13. See McGinn, *Sport*, especially the final chapter, "Athletic Investigations," for the stress on limits and self-knowledge.

14. Jan Boxill, "Beauty, Sport, and Gender," in *Philosophy of Sport*, edited by Holowchak, 127–37.

15. Novak, "The Natural Religion," chap. 2 in *Joy of Sports*, 18–34; Mandelbaum, *Meaning of Sports*, 4; McGinn, *Sport*, 23.

16. Jan Boxill, "Title IX and Gender Equity," in *Philosophy of Sport*, edited by Holowchak, 397–98. In an earlier essay, Keith Algozin also describes sport as "unalienated action." "Man and Sport," in *Philosophic Inquiry in Sport*, edited by Morgan and Meier, 183–87.

17. Novak, *Joy of Sports*, xi.

18. Feezell, *Sport, Play, and Ethical Reflection*, 30–31; Peter Heinegg, "Philosopher in the Playground: Notes on the Meaning of Sport," in *Sports Ethics: An Anthology*, edited by Jan Boxill (Malden MA: Blackwell, 2003), 54.

19. Peter Finley and Laura Finley, *The Sports Industry's War on Athletes* (Westport CT: Praeger, 2006).

20. See Jay J. Coakley, *Sport in Society: Issues and Controversies*, 6th ed. (Boston: McGraw-Hill, 1998); John Underwood, *Spoiled Sport* (Boston: Little, Brown, 1984); Murray Sperber, *Beer and Circus: How Big-Time College Sports Is Crippling Undergraduate Education* (New York: Owl, 2000); Dennis Perrin, *American Fan* (New York: Avon, 2000); Jeff Benedict, *Public Heroes, Private Felons* (Boston: Northeastern University Press, 1997); and D. Stanley Eitzen, "The Dark Side of Competition," in *Philosophy of Sport*, edited by Holowchak. See also Christopher Lasch's discussion of social critics of sport in *The Culture of Narcissism* (New York: Warner Books, 1979), chap. 5.

21. McGinn, *Sport*, 119, 120.

22. See Finley and Finley, *Sports Industry's War on Athletes*, final chapter.

23. Arthur Schopenhauer, *The World as Will and Representation*, translated by E. F. J. Payne (New York: Dover, 1969), 1:311–12, 313–14, 315.

24. See Kahneman, Diener, and Schwarz, *Well-Being*.

25. T. Ben-Shahar, *Happier: Learn the Secrets to Daily Joy and Lasting Fulfillment* (New York: McGraw-Hill, 2007). The quote appears in David Light Shields and Brenda Light Bredemeier, *True Competition: A Guide to Pursuing Excellence in Sport and Society* (Champaign IL: Human Kinetics, 2009), 74–75.

26. See Feezell, *Sport, Play, and Ethical Reflection*, chap. 3, "Sport, the Aesthetic, and Narrative," 32–45.

27. Luper, *Invulnerability*, 64.

28. Kohn, *No Contest*, 4, 9.

29. Kohn, *No Contest*, 114. See the chapters for Kohn's detailed defense of these claims.

30. Shields and Bredemeier, *True Competition*, 21. The authors agree with Kohn's criticism of what they call "decompetition," which is not "true competition." They nicely explain and defend an ethically defensible ideal of competition.

31. Bob Knight, with Bob Hammel, *Knight: My Story* (New York: Thomas Dunne Books, St. Martin's Press, 2002), 65.

32. Novak, *Joy of Sports*, 47.

33. Novak, *Joy of Sports*, 24.

34. Kohn, *No Contest*, chap. 6. See Shields and Bredemeier, *True Competition*, 10–17, for a tidy discussion of "competition research." They say, "In fact, it is one of the most carefully and thoroughly researched topics in all of the social sciences" (10).

35. Luper, *Invulnerability*, 67 (quote); Drew Hyland, "Competition and Friendship," in *Philosophic Inquiry in Sport*, edited by Morgan and Meier, 231–39.

36. See McGinn, *Sport*, 75–87, 102–4, for an interesting account of his attempt to become adept at windsurfing. See also his various com-

ments on competition, including this: "To me, competition is incidental to sport, a means rather than an end, and in truth I rather dislike it as an overriding motive" (22).

37. Luper, *Invulnerability*, 23, 167.

## 3. Losing Is Like Death

1. See G. F. Schueler, *Desire: Its Role in Practical Reason and Explanation* (Cambridge MA: MIT Press, 1995), chap. 1, "What Are Desires?," 9–41, for a helpful discussion.

2. Schueler, *Desire*, 12.

3. Thomas Nagel, *The Possibility of Altruism* (Princeton NJ: Princeton University Press, 1970), 29.

4. Martha C. Nussbaum, *The Therapy of Desire: Theory and Practice in Hellenistic Ethics* (Princeton NJ: Princeton University Press, 1994); Kohn, *No Contest*, 87–95.

5. Luper, *Invulnerability*, 46.

6. I attempt to show some of the consequences of unreflective acceptance of religious beliefs in "Religious Ambiguity, Agnosticism, and Prudence," *Florida Philosophical Review* 9, no. 2 (2009).

7. Luper, *Invulnerability*, 81, 85.

8. See William Rowe, "The Problem of Evil and Some Varieties of Atheism," in *Contemporary Perspectives on Religious Epistemology*, edited by R. Douglas Geivett and Brendan Sweetman (New York: Oxford University Press, 1992), 33–42. Rowe defends the reasonableness of atheism in light of the lack of justification for some instances of intense suffering, like intense animal suffering. The added claim about wishful thinking is not his.

9. See H. J. McCloskey, "God and Evil," in *To Believe or Not to Believe: Readings in the Philosophy of Religion*, edited by E. D. Klemke (New York: Harcourt Brace Jovanovich, 1992), 471–76.

10. Luper, *Invulnerability*, 86.

11. Luper, *Invulnerability*, 91; Philip J. Ivanhoe, trans., *The Daodejing of Laozi* (Indianapolis: Hackett, 2002), chaps. 37, 19, 64.

12. Irvine, *On Desire*, 1, 2, 5–6.

13. Joel Kupperman, *Classic Asian Philosophy: A Guide to Essential Texts* (New York: Oxford University Press, 2001), 30, 33, 139.

14. Ivanhoe, *The Daodejing of Laozi*, xvii–xviii.

15. Ivanhoe, *The Daodejing of Laozi*, xviii; Kupperman, *Classic Asian Philosophy*, 34 (quote), 35.

16. Ivanhoe, *The Daodejing of Laozi*, xviii.

17. I am referring to Eknath Easwaran, trans., *The Bhagavad Gita* (Tomales CA: Nilgiri Press, 2007), sec. 2, paras. 47–48, 49–50, sec. 4, paras. 19–20, 22–23.

18. See Mihaly Csikszentmihalyi, *Flow: The Psychology of Optimal Experience* (New York: Harper Perennial, 1990).

19. Kupperman, *Classic Asian Philosophy*, 52–53.

20. See Feezell, *Sport, Play, and Ethical Reflection*, chap. 4, "Play and the Absurd," and chap. 5, "Sport and the View from Nowhere."

21. Susan Wolf, "Meaning in Life," in *The Meaning of Life: A Reader*, edited by E. D. Klemke and Steven M. Cahn, 3rd ed. (New York: Oxford University Press, 2008), 233.

22. Jim Bouton, introduction to *Ball Four* (New York: Dell, 1970). All of his comments come from the introduction.

23. See Luper's discussion of conditional desires in *Invulnerability*, esp. 114–18 and 140–49.

24. Shields and Bredemeier, *True Competition*, 173.

25. Harry Frankfurt, "Identification and Externality," in *The Importance of What We Care About: Philosophical Essays* (New York: Cambridge University Press, 1988), 58–68.

26. McGinn, *Sport*, 39.

27. McGinn, *Sport*, 39.

## 4. The Pitfalls of Partisanship

1. Nicholas Dixon, "The Ethics of Supporting Sports Teams," *Journal of Applied Philosophy* 18, no. 2 (2001): 149–58. I will refer to the paper as it appeared in *Ethics in Sport*, edited by William J. Morgan, 2nd ed. (Champaign IL: Human Kinetics, 2007), 441–49. I will cite all specific references to the paper in the body of the text.

2. I am using the term *absurd* in the sense that Thomas Nagel uses it in his classic paper "The Absurd," in *Mortal Questions* (New York: Cambridge University Press, 1979). "In ordinary life a situation is absurd when it includes a conspicuous discrepancy between pretension or aspiration and reality" (13) For example, fervent desire for an impossible object is futile, hence absurd. In the case of a fan's desire for her team to win, there is a discrepancy between the strength of the desire and the value of the object. I have discussed this at length in my book *Sport, Play, and Ethical Reflection*, chap. 4, "Play and the Absurd," and chap. 5, "Sport and the View from Nowhere."

3. See Kupperman's discussion of Buddhism in *Classic Asian Philosophy*, chap. 2.

4. See James O'Toole, "Money Fixation Is Harmful to College Sports," *Omaha World-Herald*, June 27, 2010. The essay was written for the *Los Angeles Times*. In response to the frenzied events in the summer of 2010 associated with the conference realignment among powerhouse college athletic programs, O'Toole offers the standard but important call to rethink our priorities. "In effect, universities now suit up unpaid mercenaries in the school colors, then cash in on their efforts. . . . There is nearly a complete disconnect at some universities between their academic missions and the practices of their athletic departments. At worst, the system amounts to the exploitation of vulnerable adolescents who, in fact, are likely to end up with neither a college degree nor a professional contract." O'Toole calls for the creation of a new conference of academically elite schools (Notre Dame, Stanford, Northwestern, Duke, Boston College, Pittsburgh, Brigham Young, and USC) who "should be willing to forgo a few dollars made off student-athletes in order to regain their integrity and enhance their academic reputations." He appeals to an ethical principle suggested by the moderate purist's final argument: "An important ethical principle is involved here: Whenever one finds oneself part of a compromised situation, and one lacks the power to change it, there is a moral obligation to absent oneself from the system."

### 5. Sport, Dirty Language, and Ethics

1. In this chapter I will typically use the words *cussing* and *swearing* as the most general terms referring to the central topic of the chapter. One of my colleagues suggested to me that *swearing* is the preferred term on the East Coast, where he grew up. Perhaps *cussing* is the preferred term in the Midwest and the South. The Australian linguist Ruth Wajnryb seems to prefer to use *swearing* as the most general term. I will also speak generally of "bad language," "dirty language," and "foul language" to avoid the monotony of using only one term. Nothing hinges on the use of different terms. I will comment on the "metalanguage" of cussing later.

2. I will define these terms later.

3. Harry Frankfurt, "On Bullshit," in *Importance of What We Care About*.

4. I found this review, by Peter Edidin, online. See the *New York Times* website, Feb. 14, 2005.

5. Timothy Jay, *Cursing in America: A Psycholinguistic Study of Dirty Language in the Courts, in the Movies, in the Schoolyards, and on the Streets* (Philadelphia: John Benjamins 1992), 85–89.

6. Rick Reilly, *Sports Illustrated*, Sept. 26, 2006; James V. O'Connor, *Cuss Control: The Complete Book on How to Curb Your Cussing* (New York: Universe, 2006).

7. I am using the notion of "ethical reflection" quite broadly. Both J. L. Mackie, in *Ethics: Inventing Right and Wrong* (New York: Penguin Books, 1977), and Bernard Williams, in *Ethics and the Limits of Philosophy* (Cambridge MA: Harvard University Press, 1985), distinguish morality in a narrow sense and morality or the "ethical" taken much more broadly. In a narrow sense, morality typically is understood as a particular kind of normative system, essentially involving the consideration of others' interests. William Frankena offers a quintessential formulation of the moral point of view, in *Thinking about Morality* (Ann Arbor: University of Michigan Press, 1980). On the other hand, as Mackie says, "a morality in the broad

sense would be a general, all-inclusive theory of conduct" (106), which might or might not interpret morality in the narrow sense as overriding. Williams uses the term *ethical* in a broad sense, as I do. For example, Nietzsche's interests were ethical, although he was, in an important sense, a critic of "morality." Ayn Rand's ethical egoism recommended how we ought to live, although some have wondered whether ethical egoism is compatible with morality. Aristotle's concerns were much broader than what we may think of as "morality." Some may wonder whether ethical reflection about swearing could ever rise to the level of "moral" concern because they do not make the distinction between the broad and narrow senses of "morality" and the "ethical," as I do. It will depend on the perceived weight of the normative concerns involved. Some appeals to possible harm involved in swearing may rise to the level of morality in a narrow sense, while some may not. Insofar as normative appeals are made concerning prudence, civility, manners, self-expression, or other factors, however, ethical reflection in a broad sense is required. Even in a narrow sense, it is an open question whether appeals to good manners might involve morally thicker concerns. Sarah Buss has argued that "good manners have an essentially moral function and that function is essential to treating persons with respect." "Appearing Respectful: The Moral Significance of Manners," *Ethics* 109, no. 4 (1999): 804. Here I am not endorsing her view. I am simply commenting on the misleading initial assumption that considering the ethics of swearing raises no substantive ethical or moral concerns. Of course, these remarks raise large and significant issues in moral philosophy, requiring much more discussion.

8. Ruth Wajnryb, *Expletive Deleted: A Good Look at Bad Language* (New York: Free Press, 2005), 16; Jay, *Cursing in America*, 1, 2.

9. Wajnryb, *Expletive Deleted*, 118.

10. Jay, *Cursing in America*, chap. 5.

11. In the text from which I am quoting, these words are capitalized. I do not do this for shock value.

12. Wajnryb, *Expletive Deleted*, 24, 55.
13. See Wajnryb, *Expletive Deleted*, chap. 2; Jay, *Cursing in America*, chap. 1; and Richard Dooling, *Blue Streak: Swearing, Free Speech, and Sexual Harrassment* (New York: Random House, 1996). See Dooling's book for an informative and amusing discussion of obscenity by a lawyer and very fine writer.
14. Jay, *Cursing in America*, 5.
15. One can find references to Carlin's famous routine in many places. Wajnryb mentions the specific words on page 12 of her book.
16. Jay, *Cursing in America*, 9.
17. Scholars of dirty words do attempt to explain the sources of the taboos and the level of offensiveness. See Wajnryb, *Expletive Deleted*, 66; and Dooling, *Blue Streak*, 17–37, 38–54. Wajnryb has separate chapters on the etymology and history of various words, including the *F* word and the *C* word.
18. J. L. Austin, *How to Do Things with Words*, 2nd ed. (Cambridge MA: Harvard University Press, 1975); Ludwig Wittgenstein, *Philosophical Investigations*, translated by G. E. M. Anscombe, 3rd ed. (New York: Macmillan, 1968); John Searle, *Speech Acts: An Essay in the Philosophy of Language* (Cambridge: Cambridge University Press, 1970).
19. Wittgenstein, *Philosophical Investigations*, 11–12; Wajnryb, *Expletive Deleted*, 14–15, 24.
20. Jay, *Cursing in America*, 1, 10.
21. Wajnryb, *Expletive Deleted*, 25, 36.
22. I once coached with someone who allowed his players to vent in the locker room (a few steps up a tunnel from the dugout, underneath the stands) during the game. After a strikeout you might hear a muffled but fairly clear scream, usually the so-called *F* bomb. My coaching colleague found this need for venting excess emotion natural, useful, and even necessary. Later I will briefly explain why I think such an arrangement is a bad idea, apart from the possibility that a grandmother seated in the stands might hear these outbursts.
23. Wajnryb, *Expletive Deleted*, 48.

24. John Feinstein, *A Season on the Brink: A Year with Bob Knight and the Indiana Hoosiers* (New York: Macmillan, 1986), 40–41.

25. Feinstein, *Season on the Brink*, 286, 89, 141, 142, 250, 285, 7.

26. Kevin Kerrane, *Dollar Sign on the Muscle: The World of Baseball Scouting* (New York: Beaufort Books, 1984), 90, 91; Feinstein, *Season on the Brink*, 138, 264, 284, 293.

27. John Feinstein, *A March to Madness: The View from the Floor in the Atlantic Coast Conference* (Boston: Little, Brown, 1998), 36–37. Feinstein is referring to Dean Smith and Mike Krzyzewski, respectively.

28. Wajnryb, *Expletive Deleted*, 34–35, 37.

29. Feinstein, *Season on the Brink*, 74, 65.

30. Dooling, *Blue Streak*, 28.

31. See Austin, *How to Do Things with Words*, esp. 94–108.

32. See Alasdair MacIntyre, *After Virtue*, 2nd ed. (Notre Dame IN: University of Notre Dame Press, 1984), 111–13, for an interesting discussion of the Polynesian word *taboo*. MacIntyre's larger point, however, concerns the need for historical reflection in order to understand key normative concepts.

33. Colin McGinn, *Moral Literacy; or, How to Do the Right Thing* (Indianapolis: Hackett, 1992), 11.

34. See O'Connor, *Cuss Control*, 141, for a discussion of the view that cussing "isn't necessary."

35. The denial of the "necessity" of using bad language contrasts with claims about the function of bad language to express complex aspects of our internal life. Dooling comments, "Even Freud knew that dirty words and anal-emissive speech are more than substitutes for sexual aggression. Vulgar speech may be verbal fallout from primal scenes and polymorphously perverse childhood traumas, but swearing is also the close cousin of magic, ritual, laughter, dreams, neurosis and reflex—all indispensable expressions of instincts and impulses. Repressed instincts usually signal their presence by slips of the tongue, by jokes, and by dirty words" (*Blue Streak*, 39).

36. O'Connor, *Cuss Control*, 76–79, 80.

37. O'Connor, *Cuss Control*, 83–113.

38. Feinstein, *Season on the Brink*, 65.

39. O'Connor, *Cuss Control*, 80.

40. See Kupperman, *Six Myths about the Good Life*, 26–31, for an interesting discussion of self-esteem and happiness, in the context of a critical examination of the "myth" that the best kind of life or the good life is the one that is most happy.

41. Feinstein, *Season on the Brink*, 4, 210.

42. Feinstein, *Season on the Brink*, 7, 307. The final comment seems to combine prudential or virtue concerns with the explicitly moral concerns raised in the passage.

43. O'Connor, *Cuss Control*, 77, 80.

44. Wajnryb, *Expletive Deleted*, 66. Here are Dooling's remarks on the comparative offensiveness of certain words: "For centuries, 'fuck' was the most objectionable word in the English language, but now 'nigger' and 'cunt' are probably tied for that distinction, and 'fuck' has at long last stepped down. Finally, hatred is more dangerous than sex" (*Blue Streak*, 18).

45. Feinstein, *Season on the Brink*, 143; O'Connor, *Cuss Control*, 193–207.

46. I am not claiming that the social argument is necessarily consequentialist. See Buss, "Appearing Respectful," for an interesting and important defense of "good manners" based on respect for persons' intrinsic value.

47. O'Connor, *Cuss Control*, 79, 80, 84.

48. Rosalind Hursthouse, "Applying Virtue Ethics to Our Treatment of the Other Animals," in *The Practice of Virtue: Classic and Contemporary Readings in Virtue Ethics*, edited by J. Welchman (Indianapolis: Hackett, 2006), 136; O'Connor, *Cuss Control*, 76.

49. O'Connor, *Cuss Control*, 80, 76.

50. Kupperman, *Six Myths about the Good Life*, 113–14.

51. Kupperman, *Six Myths about the Good Life*, 82, 104.

52. Kupperman, *Six Myths about the Good Life*, 104–5.

53. O'Connor, *Cuss Control*, 18, 137.

54. Jay, *Cursing in America*, 13.

55. Wajnryb, *Expletive Deleted*, 97; O'Connor, *Cuss Control*, 10–12; Wajnryb, *Expletive Deleted*, 42.

56. I am not claiming that a "puritan" position on swearing has any relation to Protestantism or a group of English Protestants in the sixteenth and seventeenth centuries.

57. O'Connor, *Cuss Control*, xvii.

58. O'Connor, *Cuss Control*, 10, 19, 24.

59. Some may think that my thesis is uncontroversial—obvious and thus rather uninteresting, since the extreme positions are clearly indefensible. I agree in one sense; they are indefensible. There are people, however, both inside and outside of sports, who deny what I take to be obvious. There are people whose attitudes and speech behavior instantiate the extremes. There are expectations and codes of behavior that embody the puritan extreme, and the Internet (as well as other cultural loci) is full of vulgarian excesses. Likewise, I would deny that the "only matter over which debate can reasonably occur concerns which variety of moderate view is best, and that seems essentially a skirmish between friends," as one of the astute reviewers of the chapter maintained. When it comes to swearing, O'Connor and Knight are not friends. Their fundamental attitudes toward cussing are quite different, as I have argued.

60. Hursthouse, "Applying Virtue Ethics," 151. I am also inclined to relate the ethics of swearing to the discussion of moral particularism in contemporary moral theory. The moderate vulgarian may be a particularist with respect to cussing. I do not have the space, however, to develop such arguments, and they may not even be needed, since both a virtue approach and a nuanced form of moral generalism may stress the complexity and context-dependent nature of ethical reflection on these issues. For some informative discussion of moral particularism, see Mark Timmons, *Moral Theory: An Introduction* (Lanham MD: Rowman and Littlefield, 2002); David McNaughton, *Moral Vision* (Oxford: Blackwell, 1988); and Margaret O. Little, "On Knowing the 'Why': Particularism and Moral

Theory," *Hastings Center Report* (July–August 2001), 32–40. Mark Timmons's overview (245–66) is particularly useful.

61. Nicholas Dixon, "Trash Talking, Respect for Opponents, and Good Competition," *Sport, Ethics, and Philosophy* 1, no. 1 (2007): 96–106. Like Dixon, I do not believe that trash talking can be defended by appeals to a broader notion of good athletic competition. As Dixon says, such tactics introduce "another source of pressure, but the way it does so is gratuitous and entirely unrelated to a reasonable conception of athletic excellence" (102). But there is no necessary relationship between trash talking and swearing.

62. See Craig Clifford and Randolph Feezell, *Sport and Character: Reclaiming the Principles of Sportsmanship* (Champaign IL: Human Kinetics, 2010).

63. See *USA Today*, Nov. 2, 2007. The story reports: "I don't know any coaches who don't use profanity," says ESPN analyst Jay Bilas, a former Duke player. "It's part of the competition."

64. Wajnryb, *Expletive Deleted*, 150. The context within which Wajnryb offers these comments is a discussion of swearing and gender (133–57). I have avoided these issues because of empirical complexities and questions about the ethical implications of disputed facts. Here are some of Wajnryb's summary comments:

> People *believe* that men swear more. Indeed, widespread folk-linguistic beliefs abound: Men swear more, in quantity and severity, than women; men are more comfortable with swearing than women; social expectation is more permissive of male swearing; female swearers are judged more negatively than equivalent male swearers. Over the last three decades, these beliefs have been subjected to a range of empirical tests. We now know that while men show a statistical tendency to swear more than women, the issue of gender variation is nowhere near as clear-cut as folk linguistics would have us believe. . . .
>
> Do men swear more than women? Do they use different swear words? Are the genders still subject to different social con-

straints? The view from the folk-linguistics camp is satisfyingly simple but not hugely credible. The view from the research camp offers a picture that is so complex it sends us back, yearning, to our intuitions. Eventually, the influence of postmodernity, in its tolerance of ambiguity and blurry edges, may ameliorate some of the discomfort of inconclusiveness. (145, 155–56)

65. I want to thank my colleagues in the Philosophy Department at Creighton University for some helpful discussions about these issues. Chris Pliatska offered some insightful comments. Kevin Graham, a former soccer referee, provided some interesting examples from a sport with which I am largely unfamiliar. As a soccer referee, he was instructed to distinguish between what I would call abusive and cathartic uses of *fuck* for the purpose of giving a red or yellow card. The severity of the penalty appears to express the ethical distinctions I made earlier. He also alerted me to the international character of the issues. As reported in the *Guardian Weekly*, soccer coach José Mourinho was forced to defend his use of *filho da puta* in berating a referee. Wajnryb also mentions an incident, sensationalized in the media, in which an Australian cricketer used a vile term abusively in a match with Sri Lanka. *Expletive Deleted*, 246. See Wajnryb's fascinating discussion of the apparently universal presence of swearing in all cultures and languages in her chapter "Cross-Culturally Foul" (204–36).

## 6. Celebrated Athletes and Role Models

1. Christopher Wellman, "Do Celebrated Athletes Have Special Responsibilities to Be Good Role Models? An Imagined Dialog between Charles Barkley and Karl Malone," in *Sport Ethics: An Anthology*, edited by Boxill, 333. Wellman begins his piece by including the following remarks. Charles Barkley says, "I'm not a role model. . . . The ability to run and dunk a basketball should not make you God Almighty. There are a million guys in jail who can play ball. Should they be role models? Of course not." Karl Malone

says, "Charles, you can deny being a role model all you want, but I don't think it's your decision to make. We don't choose to be role models, we are chosen. Our only choice is whether to be a good role model or a bad one." For our purposes, the references to Barkley and Malone are unimportant. They are placeholders, and those who are unfamiliar with these professional basketball players may substitute other well-known athletes from other sports.

2. Wellman, "Do Celebrated Athletes Have Special Responsibilities?," 334.

3. It is reasonable to read the dialogue as the attempt to develop, explain, and defend the position I call exemplarism. My reference to "Wellman/Malone" is analogous to the kind of references scholars and teachers make to "Hume/Philo" in Hume's *Dialogues Concerning Natural Religion*, assuming that Philo expressed Hume's skepticism. Some have denied this. I leave open the possibility that Wellman may not actually hold the position that I have called exemplarism, but many others apparently do. Also, it is an open question whether exemplarism might be explained and defended in a different manner. In the context of this chapter, I am simply referring to the way the position is explained and defended by Wellman.

4. Wellman, "Do Celebrated Athletes Have Special Responsibilities?," 335.

5. Wellman, "Do Celebrated Athletes Have Special Responsibilities?," 335.

6. Wellman, "Do Celebrated Athletes Have Special Responsibilities?," 336.

7. Wellman, "Do Celebrated Athletes Have Special Responsibilities?," 336 (emphasis added).

8. Wellman, "Do Celebrated Athletes Have Special Responsibilities?," 336.

9. MacIntyre, *After Virtue*, 201.

10. See Rosalind Hursthouse, *On Virtue Ethics* (New York: Oxford University Press, 1999), 25–32, for a discussion of this argument structure.

11. Robert Louden, "On Some Vices of Virtue Ethics," in *Virtue Ethics*, edited by Roger Crisp and Michael Slote (New York: Oxford University Press, 1958), 210.

12. Huizinga, *Homo Ludens*. See Schmitz, "Sport and Play," 22–29, for a view of sport that is a natural extension of Huizinga's approach. In the following, references to the distinction between "real" life and the "illusion" associated with the play world should be understood primarily in terms of the conventions that are put in play when we attend to these uniquely ordered experiences. The analogy with our experience of artworks is important.

13. David Best, *Philosophy and Human Movement* (London: Allen and Unwin, 1978). Best's views are included in a number of widely accessible anthologies. I will refer to "The Aesthetic in Sport," anthologized in *Philosophy of Sport*, edited by Holowchak, 109–37.

14. Best, "The Aesthetic in Sport," 120, 122.

15. See Christopher Cordner, "Differences between Sport and Art," *Journal of the Philosophy of Sport* 15 (1988): 31–47, for an important response to Best's position. Cordner's article is also anthologized in *Philosophy of Sport*, ed. Holowchak, 138–52, to which I will refer for convenience.

16. Cordner, "Differences between Sport and Art," 147.

17. Novak, *Joy of Sports*; A. Bartlett Giamatti, *Take Time for Paradise: Americans and Their Games* (New York: Summit Books, 1989); Lasch, *The Culture of Narcissism*.

18. Novak, *Joy of Sports*, 24.

19. Giamatti, *Take Time for Paradise*, 47, 55–66, 67.

20. Suits, "The Elements of Sport," 8–15.

21. Novak, *Joy of Sports*, 8–9.

22. *Lincoln Journal Star*, May 23, 2004.

### 7. Coach as Sage

1. I use the term *Character* rather loosely, to refer to recognizable types of authors. I am not using it precisely in the sense in which Alasdair

MacIntyre explains the significance of "stock characters" in the social world of particular cultures. See *After Virtue*, chap. 3.

2. Jim Tressel, with Chris Fabry, *The Winners Manual for the Game of Life* (Carol Stream IL: Tyndale House, 2008). I will cite all specific references to it in the body of the text. I wrote the first draft of this piece before the widespread publication of the problems that led to Tressel's resignation. I am not piling on. My arguments involve issues that are independent of the particular facts that came to light concerning violations in his football program at Ohio State and his knowledge of those violations. I leave it to the reader to reflect on the relation between his interest in explicit ethical instruction and the problems that occasioned his resignation—for example, lying to investigators.

3. See the discussion "Winners and Losers in Life?," in Clifford and Feezell, *Sport and Character*, 117–18.

4. Jonathan Glover, *Humanity: A Moral History of the Twentieth Century* (New Haven CT: Yale University Press, 2000).

5. For a critical look at the positive-thinking movement, see Barbara Ehrenreich, *Bright-Sided: How the Relentless Promotion of Positive Thinking Has Undermined America* (New York: Metropolitan Books, Henry Holt, 2009).

6. Iris Murdoch, *The Sovereignty of Good* (New York: Schocken Books, 1984), 77–104.

7. John-Paul Sartre, *Being and Nothingness* (New York: Washington Square Press, 1973), 86–116.

8. Plato, *Republic*, translated by G. M. A. Grube, revised by C. D. C. Reeve (Indianapolis: Hackett, 1992), 352d. See also Williams, *Ethics and the Limits of Philosophy*, chap. 1.

9. Peter French, *Ethics and College Sports: Ethics, Sports, and the University* (Lanham MD: Rowman and Littlefield, 2004), 38.

10. French, *Ethics and College Sports*, 38.

11. I do not ignore the primacy of aesthetic ideals in other parts of the university.

12. See Brand Blanshard, *Four Reasonable Men* (Middletown CT: Wesleyan University Press, 1984), especially the final chapter, for a judicious and insightful discussion of the virtue of reasonableness.

13. See Stanley Godlovitch, "On Wisdom." The article first appeared in *Canadian Journal of Philosophy* (Mar. 1981). I will refer to the pagination as it appears in Christina Hoff Sommers and Fred Sommers, eds., *Vice and Virtue in Everyday Life*, 2nd ed. (New York: Harcourt Brace Jovanovich, 1989).

14. Godlovitch, "On Wisdom," 275.

15. Godlovitch, "On Wisdom," 275.

16. Phillipa Foot, "Virtues and Vices," in *Virtues and Vices, and Other Essays in Moral Philosophy* (Oxford: Clarendon Press, 2002), 6.

17. Richard White, *Radical Virtues: Moral Wisdom and the Ethics of Contemporary Life* (Lanham MD: Rowman and Littlefield, 2008), 140.

18. White, *Radical Virtues*, 140; Jean Kazez, *The Weight of Things: Philosophy and the Good Life* (Malden MA: Blackwell, 2007), chap. 5.

19. French, *Ethics and College Sports*, 44.

20. Clifford and Feezell, *Sport and Character*; Dean Smith, with John Kilgo and Sally Jenkins, *A Coach's Life* (New York: Random House, 2002).

21. Smith, *A Coach's Life*, xxx, 117.

22. Smith, *A Coach's Life*, 114, 112, 114.

23. Smith, *A Coach's Life*, 256, 257.

### 8. Sport and the Meaning of Life

1. See Feezell, *Sport, Play, and Ethical Reflection*.

2. Quoted in Mandelbaum, *Meaning of Sports*, xiv.

3. In *Sport, Play, and Ethical Reflection*, I argue that there is a basic absurdity at the heart of playing sports, conceived as serious nonseriousness. Nevertheless, to claim that an activity or situation is "absurd" is not to claim that it is meaningless. Sports are, at the least, internally meaningful, and to play a sport is to be involved in the world in a meaningful way (as we will see). See especially chap. 4, "Play and the Absurd," and chap. 5, "Sport and the View from Nowhere." Sport may be both meaningful and absurd.

4. I will be primarily interested in the way sports contribute meaning to the life of an active participant—a player, athlete, or however we might describe one who is actively engaged in sports. See Mandelbaum's book *Meaning in Sports* for an interesting attempt to explain why sports are so important to people, fans and others, not just players. He summarizes his view in this way: "And team sports provide three satisfactions of life to twenty-first century Americans that, before the modern age, only religion offered: a welcome diversion from the routines of daily life; a model of coherence and clarity; and heroic examples to admire and emulate" (4). In other words, sport is a substitute for religion. For a recent attempt to describe sport from the perspective of the first-person experience of a fine philosopher and writer, see McGinn, *Sport*. McGinn writes with great gusto about the importance of sport in his life. He says, "To me, sport is an essential part of the good life, of the life worth living" (23).

5. Kurt Baier's essay "The Meaning of Life" can be found in *The Meaning of Life*, edited by Klemke and Cahn, 82–113. It was originally a lecture given at the Canberra University College, 1957. For an informative overview, see Thaddeus Metz, "Recent Work on the Meaning of Life," *Ethics* 112 (July 2002): 781–814. Metz's article "The Meaning of Life," in *Stanford Encyclopedia of Philosophy* (online) (May 2007), also provides a helpful survey of the recent literature. Metz's articles are especially useful if someone wants to see the contours of the debate as a whole or as introductions that help one sort out the main approaches. I hope to provide a different way of approaching the literature as a whole.

6. Robert Nozick, *Philosophical Explanations* (Cambridge MA: Belknap Press, 1981), 571.

7. See John Kekes, "The Meaning of Life," in *The Meaning of Life*, edited by Klemke and Cahn, 239–41.

8. David Schmidtz, "The Meanings of Life," in *Life, Death, and Meaning*, edited by David Benatar (Lanham MD: Rowman and Littlefield, 2004), 92.

9. See William Lane Craig, "The Absurdity of Life without God," in *The Meaning of Life*, edited by E. D. Klemke, 2nd ed. (New York: Oxford University Press, 2000), 40–56.

10. Albert Camus, "The Myth of Sisyphus," in *The Myth of Sisyphus, and Other Essays* (New York: Vintage, 1991), 3. For Camus, the concept of the absurd, or the notion that the human condition is characterized by absurdity, is occasioned by the disappointing awareness that we cannot know whether life has transcendent meaning.

11. See the articles by Metz, "Recent Work on the Meaning of Life" and "The Meaning of Life."

12. In this paper, I will use the term *God* to refer to the theistic interpretation of divine reality. If theism is true, then God is omnipotent, omniscient, omnibenevolent, eternal, and the creator of the universe. Insofar as God is eternal consciousness with such attributes, the God of the great monotheistic religious traditions is an infinite person.

13. Richard Taylor, "The Meaning of Life," in *The Meaning of Life*, edited by Klemke and Cahn, 134. Taylor's original discussion is found in *Good and Evil* (New York: Macmillan, 1970). Taylor revises his view, stressing creativity, in "Metaphysics and Meaning," *Metaphysics*, 4th ed. (Englewood Cliffs NJ: Prentice-Hall, 1992), 131–41. I will focus on Taylor's original discussion, as many do.

14. Susan Wolf, "The Meanings of Lives," in *Introduction to Philosophy: Classical and Contemporary Readings*, edited by John Perry, Michael Bratman, and John Martin Fischer, 4th ed. (New York: Oxford University Press, 2007), 64. Another important article by Wolf is "Happiness and Meaning: Two Aspects of the Good Life," *Social Philosophy and Policy* 14, no. 1 (1997). An edited version of this article appears in *The Meaning of Life*, edited by Klemke and Cahn.

15. David Wiggins's example of the pig farmer comes from his essay "Truth, Invention, and the Meaning of Life," *Proceedings of the British Academy* 62 (1976). Various philosophers have used examples involving aliens. For example, see Joseph Ellin, "The Meaning of Life," in *Morality and the Meaning of Life: An Introduction to Ethical*

*Theory* (New York: Harcourt Brace, 1995), 300–327. I have created some of these characters for classroom discussion.

16. Kekes, "The Meaning of Life," 245, 250.

17. This distinction will be clarified as we proceed. What I call an axiological approach denies that an appeal to some transcendent or cosmic purpose is necessary or sufficient for a meaningful life and reduces the question of meaningfulness to a question of values pursued in the natural world.

18. Craig, "Absurdity of Life without God." Craig is referring to a theistic God.

19. Craig, "Absurdity of Life without God," 47–53.

20. For example, Baier argues in his essay "The Meaning of Life" that appeals to God's purpose fail because the problem of evil cannot be solved. The traditional Christian story makes no sense, and the Christian attitude of total dependence on God is morally repugnant. (See section 2.) For a fascinating discussion of religious diversity and the hiddenness of God, see Robert McKim, *Religious Ambiguity and Religious Diversity* (New York: Oxford University Press, 2001). Recall Camus's skepticism about knowing anything about the transcendent meaning of the universe.

21. Nagel makes similar points in "The Absurd," which can be found in a variety of places, including the Klemke and Cahn anthology.

22. Baier, "The Meaning of Life," 99–102. Kai Nielsen makes this distinction in "Death and the Meaning of Life," in *The Meaning of Life*, edited by Klemke, 157, and does not even bother to refer to Baier.

23. Leo Tolstoy, "A Confession," in *A Confession, and Other Religious Writings*, translated by Kent Ish (New York: Penguin, 1987), esp. chaps. 3, 8, and 9.

24. Speaking of "death" may be ambiguous, a reference to "annihilation" less so. See Steven Luper, "Annihilation," in *Life, Death, and Meaning*, 199–219.

25. Tolstoy, "A Confession," chap. 4. An edited version of Tolstoy's "My Confession" appears in *The Meaning of Life*, edited by Klemke and Cahn, from which this quote is taken.

26. See Baier, "The Meaning of Life"; Nielsen, "Death and the Meaning of Life"; and Nagel, "The Absurd."

27. Craig's piece is particularly troubling. He offers a series of unsupported claims about how lack of immortality undermines meaning in life. Yet he ignores the Euthyphro dilemma as well as this basic point about extraordinary lives full of achievement.

28. Taylor, "The Meaning of Life."

29. Taylor, "The Meaning of Life," 135. Later, I will explain why one might challenge Taylor's initial intuitions.

30. Taylor, "The Meaning of Life," 136, 139, 140.

31. Taylor, "The Meaning of Life," 136, 140–41, 142.

32. Taylor, "The Meaning of Life," 136.

33. Taylor, "The Meaning of Life," 137.

34. Kekes, "The Meaning of Life," 250.

35. Susan Wolf, in "The Meanings of Lives," wants to develop a theory of meaningfulness that accounts for the pretheoretical judgments of ordinary people—how such language is used in ordinary life.

36. Wolf, "The Meanings of Lives," 64–65, 232.

37. See Laurence BonJour and Ann Baker, "Concluding Dialogue on the Good Life," in *Philosophical Problems: An Annotated Anthology*, edited by BonJour and Baker, 2nd ed. (New York: Pearson Longman, 2008), 626–29.

38. Wolf, "Meaning in Life," 233.

39. Suits, "The Elements of Sport," 11. For an extended account of Suits's account of game playing, see *The Grasshopper*. I examine Suits's account in various places in *Sport, Play, and Ethical Reflection*.

40. Feezell, *Sport, Play, and Ethical Reflection*.

41. Wolf, "Meaning in Life," 233.

42. Kekes, "The Meaning of Life," 251.

43. Kekes, "The Meaning of Life," 243; Wolf, "The Meanings of Lives," 67; Kekes, "The Meaning of Life," 254.

44. Susan Wolf makes this point about good lives in her well-known essay "Moral Saints," in *Virtue Ethics*, edited by Crisp and Slote.

45. Kekes, "The Meaning of Life," 243.
46. W. D. Joske, "Philosophy and the Meaning of Life," in *Life, Death, and Meaning*, edited by Benatar, 254.
47. See Nagel, "The Absurd," 145, for other examples.
48. Nagel, "The Absurd," 145.

### 9. Meaning, Sport, and Deflationary Attitudes

1. Schmidtz, "The Meanings of Life," 92.
2. Another fruitful way to reinforce the notion that meaningful activities are pervasive in life is to consider Heidegger's analysis of "world" in *Being and Time*, translated by John Macquarrie and Edward Robinson (New York: Harper and Row, 1962), 91–148. Dasein is a being-in-the world, and its primary relation to the world is practical, using ready-to-hand objects, equipment, in meaningful referential contexts. We find ourselves in contexts of everyday involvements, and, according to Heidegger, such involvements are characteristic of Dasein's being. For helpful discussions of Heidegger's notion of the "worldhood of the world," see Hubert Dreyfus, *Being-in-the-World: A Commentary on Heidegger's Being and Time, Division I* (Cambridge MA: MIT Press, 1994), chap. 5, and Stephen Mulhall, *Heidegger and Being and Time* (London: Routledge, 1996), 35–59.
3. MacIntyre, *After Virtue*, 187.
4. Nozick, *Philosophical Explanations*, 594; Peter Singer, *Practical Ethics*, 2nd ed. (Cambridge: Cambridge University Press, 1993), 328, 330, 331.
5. Nozick, *Philosophical Explanations*, 594–95.
6. Nozick, *Philosophical Explanations*, 595.
7. Nozick, *Philosophical Explanations*, 599, 595. Earlier in his discussion, Nozick attempts to understand why we think that meaning involves leaving "traces" after we die.
8. See Bernard Williams, "The Makropulos Case: Reflections on the Tedium of Immortality," in *Life, Death, and Meaning*, edited by Benatar, 331–48. I refer to this because of Williams's notion that an

immortal life, one transcending the limits of mortality, in Nozick's words, could be meaningless. I disagree, however, with Williams's notion that an immortal life would be meaningless because it would inevitably lead to boredom.

9. Bertrand Russell, "Prologue: What I Have Lived For," in *The Autobiography of Bertrand Russell: 1872–1924* (New York: Bantam Books, 1969), 3–4.

10. Anthony Skillen, "Sport Is for Losers," in *Ethics and Sport*, edited by M. J. McNamee and S. J. Parry (New York: Routledge, 1998), 180–81.

11. Owen Flanagan, *The Really Hard Problem: Meaning in a Material World* (Cambridge MA: MIT Press, 2007), 7, 10, 11, 12.

12. Flanagan, *Really Hard Problem*, 18. Here are some possible additions to his list: craft, business, the military, journalism, the humanities (more broadly—including philosophy).

13. Flanagan, *Really Hard Problem*, 12.

14. Flanagan, *Really Hard Problem*, 13.

15. Joske, "Philosophy and the Meaning of Life," 55.

16. Joske, "Philosophy and the Meaning of Life," 55.

17. Flanagan, *Really Hard Problem*, 189.

18. Robert Nozick, *The Examined Life* (New York: Touchstone, 1989), 166, 167–68.

19. Kai Nielsen, "Linguistic Philosophy and 'The Meaning of Life,'" in *The Meaning of Life: A Reader*, edited by Klemke and Cahn, 213, 211.

20. A more recent description of such an experience, strikingly similar to Tolstoy's anxieties occasioned by reflections on death, is given by Bryan Magee in *Confessions of a Philosopher: A Journey through Western Philosophy* (New York: Random House, 1997), 229.

In the face of death I craved for my life to have some meaning. I found the thought that it might just mean nothing at all—might, in a long perspective, *be* nothing at all—terrifying. However, far from assuming for this reason that there must be some point to it, I was only too aware that there might be no point in it. The whole thing could just be contingent, arbitrary, accidental, meaningless. I hungered for it to have meaning, but from the fact that I hungered no consequence followed to the extent that it *did* have meaning. The meaninglessness of everything was a real possibility. Confronted with this fact, I felt what can only be described as existential terror, a horror of nothingness.

21. Raymond Martin, "A Fast Car and a Good Woman," in *The Experience of Philosophy*, edited by Daniel Kolak and Raymond Martin, 5th ed. (Belmont CA: Wadsworth, 2002), 589. I assume that Martin would have similar comments on the "existential terror" that Magee describes.

22. Martin, "A Fast Car and a Good Woman," 594.

23. Owen Flanagan, *Self-Expressions: Mind, Morals, and the Meaning of Life* (New York: Oxford University Press, 1996), 10.

24. I have been primarily interested in the most general way of characterizing meaning in life as the basis for my deflationary attitude toward what many think is one of the most important questions a person might raise. More needs to be said about specific modes of meaning as connection or relation. Nozick identifies at least eight "different senses or kinds of meaning" in his discussion in *Philosophical Explanations*, 574–79. Some have no essential relation to what might be called "human meaningfulness" (for example, "meaning as external causal relationship" or "meaning as external referential or semantic relation"). It would be useful to describe types of connection or relation, for example, connections to narratives or relations with practice communities. It would also be interesting to relate the notion of meaning as relation to what I would call nonpurposive modes of meaningfulness. A Taoist approach to life stresses spontaneity, or a kind of passivity (*wu wei*—acting without acting, doing nothing) that seems quite different from what we normally think of as purposive (meaningful) activity, yet the point is to become more sensitive to (that is, connect with) the

inner dynamic of events occurring in the world (the Tao). Zen mindfulness may recommend an approach to life that seems to undermine the importance of purposive behavior, yet the point may be to become reacquainted with the particular details of the world. For clear and insightful discussions of Buddhism and Taoism, see Kupperman, *Classic Asian Philosophy*. For a wonderful expression of the Taoist sensibility, see Raymond Smullyan, *The Tao Is Silent* (New York: Harper and Row, 1977). To see how those notions might be related to sport, see Eugen Herrigel, *Zen in the Art of Archery*, translated by R. F. C. Hull (New York: Vintage Books, 1971). Finally, more could be said about the relation between the judgments we make about parts of our lives and a judgment about the overall meaningfulness of a life. In part, my deflationary attitude about the question of the meaning of life is based on my skepticism about such holistic judgments. I do not know how one would resolve this issue. In responding to Wolf's account of meaningful lives, Steven Cahn says this: "But does judging a person's life as meaningful or meaningless make sense? Susan Wolf thinks so. I do not." "Meaningless Lives?," in *The Meaning of Life*, edited by Klemke and Cahn, 216. I agree with Cahn.

# Index